PSYCHOLOGICAL EVALUATION AND EXPERT TESTIMONY:

A PRACTICAL GUIDE TO FORENSIC WORK

PSYCHOLOGICAL EVALUATION AND EXPERT TESTIMONY:

A PRACTICAL GUIDE TO FORENSIC WORK

David L. Shapiro, Ph.D.

VNR VAN NOSTRAND REINHOLD COMPANY
———————— New York ————————

Library of Congress Catalog Card Number: 83-3681
ISBN: 0-442-28183-8

Manufactured in the United States of America

Published by Van Nostrand Reinhold Company Inc.
135 West 50th Street
New York, N.Y. 10020

Van Nostrand Reinhold Company Limited
Molly Millars Lane
Wokingham, Berkshire, England

Van Nostrand Reinhold
480 Latrobe Street
Melbourne, Victoria 3000, Australia

Macmillan of Canada
Division of Gage Publishing Limited
164 Commander Boulevard
Agincourt, Ontario M1S 3C7, Canada

15 14 13 12 11 10 9 8 7 6 5 4 3

Library of Congress Cataloging in Publication Data

Shapiro, David L.
    Psychological evaluation and expert testimony.

    Bibliography: p.
    Includes index.
    1. Psychology, Forensic. I. Title. [DNLM:
1. Forensic psychiatry. W 740 S532p]
RA1148.S5   1983   614′.1   83-3681
ISBN 0-442-28183-8

THIS BOOK IS DEDICATED WITH LOVE
TO MY WIFE DEBRA
AND TO MY CHILDREN
SARA, LAURA, ANN, AND JONATHAN

Foreword

Psychology has maintained a dialogue with the law over a substantial portion of its formal history, although there has not been steady agreement as to the nature of the connection. A history of the relationship could begin with Muensterberg's curiosity about the law, reflected in his controversial treatise of 1908, *On the Witness Stand.*[1] Intended as a popular presentation of the application of psychological principles and findings to the law, its reception by the legal profession was less than sanguine. Muensterberg's observations of the proper role of psychology in the court room was viewed as unjustly admonishing the legal profession, with bare evidence to support his strong opinions. The flavor of his comments is exemplified in his chapter on "Suggestions in Court," in which he states that ". . . it seems indeed astonishing that the work of justice is carried out in the courts without ever consulting the psychologist. . . ."[2]

Wigmore, the noted authority on the law of evidence, challenged the scientific basis for Muensterberg's contentions regarding memory, suggestibility, and validity of testimony. Furthermore, according to Wigmore, if scientific data did in fact exist, psychology had failed to extend to the legal profession material that could be demonstrated to be relevant.[3] Wigmore goes on to criticize Muensterberg for placing the legal profession at fault for not recognizing the practical use of psychology in the courts, contending that the first such observations had not been published until 1902.

In spite of expected resistance by a profession with an ancient tradition to the claims of an infant discipline, Wigmore's critical review, written in an adversary style, invited further exploration of possible common ground between the two areas.

[1] Münsterberg, H. *On the witness stand.* New York: Doubleday, Page & Co., 1908.
[2] Id. at 194.
[3] Wigmore, J.H. "Professor Muensterberg and the psychology of testimony: Being a report of the case of Cokestone v. Muensterberg." *Illinois law review* 3 (1909):399–445.

In 1929, *Psychological Review* published a paper entitled "Legal Psychology," which implored psychology to gain close contact with the law.[4] Its authors, Robert M. Hutchins and Donald Slesinger, observed that as a result of the reaction to Muensterberg's work, "psychologists . . . retired from the court room and left the law to muddle along on its own." The writers encouraged psychology to come back to the courts, noting that for centuries the law had grappled with the prediction and control of human conduct, the very subject matter of psychology as a discipline recently emerging from philosophy. This paper in a psychology journal was part of a series of articles by Hutchins, then a law professor, analyzing the law of evidence on the basis of psychological assumptions. Hutchins' reputation for intellectual breadth and vision would subsequently be enhanced by his innovative approach to higher education as Chancellor at the University of Chicago.

In 1931, Lewis M. Terman, Professor of Psychology at Stanford University, referring to the Muensterberg-Wigmore debate in an address before the Los Angeles Bar Association, stated that "Muensterberg's error was not so much in exaggerating the importance of psychology for law as in exaggerating the importance of the contributions then at hand."[5] Terman, a distinguished authority on the measurement of intelligence, shared with Muensterberg, Wigmore, and Hutchins a fascination with the relationship between law and psychology. He recognized the potential value of clinical psychology and behavioral research in matters relating, for example, to the credibility of eye witness testimony and memory. Commenting in this same address on the clinical application of psychology to the law, he observed that ". . . legal procedures take very little account of the mental traits of the offender, except insofar as to pronounce him sane or insane" and that ". . . gross mental defect is often not recognized by the court.

Academic psychologists perceived the interrelationship between law and psychology as being limited to the observation and analysis of human behavior in the court room. Few psychologists had ven-

[4] Hutchins, R.M. & Slesinger, D. "Legal psychology." *Psychological review* 36 (1929): 13-26.

[5] Terman, L.M. "Psychology and the law." *The Los Angeles Bar Association bulletin* 6 (1931):142-153.

tured into the clinical area, and those who had would be most unlikely to enter the forum of the court. That was the domain of the
alienist, as the forensic psychiatrist was then called. In the period
following the Second World War, the professional identity of psychologists as clinicians expanded to include expertise in testing and
treating abnormal behavior.

The importance of clinical psychology to the law gained judicial
recognition in the landmark case of Jenkins v. The United States.[6]
Judge David Bazelon, speaking for the United States Court of Appeals,
reversed the decision of the trial court and confirmed that psychologists could offer expert testimony on matters of mental disease or
defect. In overturning the ruling of the lower court that would have
restricted such opinion to physicians, the Court clearly and formally
acknowledged the substantive contributions of psychology to the
law. The decision symbolized the growing stature of psychology as a
profession.

This volume exemplifies the clinical method and analysis employed
in recent years to identify and present psychological issues in a manner relevant and useful to the legal process. Psychologists are now
prepared to go to court as forensic specialists with an understanding
and appreciation of the law that Wigmore could approve. The forensic clinician can offer a much-needed service to the court and do so
with professional maturity. Recognizing and properly presenting
the clinical and evidentiary material in such legal concepts as competency to stand trial, criminal responsibility, and dangerousness is
now of central concern to the forensic psychologist.

During the past 20 years, departments of psychology and law
schools have taken an increased interest in the interdisciplinary
aspects of law and psychology. The American Psychology–Law
Society, founded in 1961, encouraged exchanges in teaching, research, and practice, reflecting the growing awareness of the importance of collaboration between the professions. The Society, in 1976,
appointed a committee to develop standards for a specialty in forensic
psychology. A natural sequel to the identification of the specialty
was the development of a credentialing body with powers to confer
diplomate status upon psychologists who demonstrate excellence in

---

[6] Jenkins v. The United States, 113 U.S. App. D.C. 300, 307 F2d 637 (1962).

the forensic area. In 1978, the American Board of Forensic Psychology was founded as a result of these efforts, and within two years, the American Psychological Association established a new division, Psychology and Law.

This volume represents a natural progression in the evolution of psychology in the court room. Dr. Shapiro shares a wealth of experience gained during 14 years as a forensic psychologist, spanning three-fourths of the period since the Jenkins case. A pioneer in the field, Dr. Shapiro has been directly involved in the accelerated progress of the forensic area as a founding Director of the American Board of Forensic Psychology. The material in this book brings to life the practice of a specialized area of psychology with a distinct body of knowledge. An understanding of the substance and the process of the law are here integrated with the skills of the clinician in the service of the individual and society.

PAUL D. LIPSITT, LL.B., PH.D.
HARVARD MEDICAL SCHOOL

Preface

Mental health professionals are being called upon more frequently to address forensic issues these days. While most are well trained in traditional clinical approaches, they frequently do not know how to modify their training so that they can address the needs of the legal system. This book is intended to provide a comprehensive practical guide to dealing with a variety of forensic issues, by specifically addressing the modifications in technique that clinicians must follow to be effective in the forensic arena. It will also provide information that can assist legal professionals who must utilize psychological and psychiatric data.

Performing a forensic evaluation requires not only modification of previously acquired clinical skills to incorporate forensic issues, but also the use of additional techniques not employed in standard clinical approaches. Most of the textbooks in the field of forensic psychology are based on theory or research, as opposed to being clinically oriented. This book approaches forensic psychology from a different point of view. Rather than discussing theory extensively, with occasional case illustrations, the presentation of cases generates much of the data that are discussed. That is, no attempt is made to cover either the whole field of forensic psychology in exhaustive detail or all landmark cases with scholarly conclusiveness. Instead, various areas of importance to the practicing forensic clinician are highlighted. The information presented is based on examinations of several thousand patients over the course of 14 years — in both criminal and civil settings — with both inpatients and outpatients being involved.

The book consists of nine chapters, each of which deals with a major substantive area and the specific techniques necessary to investigate it adequately. As noted, the particular features distinctive to forensic examinations will be highlighted. All case examples are derived from the author's own practice.

Much stress will be laid on specific techniques of evaluating distinctively forensic issues such as malingering and amnesia, and on assessing the adequacy of one's data base in terms of responding to issues posed by the court. Ways of maintaining impartiality and objectivity within an adversary system are also discussed extensively.

This book will be of value to the practicing clinician who works in the forensic area, as well as to those contemplating such involvement. For both groups, it should provide a sense of the complexity of the issues involved and of the need to clearly identify the specific parameters within which one is working.

For attorneys, this book should serve as a guide to those questions which can legitimately be asked of mental health professionals, as well as to those areas which are beyond the scope of their expertise. It will also indicate to the attorney the areas in which the mental health professional can make some distinct contribution.

Acknowledgments

This book represents the product not only of 14 years of practical experience in the forensic field, but also of contact with many individuals in both the mental health and the legal professions. These interactions have taught me a great deal and, on frequent occasions, have demonstrated the need for practical knowledge in this area, which has prompted me to write this book. To all of those people — the professionals with information to impart and those with the courage to ask — I say thank you.

In particular, I would like to mention the following:

Frank Shapiro, Attorney-at-Law — my father, whose legal scholarship piqued my curiosity in law and whose compassion for human beings perhaps led me to the choice of my profession.

Ames Robey, M.D., whose enthusiasm about forensic issues was contagious and from whom I learned many of the basics of forensic work.

Joseph Henneberry, Director of the Forensic Programs Division at St. Elizabeth's Hospital, as well as the many staff members at St. Elizabeth's with whom ideas were constantly interchanged, who provided me with the opportunity to expand my earlier learning.

The many attorneys with whom I have worked over the years, who have provided me with a variety of perspectives, insights, and stimulations.

The members of the American Board of Forensic Psychology, whose varied perspectives and experiences have been a constant source of new ideas and new orientations to old issues.

Harold M. Boslow, M.D., Chief Psychiatrist, Forensic Programs Division, St. Elizabeth's Hospital, whose wisdom, maturity, encouragement, and assistance in researching legal cases led to the completion of this work.

Ann Inge, Barbara Lader, and Lucille Wilson, for their secretarial assistance and willingness to adjust their schedules to accommodate my deadlines.

Most of all, to my wife, Debra, who gave me the encouragement to write this book, discussed the ideas with me as they emerged over several years, provided continual feedback and proofreading as the work progressed, and gave me the love and support I needed to complete it.

Contents

PSYCHOLOGICAL EVALUATION AND EXPERT TESTIMONY:

A PRACTICAL GUIDE TO FORENSIC WORK

1
Competency to Stand Trial

BASIC CONCEPTS

Competency to stand trial refers to a defendant's mental state at the time that the practitioner is examining him. It does not refer to his past behavior or to anything that occurred at the time of the offense. Behavior at the time of the offense is a separate issue, namely, the issue of criminal responsibility.[1] Despite this relatively clear-cut differentiation, the number of people, in the fields of both law and mental health, who use these terms interchangeably is remarkable. One will hear people refer to "competency at the time of the offense" or to the fact that a person is incompetent because "he doesn't know the difference between right and wrong." When competency and criminal responsibility are inappropriately interchanged, it tends to confuse the issues dealt with by the courts. Chapters 1 through 3, therefore, will attempt to delineate the differences between these two concepts and those legal issues impacting on each of them.

Although statutes vary slightly from state to state and across various jurisdictions, there are two dimensions which are common to most of them: an understanding of the charges and an ability to assist in one's defense. A good example of a frequently used and comprehensive standard is the Duskey standard[2] presently in use in the District of Columbia. Under the Duskey standard, a person is considered competent to stand trial if he or she possesses a factual understanding of the proceedings, has a rational understanding of the proceedings, and is able to consult with counsel with a reasonable degree of rational understanding.

Factual understanding refers to a person's being able to state the charges against him. The patient should be able to provide a relatively

---

[1] Issues of criminal responsibility are discussed in Chapters 2 and 3.
[2] Duskey vs. United States, 362 U.S. 402 (1960).

intact statement about the actual facts of what allegedly occurred. Whether the patient did or did not commit the crime is irrelevant. That is, as long as the patient is able to recognize that he is charged or that the formal indictment against him states that he committed a particular crime, he possesses a factual understanding of the offense.

Of the three criteria — factual understanding, rational understanding, and ability to consult with counsel — the least stringent requirement is factual understanding. That is, most defendants, except the most seriously psychotic and disorganized, are able to meet the criterion of having a factual understanding of the proceedings. However, as is noted in the following example, even the factual understanding at times may be impaired by a patient's psychotic process.

EXAMPLE:

The patient was a 27-year-old male who was charged with rectal sodomy with a young boy. Clinical evaluation and testing showed him to be seriously psychotic, with a marked breakdown in reality testing and a very concrete manner of reasoning. The concrete reasoning was evident when the patient was asked what it was he was charged with and he replied, "Breaking and entering."

Determining whether a patient possesses a rational understanding of the proceedings is somewhat more complex. It involves several dimensions, the first of which is whether or not the person can appreciate the severity of the charge against him. That is, does he know whether he is charged with a misdemeanor or a felony, and in general, can he appreciate the appropriateness or inappropriateness of various forms of penalties as the outcome of various crimes?

EXAMPLE:

A mentally retarded late adolescent, who was functioning in the moderately mentally retarded range, was charged with a variety of petty offenses, involving stealing a carton of cigarettes from one store and some canned goods from another. When asked what would happen if he were convicted of these offenses, the individual exhibited relatively little understanding of the relationship of the possible sentence to the severity of the offense. The patient stated that if convicted of stealing the carton of cigarettes, he could be placed on probation; he could be given a month in jail, a year in jail, five years in jail, or life imprisonment; or he could be executed.

Another dimension of the concept of rational understanding is the extent to which the mental disease, defect, or illness intrudes into the patient's understanding of the criminality of the conduct itself.

EXAMPLE 1:

A patient was charged with robbing a liquor store, taking several bottles of red wine. The patient insisted that he should not have been charged with anything since certain cosmic forces were draining his body of blood. He felt that since he was Jesus Christ and wine was blood, he was merely replenishing his blood supply. Therefore, he felt that what he did was not a crime at all, but a matter of self-preservation.

EXAMPLE 2:

A patient was charged with robbing a fast-food counter in a restaurant. He indicated that he really should not be charged with a criminal offense because "the lady behind the counter and me had an understanding." When asked to explain this, the patient stated, "I told her that it was a holdup, but she saw I had no weapon; therefore, when she gave me the money, and I had not threatened her, it must have meant that we had an understanding." According to the patient, no crime was committed; he could not understand that whether or not he possessed a weapon, his statement of a robbery constituted a criminal offense.

The final dimension involved with competency to stand trial is the ability to consult with counsel with a reasonable degree of rational understanding. Obviously, this dimension overlaps with the first two aspects of competency to stand trial, but it involves another very important consideration: the interpersonal aspect. How well can the defendant or patient actively cooperate in preparing a defense? There are any number of delusional systems which could encompass a lawyer and his legal representation. If the patient has developed a paranoid delusional system about his attorney that would render him incapable of working with the attorney, or if he feels that the attorney is in conspiracy with the government and is just going through the motions of defending him, some serious questions can be raised about the patient's ability to rationally assist counsel in his own defense. One practical matter should be considered: the examiner has to take into account the fact that court appointed lawyers frequently do not represent their clients very adequately. At times it becomes somewhat difficult to determine to what extent the patient's statements about his attorney are accurate reflections of what the attorney is or is not doing, and at what point the statements cross over into delusion. One interview technique which is often helpful in distinguishing adequacy of represenation from actual delusion, is to inquire whether the patient feels simply that his attorney is inadequate, lazy, and unmotivated or, rather, that his attorney is actively conspiring against him.

COMPETENCY CRITERIA IN MORE DETAIL

One very helpful monograph, which delineates the different dimensions of competency to stand trial in far more detail than the broad criteria just discussed, is a work by A. Lewis McGarry and his associates entitled *Competency to Stand Trial and Mental Illness*.[3] In McGarry's work, a general interview format and a sentence completion test are provided; these are scored according to the patient's level of abstraction in understanding the different dimensions. McGarry's work specifies a number of areas of competency to stand trial.

The first issue presented is the patient's or defendant's ability to appraise the available legal defenses. This refers to whether or not the defendant is aware of the various options that he has if he goes to court. That is, is he aware of and does he understand the pleas of guilty, not guilty, not guilty by reason of insanity, no contest, etc.? The patient needs to be cognizant not only of these options but of the outcome associated with each one. Does he know, for instance, what happens if he pleads guilty, giving up the right to trial and the right to appeal, or what might happen to him if he

---

[3] McGarry, A.L. et al. *Competency to Stand Trial and Mental Illness.* Center for Studies for Crime and Delinquency, National Institute of Mental Health (Publication HSM 73-9105).

successfully pursues a defense of not guilty by reason of insanity (acquittal resulting in commitment to a mental institution)? One of the difficulties most frequently noted in a patient's ability to deal with this criterion is the fact that often an individual is so impaired, and his reasoning so concrete, that he cannot separate his own situation from the broader situation posed by the legal system. That is, if he feels that he is not guilty, then he cannot even conceive of alternative pleas such as guilty, not guilty by reason of insanity, or no contest. In short, he does not possess the level of abstraction necessary to rise above his own limited perception of the events.

A second dimension has to do with the degree of unmanageable behavior manifested by the patient, namely, whether or not the patient will maintain appropriate courtroom decorum. While some critics question whether or not this is actually relevant to competency (i.e., whether the patient will appear to be hostile or angry, or will exhibit inappropriate responses in the court), there is another school of thought that talks about which kinds of behavior are indeed appropriate in a courtroom situation. In practical terms, it is relatively rare that a judge will tolerate disruptive behavior on the part of the defendant and still regard him as competent to stand trial. One notable exception is the case in which the examining psychologist or psychiatrist finds that the patient is without mental disorder but may deliberately and willfully attempt to disrupt the proceedings. Under these circumstances, such information should be provided to the court in advance, and the court may take this into consideration in its examination of the competency issue.

A third dimension concerns the quality of the patient's relationship to his attorney. This refers to his ability to trust and communicate with the attorney in a relevant and coherent manner.

The planning of legal strategy is another important dimension. It includes the person's understanding of his ability to plead to a lesser offense when a plea bargain option is offered by the prosecution, as well as the rights he surrenders by taking the plea.

A fifth dimension involves the roles of various people within the court system. Does the patient know what function the defense attorney serves, what function the prosecutor serves, what the roles of a judge and jury are, and what his own role is in reference to the proceedings? Furthermore, can the patient understand the function of witnesses, and can he intelligently and rationally deal with these dimensions? This does not call for a terribly high level of abstraction, but instead involves a fairly minimal understanding. For instance, an adequate response to a question regarding what the prosecutor is there to do, is that "he is there to try to convict me," or a question as to the role of the defense attorney could be appropriately answered by a statement as simple as "he is there to try to help me."

The sixth dimension is concerned with the patient's ability to retain and understand what he learns. A patient, by virtue of the fact that he has not been involved in the judicial system before, may not understand many matters with which he is confronted; this does not result in incompetency. This dimension, rather, involves the ability or lack of ability to understand and appreciate these matters once they have been explained to him.

EXAMPLE:

The patient was a 62-year-old male, suffering from a chronic brain syndrome secondary to many years of alcohol abuse, who was charged with first degree murder. On interview, he would continually confuse the role of his defense attorney and prosecutor. He was told on several occasions that his defense attorney was there to assist him and that the role of the prosecutor was to try to convict him. If one returned to this topic several moments later, after a discussion of other areas, and asked the patient what the job of his defense attorney was, he would once again confuse the roles. This addressed his inability to comprehend the dimensions even when he was instructed about them. Questions, therefore, arose about his ability to concentrate on and follow the criminal proceedings at a trial.

The seventh dimension is the patient's understanding or lack of understanding of court procedures. Does the patient understand the sequence of events in a trial? Does he understand what direct examination is, that every witness that testifies can be cross-examined, and that he, through his attorney, would have a chance to subject a witness's statement to question?

The next three dimensions refer to what has been described as the rational understanding of the proceedings, namely, the patient's appreciation of the nature of the charges, the range of possible penalties, and the appraisal of likely outcomes.

The eleventh dimension is an exceedingly important one: the capacity to disclose to one's attorney the available pertinent data that will assist the attorney in the preparation of a defense. More directly stated, this dimension speaks to the patient's ability to disclose material to the attorney, and whether or not that ability is impaired by his delusional system or, in more general terms, by his mental disorder.

EXAMPLE:

A patient was charged with first degree murder and refused his attorney access to the one person who could establish the fact that he was indeed quite disturbed at the time of the offense, namely, his wife. His wife was present with him at the time of the shooting, yet the patient was so paranoid that he projected his own fears onto his wife, telling his attorney that his wife could not stand the emotional stress of being interviewed. For over eight months, he refused to let his attorney talk with his wife, though she was the only one that could provide the requisite information. It was clear from the patient's history that he had a valid defense of not guilty by reason of insanity, and the patient was repeatedly adjudicated incompetent to stand trial. Gradually, with treatment, the patient was able to recognize that he was projecting his own fears onto his wife, and he eventually granted his attorney access to his wife who, parenthetically, had been willing to talk to the attorneys all along but had deferred to her husband's wishes. Once the wife's statements were obtained, the case became very clear, and the man was found not guilty by reason of insanity in an uncontested trial.

The twelfth dimension is the patient's capacity to realistically challenge a witness's testimony. Can the patient assist his attorney in cross-examining a witness, without the intrusion of some paranoid belief about the particular witness in question?

A thirteenth dimension involves the patient's capacity to testify in a realistic, relevant, and coherent manner. The defendant always has the right to testify in his own behalf, but it is a right that he can waive if he so chooses. This dimension addresses itself to whether or not the patient can testify relevantly and coherently in his own behalf.

EXAMPLE:

The patient, a 55-year-old, male, was charged with bank robbery. He had the delusion that for the past ten years, the Republican party had been persecuting him and had been implanting in his mind obsessive thoughts of his jumping into a live volcano and committing suicide. One day, he robbed a bank in order to get money to buy a lie detector machine, intending to then take the machine, hook up the leaders of the Republican National Committee to it, and on national television, expose to the country the fact that he had been plotted against in this manner. In consulting with this patient's defense attorney, the issue was raised concerning the jury's response when the patient tried to testify about his delusional system. The defendant had refused an insanity defense. The attorney wondered whether allowing the patient to testify and describe his delusions would be an effective tactic in establishing a lack of "requisite specific intent," i.e., there was no profit motive in the robbery. The patient insisted that he wanted to explain to the jury that there were mitigating circumstances. Of course, the patient's idea of mitigating circumstances and his lawyer's idea were far different.

One final dimension does not often appear, but when it does, it may manifest itself in an exceedingly dramatic form; this is the idea of self-defeating as opposed to self-serving motivation. In the legal sense, self-serving motivation refers to whether or not a person can understand in a fairly rudimentary sense the legal safeguards that he has. Self-defeating motivation may become manifest when the crime involves some form of domestic dispute, e.g., when an individual kills his spouse.

Frequently, at the time of examination, such individuals are in a state of profound reactive depression, and will tell both their lawyer and the examining individual that they have no desire to defend themselves in court; that they merely want to die, be put to death, or be locked up for the rest of their lives; that they are not going to participate in their own defense at all. Such people are usually adjudicated incompetent to stand trial and remanded for treatment until such time as the severe reactive depression is alleviated.

Two examples bring another aspect of this dimension into focus. In these, a delusional system results in an individual's lack of "self-serving motivation":

1. A patient was quite delusional, feeling that he was related to Christ or a Christ-like figure and that his goal in life was to be martyred. He felt that the whole purpose of the criminal proceeding was to have him sent to a correctional facility where he, a white individual, would be murdered by black inmates, so that he would ascend to heaven and become a second Christ. The whole legal proceeding was totally irrelevant to him, and for that reason he refused to participate in his own defense. He stated that he would sit in court, be convicted, go to jail, be martyred, and die. He refused, on the basis of his delusional system, to participate in the preparation of a defense.

2. The patient, an 18-year-old man, had been charged with an attempted rape and had been released on bond pending trial. He had fled the state and, while in another state, had undergone an acute psychotic episode, that is, *following* the commission of the offense. During the course of this psychotic episode, he converted to Islam and assumed a different name as well as a different identity, which is quite common in Islamic belief. However, when later extradited back to his home state to stand trial, he insisted that since his former self was responsible for the offense and he had since changed his identity, he could not in fact be tried for a rape committed by his previous self. What made this case particularly intriguing was the fact that the patient was intelligent enough to recognize that a number of secondary gains accrued to him in his never going to trial. On the other hand, there were repeated psychiatric evaluations, as well as several batteries of complete psychological testing, which established definitively that the patient was indeed severely mentally ill and that, while there may have been some element of secondary gain involved, the belief that he could not be tried for what his former self did was a delusional one. The recommendation of the staff was that the patient be adjudicated incompetent to stand trial. The judge in this particular case overruled that recommendation, declared the patient competent to stand trial, and shackled him to his seat during the course of the trial.

One additional criterion for competency, which is an important one but is generally not formally written into any of the competency statutes, is the patient's susceptibility to decompensation. That is, while a patient may appear competent at the time of examination, one needs to raise the question of whether or not the competency will remain during the course of a stressful proceeding, namely, a trial. There are a number of critics who state that this is not a relevant dimension in terms of competency to stand trial. On the other hand, in practical terms, it is one which virtually always has to be addressed. In those cases in which one feels that there is a strong likelihood of substantial deterioration during the course of the trial proceedings, it is incumbent on the professional doing the evaluation to inform the court of this and to suggest certain modes of handling the case that would prevent the patient from deteriorating. Such statements may be contained within the letter to the court. For instance, if an individual is being examined, and one feels that the competency is somewhat tenuous and that the stress of trial proceedings may well render the patient incompetent, one might state the following: "Prolonged incarceration preceding trial or prolonged trial proceedings may well alter the mental capabilities of this defendant. Competency to stand trial is contingent upon his continuing to receive medication or remaining in the hospital pending or during trial proceedings." In certain correctional settings where psychotherapy and psychiatric treatment such as medication are available, recommendations along these lines should be made.

One of the practical difficulties that arises from this is that judges will speak in a negative manner about the patient having "drug induced competency." Such an approach is generally handled by explaining to the court that the competency is not drug induced; instead, without the medication, the anxiety would be so overwhelming that the patient could not effectively participate in the proceedings. Competency is not being induced. Rather, anxiety is being reduced so that the competency, which has been there all along, can emerge. Therefore, while it does not apply in all cases, when one feels that the likelihood of future decompensation and deterioration is great, the court should be informed of this. If possible, a probability statement as to how likely this might be, or the form the behavior might take, should be given. That is, might the patient act out violently or become acutely psychotic; might he become severely depressed and suicidal when some of the trial evidence comes out, or will he regressively withdraw and pull into himself, becoming comatose or catatonic? If, from an evaluation of the patient, the professional sees any of these as likelihoods, the court should be so informed.

The vast majority of cases in which the issue of medication has come up have been decided in favor of allowing the patient to be on medication during the course of trial proceedings. There are, however, a number of exceptions that should be noted. In the case of Washington vs. Murphy[4], the defendant Mr. Murphy was given heavy doses of three tranquilizing drugs shortly before he took the witness stand in his own behalf. The combination of these drugs enabled him to appear relatively detached, calm, and cool as he related the bizarre details of the murder for which he was on trial. The manner in which he appeared in court contrasted sharply with his prior agitated and psychotic appearance. He was convicted, and following an appeal, the Supreme Court of the state of Washington reversed the conviction, stating that there was a reasonable possibility that the defendant's appearance, attitude, and demeanor, and consequently his impact on the jury, had been substantially influenced or affected by circumstances over which he had no control, namely, the effects of the drugs. The court noted in its decision that the undesirable consequences in terms of the law that may come from "drug induced demeanor" could be eliminated, or at least minimized, if the effect that the drug can have on the defendant is known to the other trial participants, especially the jury. The judge and the jury, in short, should be told that the defendant is under the influence of medication, what the medication is, what the dosage is, and what the mental status of the individual was prior to the administration of the medication or without the medication. It was felt by the court that informing the triers of fact in this manner would avoid the negative emotional response which the jury apparently had to Murphy's "cool and calm demeanor."

THE ISSUE OF MALINGERING

The question of malingering — that is, an individual's attempt to deliberately deceive, to create an impression of a mental disorder

---

[4] State vs. Murphy, 56 Wash. 2d 761, 768, 355 P.2d 323, 327 (1960).

where none exists, or to create the impression of a lack of competence or a lack of criminal responsibility — is perhaps one of the most difficult issues which the mental health practitioner must face when doing forensic evaluations. It is certainly one of the most difficult aspects of the forensic evaluation process for an individual trained in traditional clinical approaches to comprehend. It involves a totally different "set" or "cognitive map" than one has in the traditional office setting where one is performing psychotherapy or psychological testing. In such traditional settings, what the patient says is taken in a fairly straightforward manner, though certainly various interplays of defenses and impulses are noted. However, rarely if ever is the assessment of genuine and deliberate deception a significant part of the traditional clinical psychological undertaking. On the other hand, such an approach is essential when doing a forensic examination. In the area of criminal proceedings, of course, there are many gains to be made by the avoidance of prosecution; even in civil litigation, if one is able effectively to deceive an examiner into thinking he is disabled, or more disabled than he really is, significant monetary awards can be made.

In assessing malingering, there are many different avenues of approach, some of which will be spelled out and considered here. The first approach deals with the necessity of doing a comprehensive examination, over a period of time, in a controlled institutional setting. As a practical matter, such examinations often cannot be made. That is, one has a limited period of time and can see the patient on only one or two occasions for relatively brief interviews. On such occasions, collateral material is crucial to gain a picture of whether or not the patient in question acted in a similar manner prior to and following the evaluation. There is no better way to detect malingering than prolonged inpatient observation. Many patients who come into a doctor's office for an examination will try to appear far more disturbed than they are. However, if the practitioner who is working in a hospital setting is careful not only to document the impressions given in a clinical interview, but also to compare and contrast them with the behavior noted on the ward, in interaction with family and friends during visiting hours, and in the behavior documented in the nursing notes, the issue can often be elucidated. If a patient, for instance, interacts coherently with staff, participates actively in all ward activities, and is sometimes even able to discuss his charges with staff members, but never with the doctors, one needs to raise the question of possible malingering. When such discrepancies occur and one can predict that the patient will try to appear disturbed in court, all of the different behaviors that one might expect should be documented in the court report, and it should be pointed out that such pieces of behavior are deliberate attempts at deception rather than the outgrowth of a mental disease or defect.

In one case, the patient very dramatically started jumping up and down, screaming about the snakes that were crawling all over his body, and proceeded to take off his clothes in the courtroom. However, his behavior had been carefully observed over a period of two months on the ward, and careful examination in terms of psychiatric interview, psychological testing, and neurological workup had established the fact that the patient was without mental disorder. Therefore, all of the behavior which appeared in court was clearly seen as a deliberate attempt to avoid the court proceedings, and the patient did not succeed in such deception.

If an outpatient examination is being conducted and the issue of malingering arises in one's mind, no final opinion should be rendered. A preliminary letter should be sent to the court, indicating that such an issue needs to be considered and that a prolonged period of inpatient hospitalization would be helpful in determining this.

One of the difficulties, parenthetically, that one encounters in such recommendations, in a purely practical sense, is the opposition of a number of attorneys concerned with the civil liberties of their clients because of their feeling that prolonged inpatient observation is a deprivation of their client's constitutional rights. As distinguished a critic as Alan Stone, a professor of law and psychiatry at Harvard University, and past president of the American Psychiatric Association, has pointed out that in his opinion such inpatient observations are indeed a deprivation of constitutional rights since the vast majority (well over 90%) of defendants are found competent.[5] The argument from the other side is that doing only a brief outpatient examination equally deprives the individual of his rights in the sense that it does

---

[5] Stone, A. *Mental Health and Law: A System in Transition.* New York: Jason Aronson, 1976, pp. 199–217.

not provide the basis for the most well-informed and comprehensive opinion about competency and criminal responsibility. The expert witness must learn to become comfortable with the fact that whichever approach he or she adopts will be subject to attack from the proponents of the opposite philosophy.

When circumstances prohibit the professional from actually observing the patient over the course of a substantial amount of time in an inpatient setting, secondary sources are very valuable. If the patient is hospitalized, the mental health professional should be very careful to have the attorney subpoena all available hospital records, especially the day-to-day nursing notes which frequently contain very important insights regarding the patient's daily behavior, and how well he interacts with staff and other patients. If the patient is incarcerated in a correctional setting, the practitioner should attempt to obtain whatever jail medical records are available and to interview, to whatever extent possible, the various correctional personnel who have had contact with that individual. Certainly, family members and employers as well should be contacted for their input regarding the patient's behavior in settings other than the one in which the examination is being conducted.

Some indication of the impact of careful observations of the nursing staff on a professional opinion regarding competency to stand trial is contained in the following examples.

EXAMPLE 1:

The patient was charged with a homicide and, during the course of the examination in the doctor's office, appeared totally disoriented, confused, and unable to remember his name, the date, where he was, or anything to do with his charges. Indeed even on psychological testing, the patient produced some test results that were highly suggestive of an organic brain syndrome. However, during the course of one of the change-of-shift meetings with the nursing staff, it was noted that the patient had been playing an excellent game of chess on the ward, beating virtually every other patient there. Certainly, if a patient were suffering from a brain syndrome as severe as that manifested on clinical interview and psychological testing, he most likely would not have the concentration necessary to play even an adequate, much less an outstanding, game of chess.

With this piece of information in mind, the patient's behavior both in and out of the doctor's office was subjected to closer scrutiny, and indeed the opinion of the hospital regarding the man's competency was changed from a feeling that the patient was incompetent to feeling that he was competent and was malingering. Furthermore, with this suspicion in mind, the patient was subsequently observed far more carefully, and it was noted that during the course of meetings the patient had with his fiancée, he conversed in a far more coherent and goal directed matter. It is very difficult, indeed virtually impossible, to state from one or two observations or interviews just what the patient is really like in other circumstances.

EXAMPLE 2:

A similar kind of situation was presented in the case of an individual who did indeed have some discernible degree of brain damage. He was charged with armed robbery and assault on a police officer, but claimed to have no memory whatsoever of the alleged offenses. However, his so-called amnesia became highly suspect since his memory for events on the ward was exceedingly precise, including his statements regarding the activities of various staff members who he felt were trying to hurt him. He was able to describe what staff member, at what time of day, on what day of the week and month, committed some particular action against him. However, in the very next breath, the patient would deny having any memory of any criminal offense whatsoever.

One of the other issues that can alert the practitioner to the issue of malingering is the nature of the symptom picture which the patient presents. It is relatively rare, for instance, for someone trying to feign mental disorder to know some of the subtleties of which mental health professionals are aware in their understanding of various clinical syndromes. For example, one notable feature of schizophrenia is auditory hallucinations; most of the patients who are trying to malinger, trying to appear schizophrenic, are unaware that it is very rare for a schizophrenic to experience visual hallucinations. These, of course, are more characteristic of drug induced psychoses and of organic psychoses. When a patient enters the examining room and begins to describe the little green men who are running around the room, or the blue horses which come into his room and terrify him, one needs to take note of the symptoms being presented. In the absence of a drug history or symptoms suggestive of central nervous system impairment, one must suspect malingering.

EXAMPLE:

A patient spoke about a little man dressed in a red velour suit, that he would hold in the palm of his hand, who would talk to him, telling him what to do and what not to do. The very nature of the symptoms alerted the examining physician to the likelihood of malingering, and indeed sustained observation of this patient substantiated that opinion. A report was sent to the court that the patient was competent to stand trial and that the alleged symptomatology was the result of deliberate attempts at deception and malingering.

In this particular case, one other diagnostic tool proved quite helpful. The patient was administered the Minnesota Multiphasic Personality Inventory on several occasions. The use of various MMPI scales can help to detect malingering. One can utilize the validity scales, that is, the comparison of the F and K scales, which is sometimes referred to as a "dissimulation index." In addition, Weiner and Harmon have performed a subscale analysis on what they call the subtle and obvious scales, in which some pathology associated with a particular syndrome is very grossly apparent and some of it very subtle.[6] If someone is deliberately trying to feign or "put on" a mental disorder where there is none, he will probably endorse most of the obvious items and miss a large number of the subtle ones. One can tell by looking at the MMPI profile, how far apart on the profile the subtle and obvious items are. If the obvious items are exceedingly elevated and the subtle items depressed, it should raise some doubt in the examiner's mind about the validity of the symptom presentation. In the case described here, on two repeated observations of the MMPI, the patient had widely discrepant subtle and obvious items, and an

[6]Weiner, D. N., and Harmon, L. R. Subtle and obvious keys for the MMPI – their development. *Advisement Bulletin No. 16*. Minneapolis, Minn.: Regional VA Office, 1946.

F-K (dissimulation) score of approximately 40, indicating an invalid "fake bad."

The patient eventually returned to the hospital, having been found not guilty by reason of insanity based on the testimony of an independently retained mental health professional. Following the acquittal by reason of insanity, the MMPI was administered once again. Here, the very classic profile of the "4-9" (i.e., the modal profile for an antisocial personality) emerged, with the subtle and obvious items being exceedingly close together. Clearly, then, the evaluation revealed that the patient did manage to malinger and deceive, and once he achieved what he was seeking — namely, the acquittal by reason of insanity — he "showed his true colors."

In considering the nature of the symptoms presented, one often has to go into very minute detail. For instance, when a patient claims to be experiencing auditory hallucinations, one frequently needs to inquire just what the "voices" tell the individual. Most often, auditory hallucinations contain some sort of negative self-reference or derogatory kinds of statements. Theoretically, they represent the return of the repressed which the person is unable to "keep buried" any longer. If the patient states that the voices tell him to "bury the money," "run away," "lock the door," or any other variety of self-serving statements, one should start to question seriously the validity of these reported hallucinatory experiences.

There is, however, a final note of caution before leaving the discussion of malingering. There may be certain sets of symptoms or constellations of symptoms, which are manifest in pretrial examination, that do not manifest themselves following an acquittal by reason of insanity. In and of itself, this does not necessarily mean that the patient has been malingering. One must bear in mind that the pretrial situation is an exceedingly stressful one which may exacerbate much underlying psychopathology. The fact that such psychopathology is not evident following an acquittal by reason of insanity does not necessarily mean that the symptoms observed previously were malingered or feigned; rather, they may have been made manifest by the stress of pretrial proceedings. Clearly, this dimension must be considered at the time one is evaluating the possibility of malingering.

The case noted earlier in which the individual experienced a change of identity and refused to accept responsibility for what his previous self had done also highlights the above point. That is, one could easily have stated that since there were secondary gains in the patient's refusing to accept responsibility for what his prior self had done, he must have been malingering. This would overlook the fact that the patient was genuinely mentally ill and that the willful noncooperation was superimposed on an underlying delusional system. In short, in such cases, one must make a "judgment call" in terms of whether it is the secondary gain or the underlying delusional system that is the more prominent determinant of the behavior being presented, though one must also clearly acknowledge the other determinants.

THE PROBLEM OF AMNESIA

Closely related and frequently overlapping with the problem of malingering is the question of amnesia. Clearly, not everyone who professes amnesia for an alleged offense really does not remember, nor does amnesia, in and of itself, automatically render an individual incompetent to stand trial.

When evaluating the impact of amnesia on competency, several issues must be considered. First, is the amnesia real or feigned (self-serving)? The practitioner needs to assess the extent to which an individual can remember other things outside of the offense itself. Here again is an example of where an inpatient setting can be of great value, for one can always check with the nursing staff regarding how well the individual appears to remember things on the ward. The example of the individual who feigned mental illness but played an excellent game of chess provides a good illustration.

A second issue is: If the amnesia is real, what are its causes? Is it some sort of functional process (perhaps a repression of some severely upsetting materials which could conceivably remit once the person is psychically able to handle the material), or is it some sort of an organic process? If organic, is it an acute reversible process, or is it some manifestation of a chronic brain syndrome in which the person is unlikely ever to regain his memory? Is it a failure of registration (e.g., the patient was so intoxicated that no memory trace was ever laid down, and conceivably, he can never deal with the issue)? One needs to assess from careful history taking whether it is anterograde or retrograde amnesia, what part of the individual's life is really blocked out, and what sorts of parameters must be taken into account. If it is a temporary amnesia, is it treatable (some people for instance will use hypnosis or various narcoanalyses in a treatment setting to help the patient regain some of the memories)? A final issue is whether or not the memory of the events is critical to the case itself. In United States vs. Wilson,[7] the opinion stated that but for the amnesia, if a man would otherwise be found competent, then he should indeed be found competent to stand trial. A series of criteria, that is, several different aspects to the amnesia, were proposed on which a decision regarding competency could be based:

1. The extent to which the amnesia affects the ability to consult with counsel. Several dimensions are considered. With the exception of the amnesia, is the patient rational and coherent? Can the evidence be reconstructed from secondary sources? Can the defendant understand it from listening to other people's accounts of the offense? If all these are answered in the affirmative, then the amnesia itself is not regarded as critical to the case.

2. The extent to which the amnesia affects the individual's ability to testify in his own behalf (if that is an essential part of the trial).

3. The extent to which the evidence can be extrinsically reconstructed. If, for example, people can describe the evidence, and the man's defense is his alibi that he was somewhere else at the time, are there other people who can testify to his presence at the other place? In such a case, his memory deficit would not be that critical.

4. Finally, the Wilson decision spoke about the strengths of the government's case. Will the strengths of the government's case, in the words of the decision, "negate all reasonable hypotheses of innocence"? These issues then must be evaluated, along with whether the amnesia is temporary and treatable, or permanent and untreatable. Along these lines, it has frequently been decided that if the amnesia is temporary and treatable, the patient should be found incompetent until such time as he recovers his memory, and then can be found

---

[7] United States vs. Wilson, 263 F. Supp. 528 (D.C. Circuit 1966), 391 F. 2d 460.

competent to stand trial. If, on the other hand, it appears to be a permanent amnesia, but in all other regards the patient would be competent (according to the criteria in the Wilson decision), then he should be regarded as competent for trial.

Amnesia in and of itself, "without accompanying mental disease or defect," does not render the person incompetent to stand trial. Several recent cases basically reinforce the Court's position in the Wilson case. For example, the fifth Circuit recently reaffirmed that amnesia does not constitute incompetency to stand trial per se, but the circumstances in each individual case have to determine the propriety of trying an amnestic defendant.[8]

To address some of the criteria used in the Wilson case, permanent amnesia which prevents recall of events of the crucial period may preclude a fair trial and merit the dropping of charges. In the case of Massachusetts vs. Lombardi,[9] it was noted that several factors should be taken into account in making the case-by-case assessment, including the nature of the crime, the sufficiency of the prosecution's evidence, and the degree of disclosure of that evidence.

LONG-TERM INCOMPETENCE TO STAND TRIAL

A number of defendants who are adjudicated incompetent to stand trial, remain incompetent for substantial periods of time. This became a matter of rather critical importance, which was eventually ruled on by the U.S. Supreme Court in 1972 in a case entitled Jackson vs. Indiana.[10]

Jackson was a severely retarded, brain damaged young man who, in the opinion of doctors, would never be able to regain competency. His lawyers filed a petition within the state courts based on deprivation of due process. This was dismissed by the state courts, appealed, and eventually found its way to the Supreme Court of the United States. The question in Jackson vs. Indiana was whether a man could be indefinitely incarcerated solely on the grounds of incompetency. The Supreme Court ruled in the negative, that one cannot confine a

---

[8] United States vs. Mota, 598 F.2d 995 (Fifth Circuit 1979).

[9] Massachusetts vs. Lombardi, 393 N.E.2d 346 (Massachusetts Supreme Judicial Court 1979).

[10] Jackson vs. Indiana, 406 U.S. 715 (1972).

man indefinitely solely on the grounds of incompetency. What the Supreme Court further ruled in the case was that the hospital would, in what was called a "reasonable period of time" (and the Court specifically stated that it was not going to specify what the time period should be), render an opinion whether the patient is likely or unlikely to regain competency within the foreseeable future. If, in the hospital's opinion, the man is unlikely to regain competency in the foreseeable future, then the hospital must either initiate civil commitment proceedings or release the individual. As is so often the case, the theoretical rationale is a very fine one, but in practical terms, it becomes a difficult standard to apply. A particular dilemma arises from the fact that many people who will remain incompetent for many years do not fit the criteria for civil commitment (in most states, the substantial likelihood of immediate danger to self or others if released from custody). A further difficulty is that, frequently, an opinion as to the propensity for immediate destructive activity to self or others must be based on "recent overt acts."

EXAMPLE:

A patient came to a pretrial evaluation unit charged with threats against people and destruction of property — two misdemeanors. He had been an inpatient at the hospital and, during the course of his stay there, had developed the delusional system that the staff members on the ward were performing black masses and were conspiring against him. He took some pool balls and threw them through the glass windows in the nursing station. There were no personnel injured, though there were many in the nursing office at the time. The patient was very delusional; there was little that could be done to treat the delusional system, since it was quite isolated and encapsulated; medication was of no assistance. The patient remained incompetent for a substantial period of time, and eventually a court order was received instructing the hospital to examine the patient in terms of criteria for civil commitment. In the hospital's opinion, the man was civilly committable, not only on the basis of the previous activity — namely, throwing the pool balls as the outgrowth of a delusion — but also in terms of a delusional system that emerged within the course of subsequent interviews. The patient felt that the Catholic church was persecuting him and that when released, he was going to go out, destroy churches, and kill priests before they could kill him.

When the case was presented to the Mental Health Commission, in Washington D.C. the commission rejected the petition, stating that the criterion for commitment was recent, overt, assaultive acts, and that the man was not therefore civilly committable, not having been assaultive for over 18 months in the hospital. The patient was discharged from the hospital and, within six weeks of the discharge, did indeed act out on the basis of his delusional system, cutting the throat of an individual whom he believed to be a paid assassin from the Catholic church. He was committed once again for pretrial examination, was again felt to be incompetent to stand trial after a substantial period of observation, and was once again released by the Mental Health Commission. This occurred, once again, because the assaultive act was not a "recent overt" one in terms of his history of hospitalization and the criminal charge had yet to be proved in a court of law and, therefore, could not be used as evidence of dangerousness.

This case and others similar to it pose a very real problem, a paradox, and an unanticipated consequence of the Supreme Court decision in Jackson vs. Indiana. Under this decision one does not seek the civil commitment until one certifies first that the man is unlikely to regain competency within the foreseeable future; this usually means eight or ten months, or even a year, after the time of the offense. During that period of time, the patient has been in a highly structured, artificial environment, frequently on substantial dosages of medication, with his behavior, in short, being highly controlled. After this long lapse of time, one is asked to civilly commit him, with the criterion for commitment being "recent overt dangerous acts." To fulfill that criterion is a total paradox because of the manner in which the system operates. One cannot file the civil commitment forms unless one has observed the patient long enough to say that he will not regain competency in the foreseeable future; yet by virtue of that same lengthy period of observation under highly controlled circumstances, one can lose the basis on which to civilly commit him, because that basis is recent, overt, assaultive, or dangerous acts.

This paradox, however, has indeed received some notice in a variety of areas. The American Bar Association Commission on the Mentally Disabled has recommended that special commitment provisions be set up for persons found unrestorably incompetent to stand trial. This special commitment proceeding would be limited to defendants charged with crimes of violence. The criteria for "special commitment" would require proof beyond a reasonable doubt that the defendant committed the specified offense. Persons who might have been acquitted had they been tried would not be subject to this form of commitment. In addition, the special commitment statute would require proof that the defendant presents a *"substantial* risk of serious bodily harm to others." This is a lesser standard than would apply in the case of ordinary civil commitment. The lower standard is justified by the determination that the defendant has actually committed a serious criminal offense involving at least the risk of serious bodily harm to others. The total period of commitment would not exceed three years or extend beyond the date by which the defendant would have become eligible for consideration for parole had he been convicted of, and sentenced to, the maximum confinement for the offense. If at some earlier time the individual was no longer "dangerous" (i.e., no longer posed a substantial risk of serious bodily harm to others), he would be released. Any requirement for treatability is omitted because the primary purpose of this special proceeding is to protect society. Secondly, the civil commitment requirement of "recent dangerous behavior" (usually within 20 days of filing the petition) would not be applicable. The individual's harmful conduct most likely had occurred several months prior to the hearing, and the lack of more recent dangerous behavior might be attributable to arrest, confinement, or treatment (e.g., the example just discussed). The special commitment statute would not require that the individual lack the capacity to make informed decisions about treatment. As with treatability, the reason for omitting this criterion in the special commitment standard is the goal of protecting society.[11]

Similar reasoning is apparent in a number of recent cases which reflect the reasoning of a variety of courts that the state does not need

---

[11] Suggested Statute on Incompetence to Stand Trial on Criminal Charges – Mental Disability Law Reporter, Vol. 2, No. 5, March–April 1978, pp. 636–650.

to prove that there was threat of physical danger to self or others, based on recent overt acts, in order to justify involuntary commitment of people charged with criminal offenses. The person is in custody because of the commission of felonious acts, and this in and of itself is a criterion for dangerousness; therefore, as a result of mental disorder, he presents a substantial likelihood of repeating similar criminal acts.

For example, a case from the District of Columbia Court of Appeals in 1979, involving Aaron Nelson,[12] spoke of the fact that criminal activity could be used as a criterion for civil commitment when the criminal activity is clearly shown to be an outgrowth of the mental disease or defect. Also, in the case of Nebraska vs. Blythman,[13] it was ruled that it was proper to use an act committed years ago to prove that Theodore Blythman was dangerous, because he had been in confinement ever since a previous offense and had not had the opportunity to repeat similar acts.

CRITICISM OF COMPETENCY EVALUATIONS

As we have noted, one of the primary lines of attack against extended competency evaluations is that they involve deprivation of liberty, especially in the case of an individual who might otherwise be released on bond, had it not been for the competency study. In such cases, if an individual is found to be incompetent, it could conceivably result in his being incarcerated longer than the maximum sentence, as is very frequently the case on a misdemeanor charge. Often, forensic facilities constitute the least well-staffed and the least physically attractive part of an institution. In most states, more people are confined by virtue of their being examined for competency or having been found incompetent to stand trial, than for having been found not guilty by reason of insanity. In short, their guilt or innocence has never had a test in court; they are confined pretrial, with the possibility of almost indefinite confinement.

The state of Massachusetts can utilize, according to statute, "provisional trials."[14] This would occur when a person is sent for evaluation

---

[12] In re Nelson, 408 A.2d 1233 (D.C. Court of Appeals 1979).

[13] Nebraska vs. Blythman, 302 N.W.2d 666 (Nebraska Supreme Court 1981).

[14] In practice, such trials have not been utilized (personal communication from Paul Lipsitt, Ph.D.).

for competency to stand trial and is found, as a result of the evaluation, incompetent. The person would be given a provisional trial, regardless of his incompetence. The facts of the case would be presented, and if the defendant was acquitted by a jury on the factual basis *without the issue of mental state being involved,* he would be set free, the whole proceeding would be dismissed, and he could leave the state hospital with no further involvement in the judicial system. If he was convicted by the jury, the conviction would be set aside and he would be sent back to the state hospital for further treatment. This provision serves the function of avoiding long-term incarceration when an individual may be acquitted in the merits phase of the case.

RELATIVE DEGREES OF COMPETENCY

While there are no statutes that discuss differing degrees of competency for different crimes, this frequently becomes a practical issue which one encounters many times in assessing competency to stand trial. That is, how competent does an individual really have to be, especially when he is charged with a relatively minor offense such as shoplifting? Is one going to demand the same level of competency for a man charged with a misdemeanor as for a man charged with first degree murder? In some cases, where the charge is very minor, all an individual must do to be competent is to have the self-control to allow his attorney to present his case in court, and not speak in an inappropriate manner. There are of course different schools of thought on this matter, some stating that competency is an absolute standard regardless of the charges and others feeling very strongly that one has to use a sliding scale to assess it adequately. One must keep in mind the long-term results or outcomes if one states that a man is incompetent to stand trial. For instance, if he is found incompetent on a charge of unlawful entry, which would in most jurisdictions carry a maximum of 90 days in jail, what is the benefit to the individual of incarcerating him as incompetent to stand trial for far more than that 90-day period? On the other hand, no matter how mentally disturbed the individual is, if he is merely able to acknowledge his involvement and indicate his plea in a misdemeanor case, but does not understand the ramifications of his ability to confront witnesses and consult with an attorney, as a practical matter he may be regarded as competent to stand trial. In contrast, to defend himself adequately on a charge of first degree murder, the defendant must possess far more awareness and a far greater ability to participate actively in the trial than if he is charged with a misdemeanor.

One somewhat related issue is that, frequently, the term "marginally competent to stand trial" may be acceptable in some jurisdictions, provided an explanation is made to the court regarding what "marginally competent" means. This would involve, for instance, an individual whose competence tends to fluctuate depending on the adequacy of his remission from mental disorder at any particular point in time. It would provide an opportunity for the mental health professional to educate the judiciary to the different aspects of personality functioning that one looks for in assessing the competency issue. One frequently needs to teach the court that in the field of mental health, most things are relative, and it does not deal in the black-and-white, yes-and-no realms in which the law deals.

PROVISION OF ADDITIONAL INFORMATION

A practical issue which often arises for the mental health professional in the forensic field is how much information to provide the courts. On the one hand, there are those who feel that the professional should answer only what the court asks and should not volunteer any further information. On the other hand, there are those who feel that it is important not only to answer the questions asked, but to provide a basis for the findings and to volunteer additional information when the issues demand them.

For instance, when one is doing a competency evaluation, but becomes very concerned about a patient's potential for violent acting out, does one note this in the letter to the court, or does one choose to ignore it since the court is only requesting an opinion on competency? In the experience of the author, the former is by far the more appropriate choice. Even though courts will not specifically ask for such opinions, they welcome them when they are provided. Much of the recent litigation, in cases involving the concept of wrongful death, also bears out this position. A recent case, decided in Washington, D.C., was highly critical of a hospital which failed to provide information to the court that an individual was assaultive towards his family; in point of fact, after he was found competent, the individual was allowed out on bond and did murder a member of his family.[15] The family sued the hospital for not providing the information to the court; the hospital's defense was that the information was not requested by the court. The court strongly disagreed with the hospital's position, indicating that such information was critical and should have been provided.

This does present something of a problem for the mental health professional: defining exactly what kind of data should be presented and to what extent these data should be communicated to the court. There are many issues regarding confidentiality of communication that arise here, which could potentially subject the mental health professional to a malpractice action because of breach of confidentiality. While privilege is certainly waived in an examination setting, a point to be litigated is just what matters can and cannot be shared with a court of law. A recent very critical issue originating in the state of Texas and eventually being appealed to the United States Supreme Court involved a competency examination in which a psychiatric expert diagnosed the patient as having an antisocial personality; he defined that as someone who will repeat criminal activities with little likelihood for rehabilitation. In this case, the jury utilized this definition as justification for imposing the death penalty.[16] There is clearly a valid argument that material provided by psychological and psychiatric experts can be misused by the courts, and it must be a matter of professional judgment, how much, and what kind of, material should be provided to the court above and beyond what is requested by the court order itself.

---

[15] Hicks vs. United States, 511 F.2d 407 (D.C. Circuit 1975).

[16] Estelle vs. Smith, Cert. Granted 48 U.S.L.W. 3602 (March 17 1980).

2
Criminal Responsibility —
The Historical Background

DEVELOPMENT OF THE STANDARDS

Criminal responsibility, as distinct from competency, refers to the state of mind of the individual at the time of the offense. There are currently a variety of different tests for criminal responsibility being utilized in different parts of the country.

One of the most dominant, which dates back to England in the 1840s, is the McNaughten standard.[1] This standard, which will be discussed in more detail shortly, speaks of an individual being unable to appreciate the nature and quality of his act, or not knowing that the act was wrong, by reason of mental illness. Other tests include the so-called irresistible impulse test;[2] the American Law Institute Model Penal Code,[3] which refers to substantial capacity to appreciate the wrongfulness of one's actions and to conform to the law; and the Durham test,[4] which speaks about the alleged criminal behavior being a product of a mental disease or defect.

The first major test for criminal responsibility, of contemporary importance, which is still quite dominant in many areas, evolved from the case involving Daniel McNaughten who, in 1843, developed a delusional system concerning the government of Queen Victoria. He shot one of the lesser ministers in Queen Victoria's cabinet. It became obvious to people talking to McNaughten that he was quite delusional, and in the aftermath of his case there emerged the so-called McNaughten or "right/wrong" test. As noted, it consisted of two sections.

---

[1] Daniel McNaughten's Case, 10 Cl. and Fin. 200, 8 Eng. Rep. 718 (1843).

[2] Davis vs. United States, 165 U.S. 373, 378 (1897).

[3] American Law Institute Model Penal Code, Section 4.01 (1962).

[4] Durham vs. United States, 214 F.2d 962, 874–875 (D.C. Circuit 1954).

First, it spoke about an individual being so mentally ill that he did not know the nature or quality of his act, that is, he did not really know just what the act itself was. The example was given of an individual who strangled someone who did not think that he was strangling somebody but rather that he was squeezing a lemon; such an individual did not in the logic of this test "appreciate the nature and quality of the act." Another example given was of a mentally retarded individual who thought that it would be amusing to cut someone's head off because he thought it would be funny to watch the person get up in the morning and look for his head; he obviously did not understand the quality of the act, namely, that decapitation causes death. The second part of the McNaughten test asked whether, even if he knew the nature and quality of the act, the individual was incapable, by virtue of a mental illness, of knowing that what he was doing was wrong.

It is striking that the McNaughten standard has survived the test of time but has come into modern day thinking as "the right/wrong test," with many people forgetting that there was indeed another aspect to it, namely, that aspect dealing the the "nature and quality of the act." Especially in recent years, the McNaughten test has come under tremendous criticism, with people regarding it as an exclusively cognitive test (knowledge of right and wrong) which does not take into account the complexity of human beings. However, when one considers the ramifications of the concept "nature and quality of the act," there are ample grounds to speak of far more than mere cognitive capacities.

The McNaughten Rule more or less "reigned supreme" as the test for criminal responsibility, though there were some challenges in the late 1800s, which were refined into the so-called product tests in the 1950s.

In 1887 and later in 1897, the second major development in thinking regarding criminal responsibility emerged in the form of the so-called irresistible impulse test: the defendant lacked the willpower to control his or her behavior. Most frequently, this test is used along with the McNaughten standard, rather than standing by itself as a criterion on which to decide the issue of criminal responsibility. Often, when the irresistible impulse test is added, the test for criminal responsibility becomes an "either/or" situation. In other words, a person may be exculpated for his criminal activity if (a) he could not understand the nature and quality of his act, (b) he did not know that the act was wrong, or (c) he was irresistibly impelled to commit the act.

One can imagine of course, the vast furor and lack of consensus on just what constituted an irresistible impulse. What, for instance, is the difference between an irresistible impulse and an unresisted impulse? That is, at what point does one draw the line between a person *choosing* not to exert control and being totally *unable* to exert control?

In order to cope with this vagueness, some states attempted an operational definition of "irresistible impulse." For instance, the state of Michigan defined irresistible impulse as "the policeman at the elbow test." A criminal act could be defined as irresistible if the impulse was so overwhelming that even the presence of a law enforcement officer would not be sufficient to deter the individual. That is, the individual's delusional system would be so overwhelming that either it would eliminate his awareness of a legal authority or it would seem more important to him than the presence of a law enforcement individual. In practice, however, even this test has many problems.

EXAMPLE:

Mr. H. was a 35-year-old truck driver who experienced an acute psychotic episode. He became quite delusional while driving a truck cross-country and heard voices telling him that he had to "get a body." He pulled his truck into a truck stop and entered a restaurant where there were four off-duty policemen sitting at a table. Mr. H. walked over, pulled out the service revolver from one of the officer's holsters, and proceeded to shoot the officer to death.

While psychological evaluation and testing pointed to the delusional nature of the crime, and while there was more than ample evidence for a "policeman at the elbow" (in point of fact there were four policemen at his elbow), there was still some opposition to this opinion, for the man did indeed have a long history of antisocial behavior and had been arrested on many occasions. The government expert witness in the case stated that this was not an irresistible impulse but merely an unresisted impulse (i.e., he *chose* not to exert control) conditioned by Mr. H.'s long dislike for, and distrust of, law enforcement agents.

As noted, however, there was much dissatisfaction with the McNaughten standard even with the modifications offered by the irresistible impulse test. Many mental health professionals, especially, stated that the definitions given were too restrictive and that cognition alone — "knowing right from wrong" — was far too narrow a basis on which to state an opinion. In 1954, the courts responded with the Durham rule or so-called product test. This test was constructed by Judge David Bazelon of the United States Court of Appeals in Washington, D.C. The Durham test stated that an accused is not criminally responsible if his criminal activity is a product of a mental disease or defect. This test was intended, in Judge Bazelon's words, to give "the widest possible scope to expert evaluation and expert testimony."

However, the Durham rule was not without its own set of problems and predicaments. There were two major stumbling blocks. First, the term "product" was excessively vague. Fanciful manipulation of psychodynamic theories of personality, for example, can (and often did) result in a belief that virtually anything can cause anything. The second, and perhaps more troubling, aspect of the Durham rule was that at no point was the term "mental disease or defect" actually defined, which left each mental health professional with the task of defining it in every case.

The next major landmark decision in the field of criminal responsibility addressed itself to this very issue. This was the case of McDonald vs. United States,[5] in which a "legal definition" of mental disease or defect was given. For the purposes of the legal system, a mental disease or defect was defined as "any abnormal condition of the mind which substantially affects mental and emotional processes or substantially impairs behavioral controls." The test described a mental disease as something that could show some change (i.e., some functional process) and a mental defect as a condition which most likely would not change (i.e., some organic problem).

---

[5] McDonald vs. United States, 312 F.2d 844 (D.C. Circuit 1962).

Admittedly, the McDonald definition did narrow the scope somewhat, because it took the position that not every diagnosable condition could result in a person's exculpability. It would instead have to be a mental condition which showed evidence of substantial impairment of mental and emotional processes or substantial impairment of behavioral controls. The McDonald definition of a mental illness, coupled with the Durham criterion for exculpability, however, was not without its own limitations as well.

A rather fascinating case in the District of Columbia, which is known in legal history as the "Weekend Reversal," involved a patient named Blocker,[6] at St. Elizabeth's Hospital, who had been found competent to stand trial and responsible for his actions, having been diagnosed as an antisocial personality; personality disorders were not felt to be mental diseases or defects. Blocker returned to court, was convicted, and was sentenced to some time in the District of Columbia Department of Corrections. One weekend, St. Elizabeth's Hospital changed its position and presented a hospital policy that antisocial personality or, as it was called at that time, psychopathic personality was indeed a mental disease; the hospital cited the fact that people suffering from "psychopathic personality" were basically showing maladaptive responses to life, an inability to relate to other people in a warm manner, and an inability to form stable attachments. Therefore, this clearly showed impairment of emotional controls and would fit the definition of a mental illness. Mr. Blocker's attorney quickly filed an appeal based on the reversal in the hospital's position, and the court of appeals granted a new trial. However, this still leaves open the obvious question: What is and what is not a mental disease or defect?

As noted earlier the other thorny issue is the definition of a "product." Even to this date, in courts which utilize the product test, one can hear judges rendering opinions about "products" which range from very narrow to· exceedingly broad definitions. Some judges have stated that one needs to construe product as a "but for" test: that is, had it not been for the mental illness, the person would not have committed the offense, or but for this mental illness, the offense would not have been committed in the manner in which it

---

[6] Blocker vs. United States, 288 F.2d 853, at 859, 860 (D.C. Circuit 1961).

was committed. Some judges, in their instructions to juries, have spoken about product in a very broad sense, that is, that the jury should consider virtually anything in the patient's history that relates to the criminal behavior.

One of the unfortunate consequences of the Durham rule and the vagueness of the term "product" was the fact that mental health professionals were, in the view of the court, exerting far too much control over the outcome of court proceedings. That is, the court felt that many mental health professionals were rendering "conclusory labels," speaking about various criminal activities being products of mental illness, without adequately defining the relationship and without giving an adequate basis for these opinions. Many mental health professionals were presenting a position in court that if a patient had a diagnosis of a mental disease or defect, or in some cases even a diagnosable personality disorder, he or she should not be held responsible for criminal activity.

This problem was addressed in a decision which appeared in 1967.[7] In this decision, the court stated that the expert witness may testify to the development and adaptation of the individual, how the individual functioned, and whether the particular mental disease or defect might conceivably impair his behavioral controls; the expert witness was not to render an opinion as to whether the offense was a product of the mental disease or defect. That issue – the "product" – was regarded as a question for the trier of fact (i.e., the judge or the jury) which was supposed to evaluate all of the testimony including the expert testimony. In other words, it was up to the jury or judge to determine whether or not a causal relationship actually existed. The Washington decision contained within it an instruction to expert witnesses, which was read to the expert witness in the presence of the jury, in advance of the witness's testimony, in cases involving a defense of insanity.

To paraphrase this rather lengthy instruction, it speaks of the fact that the instruction is being given in advance of testimony as an expert witness in order to avoid confusion and misunderstanding. It states that since the person qualifies as an expert witness, his or her testimony is governed by special rules. Lay witnesses are not allowed

---

[7]Washington vs. United States, 129 U.S. App. D.C. 29 (1967).

to express opinions or conclusions based on observation. However, because of the training and experience of the expert witness, he or she can express such opinions. Nevertheless such opinions and conclusions of an expert cannot be given unless the expert also tells the jury "what investigations, observations, reasoning and theories led to the opinion." This, of course, is the court's attempt to avoid the use of what it calls "conclusory labels." The expert witness may give an opinion about whether or not the defendant suffered from a mental disease or defect, and may then explain how the defendant's disease or defect related to the alleged offense, that is, how the development, adaptation, and functioning of the defendant's behavioral processes may have influenced his/her conduct. The explanation, the court goes on, would be so complete that the jury will have a basis for an informed judgment on whether the crime was a product, but the expert is not supposed to state, himself or herself, whether the crime was a product. The opinion goes on to state that the expert is to give an opinion of whether or not the defendant suffered from a mental disease or defect because the "clinical diagnostic meaning of the term may be different from its legal meaning." An important issue here is that the expert "should not be concerned with its legal meaning." This, of course, puts the expert witness, the examiner, in a true bind. On the one hand, the expert is given the McDonald standard and asked to render an opinion as to whether or not the patient was criminally responsible, that is, whether there was a substantial impairment of mental and emotional processes or behavioral controls. At the same time, however, the instruction in the actual trial phase tells the expert witness not to concern himself or herself with the legal meaning, but only with the clinical meaning, of "mental disease and defect." Many experts feel that the court was "talking out of both sides of its mouth" simultaneously, saying essentially that when one performs an evaluation, one should concern oneself with the legal aspect so that an opinion can be rendered as to whether or not the person is responsible, but when testifying in front of a jury, one should concern oneself only with the clinical meaning of the terms involved.

The instruction to expert witnesses goes on to state some very practical issues. When the expert is asked questions which fall within the scope of his special training and expertise, he or she should "answer them if you feel confident to do so; otherwise you should not answer them, if the answer depends upon knowledge and experience generally possessed by an ordinary citizen." The expert is to try to separate expert judgments from lay judgments, and if one is unable to make a separation, one should state clearly to the jury that the answer is not based solely on one's special knowledge. The expert need not give yes or no answers, but may always feel free to explain and amplify upon a stated position. The expert should ask for clarification before answering any question that is unclear. Matters should be explained to the jury in simple language, and technical terms should be avoided whenever possible.

The next major decision which found its way into the thinking about the issue of criminal responsibility was the American Law Institute (ALI) Model Penal Code, which spoke of an individual's not being criminally responsible if, by reason of mental disease or defect, he lacked substantial capacity to appreciate the wrongfulness of his conduct (sometimes called the criminality of his conduct) or lacked substantial capacity to conform his behavior to the requirements of the law. In some jurisdictions, there were statements added to this code that allowed for the introduction of a concept of diminished capacity, namely, that "as a result of a mental disease or defect, a person lacked the requisite specific intent to commit the alleged offense."[8] This specific intent applies only to certain crimes, and in such cases the mental disease or defect is regarded as a mitigating factor. Often such a reduction of intent would be utilized in terms of sentencing or disposition rather than in the trial process itself, but recently, diminished capacity has been cropping up more frequently in the trial phase also.

A rather interesting example of a case in which diminished capacity was asserted, rather than an insanity defense, in the course of the trial itself follows.

EXAMPLE:

The patient had become involved in a "you kill my wife, I'll kill yours" arrangement with another man. While the patient was not psychotic in any sense of the word, there was a rather extreme

---

[8]United States vs. Brawner, 471 F.2d 969 (D.C. Circuit 1972).

dissociation of thought processes from affective life. The patient did not appear to have any capacity to connect what he was thinking about with any sort of feelings, and he basically thought that the planning of the homicide "was a joke." The patient truly believed that the other man was never really serious. Because of his mental illness or disorder, which was diagnosed as a severe hysterical personality, he did not actively conspire — but rather passively acquiesced — to the offense, which he really did not feel would ever happen. Practically speaking, the way the material was introduced at the trial was not in terms of an insanity defense, but rather in terms of an open-ended question from the defense attorney to "present a psychological profile" of the patient.

The ALI Model Penal Code also added a statement that diseases whose only manifestation was repeated criminal activity were specifically excluded from the purview of this test. In other words, this test eliminated the utilization of insanity defenses for people diagnosed as antisocial, psychopathic, or sociopathic personalities.

CRITIQUE OF THE STANDARDS

When one surveys all of this historical background, one is struck by a variety of issues. There is, as noted before, a critique that the McNaughten rule is exclusively dependent on cognitive functioning, and does not take into account emotional functioning and affective states. The Durham rule takes into account the broad field of mental disease or defect, but is perhaps so broad that it loses any precise meaning. The irresistible impulse test speaks of a compelling or overwhelming impulse but does not define it well. The ALI Model Penal Code refers to substantial capacity to appreciate wrongfulness, which leaves one wondering about the meaning of "substantial." One, of course, needs to ask if — from a purely practical point of view — it makes any difference.

Many expert witnesses have found, much to their chagrin, that regardless of what test is technically being used, in practice the same kind of testimony is presented. That is, in giving the basis of one's opinion, many dimensions are covered other than those specifically related to the test at hand. It is of course the latter, the discussion of the grounds for the opinion, which has the most impact on the jury.

Perhaps an even more sobering fact is that most of the research on jury simulation has found that regardless of what expert witnesses say, the jury forms its own opinion by looking at the defendant sitting at the table and deciding for itself in a rather global sense, whether or not the patient is mentally ill. It is of course a rather humbling experience for the expert witness, who prepares a great deal of elaborate testimony, to acknowledge the fact that juries frequently operate in this very global sense.

From a practical point of view, it would appear that the task of the expert witness is to integrate this knowledge of the manner in which juries function into the kind of testimony that is presented. For instance, if a defense psychiatrist or psychologist believes that the jury is impressed by an obviously distraught and somewhat psychotic individual, the testimony may be presented with an emphasis on how psychotic the individual is, or if the jury tends to see the defendant as a fairly well-integrated individual, the defense expert witness may choose to speak about how appearances can be deceiving and how people who appear intact may indeed be more disturbed when one looks underneath the surface. In a similar manner, if the defendant appears disturbed in the courtroom but the expert witness for the government has the opinion that this disturbance is feigned, he or she may stress how the patient's appearance differs from that of someone who is genuinely disturbed. If the person was not psychotic at the time of the offense and has decompensated, the government witness might emphasize to the jury the fact that one can appear psychotic at the present time, but that this represents a deterioration from a prior state of mental functioning at the time of the offense.

A very fascinating study of juries is found in a book called *The Jury and the Defense of Insanity* by Rita Simon.[9] This work came to the following conclusions:

1. A jury instructed under the McNaughten rule, as opposed to the Durham rule, is more likely to convict an individual.

---

[9] Simon R. *The Jury and the Defense of Insanity.* Chicago: University of Chicago Press, 1968.

2. If the jury is left uninstructed or just told that "you have heard the testimony, decide whether or not the person should be held responsible," but is not given a specific instruction with the wording of the particular legal test, the jury is more likely to use as its own standard — something that approximates the Durham rule — which is a very broad and global conception of mental illness.

3. Intensive and in-depth expert testimony makes very little difference to the jury. Members of the jury deliberate basically on what their emotional "gut" reaction is to the defendant sitting at the table.

4. It makes no difference in terms of its deliberations to instruct the jury regarding the disposition of the individual following the trial.

To amplify this last point, Dr. Simon used as one of her parameters whether the judge included in his instruction the disposition of the individual if he was found not guilty by reason of insanity; such patients are generally committed to a state mental hospital where they can be released, depending on the criteria, when their mental disease is in remission, or when they are no longer a danger to themselves or others. Interestingly enough, in federal crimes, if a person is found not guilty by reason of insanity, the person can indeed "beat the charge" and be totally free, unless he/she satisfies the criteria for civil commitment. However, federal jurisdictions aside, many juries are unaware of the fact that a person is committed to a mental hospital pursuant to a finding of not guilty by reason of insanity; frequently, they think that if a person is found not guilty by reason of insanity, he/she is set free. Of course, they know that if he is convicted, he goes to prison. Dr. Simon interprets her data as suggesting that it makes no difference in the number of acquittals by reasons of insanity whether or not juries are instructed regarding the disposition of the individual.

Some relatively recent cases, one especially in the state of Michigan, appear to contradict this finding. In the case of Michigan vs. Cole,[10] precisely this issue surfaced. Johnny Cole was an individual in Flint, Michigan, who in the mid-1960s committed a rather bizarre and

---

[10] People vs. Cole 382 Mich. 695 (1969).

unprovoked crime. The gas company had sent a man out to turn off Mr. Cole's gas meter, because his gas bill had been not paid. Mr. Cole went down to the basement and told the man to stop trying to turn off the meter. The gas man apparently said to Mr. Cole, in a rather derogatory manner, "Go away boy, I got my orders"; Mr. Cole shot the man to death. A defense of not guilty by reason of insanity was presented at the trial, based on the fact that there was an active delusional process going on, and that Mr. Cole had been hospitalized and diagnosed as a schizophrenic. At the time of jury deliberation, the defense attorney asked the judge to give an instruction to the jury indicating that if Mr. Cole were found not guilty by reason of insanity, he would be sent to a state mental hospital for treatment. The judge refused to give such an instruction, stating that a jury should not be aware of the disposition of the defendant. The jury convicted Johnny Cole. Jurors were interviewed following the trial and asked why they convicted a man who was obviously so delusional; many jurors stated that they did not realize that if he were acquitted by reason of insanity, he would be committed to a mental hospital. On the basis of this, an appeal was filed. After Mr. Cole had spent five years in the State Prison of Southern Michigan, he was granted a new trial. In the second trial, the same expert testimony was presented; the only difference was that the jury was instructed about the outcome of an acquittal by reason of insanity. In a very short time, the jury returned a verdict of not guilty by reason of insanity.

DIMINISHED CAPACITY

As evidenced in the historical discussion of the evolution of the insanity defense, there has been much dissatisfaction with this defense over the course of the years. One of the alternative proposals that is being considered in many states is the concept of diminished capacity or diminished responsibility. There are many proposals in various courts, in various states, dealing with just how such statutes ought to be written. They range from very conservative ideas of diminished capacity to rather radical ones.

One of the most conservative approaches noted in jurisdictions with diminished capacity or diminished responsibility statutes is that which refers to a subjective state that mitigates the offense or the sentence. This involves the concept of a reduction in "requisite specific intent." That is, a mental disease or defect is admissible in so far as it impairs an individual's capacity to form the "requisite specific intent" to commit the crime. Interestingly enough, some states which have until very recently utilized diminished capacity only at the time of sentencing, now also utilize it at the time of trial. A concrete example of requisite specific intent is some mental condition resulting in the charge of first degree murder being reduced to second degree, or second degree murder to manslaughter. Matters such as the influence of some sort of physical injury on the person, the fact that he was under the influence of drugs or was intoxicated, or the fact that he reacted out of a sense of grief would be included (e.g., someone had hurt a family member, and in his grief-stricken state, he shot the offender). All would be grounds not for an insanity defense but for diminished capacity. Certainly, there are a limited number of offenses to which this defense can apply, namely, those that involve the concept of specific intent.

A second, somewhat more liberal interpretation of the concept is the approach which advocates taking into account a vast number of personal characteristics of the individual, such as his intelligence, his excitability, anything in his past history that bears on his capacity to control his actions, and any dimensions that would bear on impulse control or understanding of wrongfulness; all these, according to this school of thought, should be admitted as evidence to the jury.

Finally, the most radical approach argues that the person's entire life history should be put in front of the jury. That is, any number of factors which may predispose a person to antisocial activity are admitted, such as the fact that the patient grew up in poverty. This school of thought says that such material is relevant to a defense of diminished capacity and that all of this should be presented to the jury along with the factual statements of the case. The jury would listen to the life history and take the life history into account in its deliberations.

It is an interesting practical observation that very frequently, even when diminished capacity is not used in this latter sense, juries tend to react in such a manner.

EXAMPLE:

A patient was charged with a series of armed rapes. Psychiatric testimony for both the defense and the government failed to establish the existence of any mental disease or defect of psychotic proportions, though a variety of neurotic problems were noted, coupled with some rather bizarre historical factors such as the fact that the family always dressed the young man in girl's clothing and told him that he would "look much better as a girl." The jury found the patient not guilty by reason of insanity, the expert testimony notwithstanding, and when the foreman of the jury was interviewed, his response regarding the rationale for the verdict was that the patient had a terrible childhood, was in need of treatment, and could not receive such treatment in a prison. The substantive issues raised in the actual trial had little or no significance to the jurors in their deliberations.

A growing school of thought regards the insanity defense as a totally unworkable concept that should be abolished entirely. Some states, as we have noted, use the concept of diminished capacity; others utilize a concept known as "guilty but mentally ill"; and still others advocate providing treatment within the correctional setting itself, following conviction on the facts of the offense. In the "guilty but mentally ill" proposals, patients are committed to a hospital for treatment until such time as their mental illness is regarded as in remission, with the time in the hospital being credited towards their jail time; they are then transferred from the hospital to a correctional facility to complete their sentence. One of the reasons that people argue for the abolition of the insanity defense is that they regard it as presumptuous to attempt to infer – from evidence presented now – what a person's mental state was months, even years ago. These critics of the insanity defense point out that people's perceptions of events can change over the months and that people could either consciously or unconsciously distort what their experience was at the time of the offense. On the other hand, some proponents of the insanity defense argue that there are certain cases in which this is actually the only defense that could be appropriately utilized, and in such circumstances, it would be a disservice to the defendant to have the insanity defense abolished entirely.

EXAMPLE 1:

A patient who had a chronic history of mental illness took a bus trip from his home in Virginia to New Jersey, where he had previously been hospitalized. As he was making the trip, his hallucinations became louder and louder. When the bus stopped in Washington, D.C., the patient got out, attempted to run away from the voices, found himself wandering around the city, and eventually ended up in an office building with a shopping arcade on the ground floor. The patient identified the voices as coming from a briefcase inside a luggage store; he seized the briefcase, went running out of the store, and attempted to take the briefcase and throw it into the Potomac River, to try to get rid of the voices. When stopped by a policeman, he got into a minor scuffle because the police officer would not believe that voices were coming out of the briefcase. He was charged with robbery and assault on a police officer.

EXAMPLE 2:

A chronically schizophrenic young man was in psychotherapy, and during the course of one session, his therapist observed that he was smoking a great many cigarettes and drinking a very large amount of coffee. His therapist interpreted his anxiety as being related to his sexual inhibitions and stated that if the patient had relationships with a woman, he would not have the need to drink so much coffee and smoke so many cigarettes. Coincidentally, following that therapy session, the patient was involved in some minor infraction of rules on his ward, and the staff put him on coffee and cigarette restriction. In his schizophrenic logic, he took this as the staff's tacit message to him to fulfill what the therapist had suggested to him: namely, to find a woman. The patient wandered over into the woman's ward and attempted to have sexual intercourse with a 75-year-old woman.

Clearly, these cases illustrate the fact that in many situations, an insanity defense is certainly an appropriate choice, though to be sure not the only one, and proponents of this defense argue that if it is abolished, patients like these will be deprived of a very legitimate defense at trial.

RECENT PROPOSALS

Some very recent changes in the laws governing the not guilty by reason of insanity defense have occured in New York State and Illinois.

In the state of Illinois, officials have proposed that the insanity defense be replaced by two alternative pleas. The first is "culpable and mentally disabled." This plea would lead to a period of treatment at a mental health facility, medium or maximum security, followed by a transfer to the Department of Corrections. The second alternative, which in essence replaces the insanity defense, is "mentally disabled, but neither culpable nor innocent." This latter plea would be for a small group of individuals who commit crimes, but commit them in such a mental state that one is unable to clearly assess mental responsibility. These people would be admitted to a mental health facility with no criminal charge. They would be civilly committed and treated in a medium or maximum security facility for as long as necessary, and then discharged to an outpatient treatment setting which would be jointly supervised by psychiatric and judicial authorities. The first half of this Illinois proposal was derived from the state of Michigan, in which the concept was called "guilty but mentally ill." The guilty but mentally ill plea attempted to divorce mental illness and insanity. Under the guilty but mentally ill (Michigan) or the culpable but mentally disabled (Illinois) plea, the jury is instructed beforehand about both legal insanity and mental illness, if the accused pleads insanity, and is told specifically what to listen for during the course of the trial. The jurors then decide whether to return a verdict of not guilty by reason of insanity or a verdict of guilty but mentally ill. If the defense cannot carry the burden of establishing exculpability, the jury is asked simply to decide whether the crime occurred and whether the defendant is currently mentally ill, that is, at the time of the trial. The convicted criminal is then turned over to the correctional system. The treatment for the mental disorder could take place either in a mental hospital or within the prison. If placed in a mental hospital, the prisoner is returned to the prison when treatment is completed to serve out the remainder of the sentence; if he deteriorates in prison, he may be returned to the hospital for treatment.

The Illinois procedure differs from that in Michigan in that the convicted criminal would go to the mental health system first and then to the correctional system. The officials in Illinois felt that by eliminating the concept of insanity, the person was made to feel that he was responsible for his actions, and the treatment program was designed to demonstrate to the individual that he should be responsible.

This same concept has been utilized most persuasively in two recent books. The treatment approach advocated by Yochelson and Samenow in *The Criminal Personality,* [11] the problem of instilling a sense of responsibility for one's own behavior following an acquittal by reason of insanity is discussed extensively. In a similar vein, Fersch, in *Law, Psychology and the Courts,* [12] advocates a period of treatment for mentally ill offenders only *after* time has been served for the offense, clearly divorcing the mental disorder and its treatment from the criminal activity and the need to be responsible for it.

In New York State in 1978, the Department of Mental Hygiene Task Force recommended that the insanity defense be abolished and replaced by a concept of diminished capacity. There had been a dramatic rise in the use of the insanity defense, and it had not been used uniformly throughout the state. Psychiatric testimony was perceived as "ambiguous, superficial and incompetent." Under the diminished capacity ruling, evidence of mental disorder would be admissible only to determine the seriousness of the crime for which the defendant could be tried. Murder, for example, which by definition requires intent or knowledge, could be reduced by the jury to a crime requiring only recklessness, such as manslaughter or criminal negligence, based on psychiatric or psychological testimony. The defendant could be convicted only for a crime that he was *mentally capable* of committing and then would be turned over to the correctional system. In the state of New York, the correctional system was regarded as providing adequate treatment facilities. The role of mental

---

[11] Yochelson, S. and Samenow, S. *The Criminal Personality.* New York: Jason Aronson, 1976.

[12] Fersch, E. *Law, Psychology and the Courts.* Springfield, Ill.: Charles C. Thomas, 1979.

health professionals on a pretrial basis was considerably reduced, with their testimony being limited to the accused's capacity for "intentional or knowing conduct," in other words, making mental illness a mitigating factor in the crime, rather than an exculpating factor.[13]

OTHER RECENT DEVELOPMENTS IN THE INSANITY DEFENSE

In the state of Maryland, a recent class action suit, entitled Dorsey vs. Solomon,[14] guaranteed people acquitted by reason of insanity a second hearing, to determine their need for treatment. This was very similar to the Bolton decision in Washington, D.C.,[15] which stated that the defendant should have a hearing 50 days following an acquittal by reason of insanity to determine the same issue.

In Wisconsin, a bifurcated (split-in-half) trial is used: the first trial to determine if the defendant actually committed the offense and a completely separate trial to assess the issue of criminal responsibility. Several recent cases point to some difficulties in the bifurcation issue.

In Florida, a 1977 bifurcated trial statute was found to violate due process under both the state and the federal constitutions. It was noted that the basis for the diminished capacity dealt with the defendant's inability to form the requisite specific intent to commit the crime. This was not allowed to be introduced until the *second* trial. The bifurcated trial procedure could only be regarded as constitutional when evidence going to the issue of criminal intent was in fact permitted in, rather than excluded from, the initial trial; since the law did not allow evidence of insanity during the guilt or innocence phase of the trial, sanity was in effect presumed, and there was an "irrebuttable presumption of the necessary criminal intent." The state therefore was relieved of its burden of proving each element of the offense beyond a reasonable doubt (one of which, of course, was intent), and this consequently was regarded as unconstitutional.[16] Similar reasoning is evident in cases in Wisconsin and California.

---

[13] These proposals are discussed in more detail in the APA Monitor, April, 1979.

[14] Dorsey vs. Solomon, 435 F. Supp. 725 (D. Md., 604 F.2d 271 (Fourth Circuit) (1977).

[15] Bolton vs. Harris, 395 F.2d 642 (D.C. Circuit 1968).

[16] State ex rel. Boyd vs. Green, No. 52, 678, (Fla. Feb. 16, 1978).

In Wisconsin, the court concluded that the combined effect of the jury instruction on presumed intent, and the exclusion of evidence of incapacity to form specific intent in the first half of a bifurcated trial, resulted in a "conclusive presumption relieving the state of its responsibility to prove one of the crucial facts necessary for a first degree murder case conviction, namely the issue of requisite specific intent."[17] In California, "evidence that rebuts an element of the crime cannot be denied merely because it also suggests insanity."[18]

New Jersey adopted a statute which dealt with the fact that persons found not guilty by reason of insanity possessed the same right to automatic periodic review of their commitment as people who have been civilly committed.[19] This, of course, is consistent with the decisions in Bolton vs. Harris and in Dorsey vs. Solomon, in Washington, D.C., and Maryland, respectively.

In another recent ruling,[20] the California Supreme Court ruled that persons committed to a state institution following an acquittal by reason of insanity cannot be retained in institutional confinement beyond the maximum term of punishment for the underlying offense for which, but for their insanity, they would have been convicted, unless the state can establish that the person remains a danger to the safety of himself or others.

A similar case in the District of Columbia involved an individual named Michael Jones who had been acquitted by reason of insanity on a misdemeanor charge and had filed an appeal of his confinement within the hospital, indicating that he was being confined longer than the period of the maximum sentence had he been convicted. The case was initially denied by the court, but the decision was reversed by a three-judge appellate court, in whose opinion he should be released if not a danger to himself or others. The reversal was appealed by the government, and the entire nine-judge appellate court, in considering the matter en banc, again denied the appeal. The case is currently before the U.S. Supreme Court.[21]

---

[17] Hughes vs. Matthews, 440 F. Supp. 1272 (E.D. Wisc. Sept. 1, 1977).

[18] People vs. Wetmore, 22 Cal 3d 318 (1978).

[19] State vs. Fields, No. A-129 (N.J. July 31, 1978).

[20] In re Moye, 584 P.2d 1097 (California Supreme Court 1978).

[21] Jones vs. United States 411 A.2d 624 (D.C. Court of Appeals 1980).

Similar reasoning is followed in the case of California vs. Words-worth[22] in which Mr. Wordsworth had been found not guilty by reason of insanity of committing a burglary. He was committed to a state hospital and paroled four years later. After eight months his parole was revoked and he was ordered to return to the hospital for further treatment, at which point he appealed. The California Court of Appeals ordered his release, stating that he had already been in confinement longer than the term of punishment would have been had he been convicted.

More recent cases point to some of the difficulties and some of the issues involved in the insanity defense and in the concept of diminished capacity. In Wisconsin,[23] an issue emerged regarding whether or not the same jury should hear the evidence in both parts of a bifurcated trial. At the beginning of the trial to determine guilt, the jury was informed that the defendant pleaded both not guilty and not guilty by reason of a mental disease or defect. The defendant argued that the jury would infer from both pleas a tacit admission of his having committed the offense. The court ruled that inconsistent defenses occur in many areas of the law, and the court made special comparisons to a not guilty/justifiable homicide situation. The court ruled that in the absence of a showing of substantial prejudice, granting a different jury for the second trial was not justified.

Evidence of diminished capacity was found inadmissible in the state of Louisiana. The state, in this case, objected to the admission of testimony made by a defense psychiatrist since the defendant failed to plead not guilty by reason of insanity. The defense stated that the purpose of the doctor's testimony was to show that the defendant did not possess the requisite specific intent to commit the crime, rather than that he was "legally insane." The court agreed with the prosecution's objection and held that the Louisiana criminal code of procedure prohibited evidence of the mental condition at the time of the defense if the defendant's plea was not guilty.[24]

Some recent cases also address themselves to the issues noted earlier in the discussion of the decision in Michigan vs. Cole. In a

---

[22] California vs. Wordsworth, 155 Cal. Rptr. 330 (California Court of Appeals 1979).

[23] Wisconsin vs. Sarinske, 280 N.W.2d 725 (Wisconsin Supreme Court 1979).

[24] Louisiana vs. LeCompt, 371 So. 2d 239 (Louisiana Supreme Court 1978).

recent case in Indiana,[25] the Court of Appeals ruled that the judge may not indicate to the jury what effect different verdicts would have on the confinement of the defendant. However, in Louisiana,[26] it was stated that the jury should be instructed as to the effects of the defendant's confinement if it returned a verdict of not guilty by reason of insanity. Nevertheless, in the state of Iowa,[27] the court held that it was improper to instruct the jury as to the consequences of an insanity verdict.

Regarding the issue of privileged communication in pretrial examinations, the Georgia Supreme Court ruled[28] that the statutory patient/psychiatrist privilege did not apply to the professional relationship established when a court orders a defendant to a state hospital for evaluation and examination. Some recent cases in Alaska and Maryland add another dimension to this issue.

In Alaska, a psychiatric expert who is retained by the defense attorney to investigate the merits of an insanity plea cannot testify as a prosecution witness should the examination results be unfavorable to the defense. The effective assistance of counsel, in respect to the preparation of an insanity defense, demanded recognition that a defendant be as free to communicate with an expert as with the attorney. If the expert is later used as a witness on the behalf of the defendant, "the cloak of privilege" ends, but when the defendant does not call the expert, the same privilege applies with respect to communications from the defendant as applies to such communications to the attorney himself.[29]

In Maryland, a defense psychiatric evaluation, which emerged as unfavorable to the defense, was subpoenaed by the government, and the psychiatrist, under threat of contempt, was forced to testify for the government and be cross-examined by the defense who had initially retained him. The court ruled that it was improper for the state to subpoena these records and to force the psychiatrist to testify.[30]

---

[25] Atkinson vs. Indiana, 391 N.E.2d 1170 (Indiana Court of Appeals 1979).
[26] Louisiana vs. Gurley, 376 So.2d 110 (Louisiana Supreme Court 1979).
[27] Iowa vs. Hamann, 285 N.W.2d 180 (Iowa Supreme Court 1979).
[28] Pierce vs. Georgia, 254 S.E.2d 838 (Georgia Supreme Court 1979).
[29] Houston vs. Alaska, No. 3339 (Alaska Supreme Court Nov. 16, 1979).
[30] State vs. Pratt 284 Md. 516, 398 A.2d. 421 (1979).

Finally, a very interesting issue was recently decided in the District of Columbia Court of Appeals. It modified the ruling in the Whalem case of 1965,[31] which stated that a trial court could interpose a defense of insanity over the objection of the defendant. The new rule in the case of Frendak vs. United States[32] stated that the judge may not impose a defense of insanity over the defendant's objections if a competent defendant "intelligently and voluntarily decides to forego a defense of insanity." A ruling of competence to stand trial did not eliminate the question of the capability of rejecting the insanity defense. Separate issues were involved. In short, a separate hearing as to the defendant's ability to knowingly and voluntarily waive a defense of insanity had to be held.

The judge in the initial Frendak case believed that sufficient question was raised concerning Paula Frendak's mental responsibility for him to apply the Whalem rule which gave him broad discretion. The court weighed the responsibility to prevent the conviction of someone not guilty against the interests of the defendant in choosing to accept a conviction rather than raising a potentially possible insanity defense. Confinement in a mental institution, for instance, could conceivably be for a longer period and have greater stigma and greater consequences attached to it. In this particular case, Ms. Frendak refused an insanity defense because she felt that the hospital was worse than any prison, and in order to avoid institutionalization, she had gone on hunger strikes, attempted suicide, and refused to take medication. If a defendant then, according to the court, has already intelligently and voluntarily decided to forego a defense of insanity, the trial court must defer to his or her decision to waive it. The trial court can still have the discretion to raise an insanity defense *sua sponte* (on its own initiative) when a defendant does not have the capacity to knowingly and intelligently reject the defense of insanity. The court should have the same degree of assurance of this lack of capacity that it has when constitutional rights are waived in other circumstances such as plea bargaining. The conclusion, to quote the court, is that "whenever the evidence suggests a substantial question of the defendant's sanity at the time of the crime, the trial

---

[31] Whalem vs. United States, 346 F.2d 812 (D.C. Circuit 1965).
[32] Frendak vs. United States, 408 A.2d 364 (D.C. Court of Appeals 1979).

judge must conduct an inquiry designed to assure that the defendant had been fully informed of the alternatives available, comprehends the consequences of failing to assert the defense of insanity, and freely chooses to raise or waive that defense. Sometimes, simply questioning the defendant will suffice, and at other times additional information and psychiatric examination may be necessary."

In practical terms, once again, we must ask what constitutes a "voluntary and knowing waiver" of the insanity defense. The following illustrations may assist in defining the terms.

EXAMPLE 1:

The patient was charged with an armed rape that clearly bore the imprint of his mental illness. The judge was considering imposing an insanity defense over the defendant's objections. In an evidentiary hearing, the defendant indicated that he did not want to utilize an insanity defense because if found not guilty by reason of insanity, he would probably spend more time in a mental hospital than he would in a prison. The judge ruled that such a rationale constituted a "knowing and voluntary waiver" and did not impose an insanity defense *sua sponte*.

EXAMPLE 2:

The patient was charged with a bank robbery, in which there was a gross misperception of reality based on a delusional system. The judge was hearing the evidence relative to an insanity defense. The defendant indicated that he was rejecting an insanity defense because he was not insane, that any attempt on the part of the judge to impose an insanity defense was evidence of the judge's being part of the conspiracy against him, and that he had committed the crime in an attempt to expose corrupt officials "just like the judge." The judge ruled that these reasons were not rational and did not constitute a "knowing and intelligent waiver"; he did impose an insanity defense over the defendant's objection.

In short, it appears that the examiner must determine, regardless of the nature of the mental disorder, the *extent* to which the mental disorder specifically impacts on the patient's reasoning capacities as regards the decision to utilize an insanity defense.

3
Practical Parameters of the Criminal Responsibility Evaluation

While Chapter 2 dealt with the theoretical and historical background of the insanity defense, this chapter will address itself to the concrete practicalities of performing criminal responsibility evaluations. It will provide guidelines for the dimensions that need to be addressed when making these assessments.

BEYOND A TRADITIONAL CLINICAL APPROACH

One of the points repeatedly made in the discussion of the abolition of the insanity defense is the fact that one never really knows what a person was like at the time of the offense. Many critics and opponents of the insanity defense therefore argue that examiners should not render any opinions whatsoever on criminal responsibility.

There are, however, many secondary sources upon which we can (and should) draw that are helpful and provide some sense of what indeed was going on at the time of the offense. It should be a rule of thumb, for anyone doing a criminal responsibility evaluation, never to prepare a report without first reviewing a complete police report, as well as statements from as many of the government's witnesses as possible, people who saw what transpired. In their own lay language they can tell how the person was behaving at the time of the offense. The defense, as well, needs to be approached for whatever insight can be provided in terms of interviews with family members, friends, etc. Of course, some practical difficulties are often encountered in terms of what parts of the data are discoverable, especially in an adversary system in which the expert is retained by one side or the other. Nevertheless, a determined effort should be made, on the part of the expert witness, to obtain as much of this information as one possibly can.

EXAMPLE:

A patient was admitted to the hospital, acutely psychotic, and required massive doses of psychotropic medication to sedate him. He had been in jail for about two months after the offense before he was admitted to the hospital. Based on that time discrepancy alone, one must evaluate whether or not there was any difference between his behavior noted at the time of the offense and his behavior at the time of examination, rather than merely assuming that since the patient appeared acutely psychotic at the time of admission, he must have been so at the time of the offense. In point of fact, the government had several witnesses who gave a rather different account of the offense from that of the patient in his delusional and psychotic state two months later. The material clearly indicated that the patient manifested no signs of psychosis at the time of the offense, but apparently had suffered an acute psychotic episode while in jail following his arrest. He had decompensated, in other words, during that two-month period of time in jail, and by any legal test, he was responsible for his behavior at the time of the offense.

As noted in this example, witness statements and police reports are highly relevant to ascertaining the nature of the behavior at the time of the offense. In addition, the expert witness should attempt to gain access to any medical records, or even anecdotal behavioral entries in the patient's chart at the jail, during the time of his waiting for admission.

Frequently, one observes a somewhat related phenomenon. Because many jails and correctional facilities are stressful environments, the patient may appear acutely psychotic in that setting, but once he is admitted to the hospital, his behavior may rapidly and dramatically improve. One of the common features of jail life, in addition to the "sensory deprivation," is homosexual acting out; frequently, the patient is admitted to the hospital in an acute homosexual panic, with many paranoid fears. Once he is in the more secure setting, he may undergo a spontaneous remission. One needs to evaluate his history carefully regarding the presence or absence of psychosis in the past, to determine whether this is merely an acute situational stress reaction to the conditions in the jail, or to the fact that he was perhaps sexually approached or sexually assaulted in jail. As noted, one should not fall into the trap of inferring that the behavior one sees at the time of examination is the same behavior which occurred at the time of the offense. Very likely it could be post-arrest behavior resulting from some sort of deterioration or decompensation, or on the other hand, there may be a certain restitutive process which occurs once the individual is placed in a hospital. That is, he may have been psychotic at the time of the offense but be psychically intact at the time of the evaluation. Whenever possible, as noted earlier, one should attempt to get jail records, interview the jail staff regarding the patient's behavior within that setting, and compare that behavior with the statements from family, from witnesses to the offense, and from the police reports.

EXAMPLE:

A patient had been charged with assault with intent to kill and with bank robbery several days subsequent to the assault. A psychologist retained by the defense completed an initial evaluation of the patient, finding him to be overtly psychotic, and reasoned that since psychosis represents a breakdown in an individual's ability to control impulses and exert appropriate judgment, the two crimes committed nine months earlier were causally related to the psychosis. No witnesses to either offense were interviewed.

An expert retained by the government also examined the patient and concluded that he was overtly psychotic at the time of examination, but felt that inferring that his condition nine months earlier at the time of the offense was the same was unwarranted; the expert proceeded to interview many witnesses to the patient's behavior around the time of the offense. First, the patient's mother was interviewed: she indicated that when her son had psychotic episodes, they were consistently characterized by withdrawal, seclusiveness, fearfulness, and a sense of preoccupation; *at no time were his actions during the psychotic episodes characterized by aggressive behavior.*

The victim of the assault was then interviewed. He was a retired police officer who had, in his career, transported "hundreds" of patients to the local state hospital for treatment. He was well aware of the variety of symptoms manifested by acutely psychotic patients and indicated that the defendant was angry, but in no way manifesting any signs of psychosis.

Two bank tellers who were present at the scene of the bank robbery indicated that the patient, at the time of the robbery, appeared "nervous" but did not seem to be preoccupied, distractible, or responding to any imaginary forces.

A variety of hospital records were reviewed, which revealed that during psychotic episodes, the patient appeared to be confused and "drifty" (i.e., seeming to be in a daze), and at times manifested inappropriate sexual behavior (i.e., exposing himself and masturbating in the presence of female staff members). Once again, no aggressive or hostile behavior, consistent with assault, was ever documented.

Interview with the patient's treating psychiatrist (the patient was on a one-day pass at the time of the first offense and had been expelled from the hospital because of inappropriate sexual behavior at the time of the second offense) revealed, again, no evidence of assaultiveness or of any apparent "command hallucinations" which might relate to aggressive behavior. In fact, the psychiatrist noted that at the time of the offenses, the patient was not on medication, because of several side effects that had been noted, and that he appeared to be far more alert, coherent, and goal oriented when off medication. According to the doctor, the only symptom was the patient's inappropriate sexual acting out.

Following the patient's arrest, he was "bounced around" among approximately six different hospitals and correctional facilities, and appeared to deteriorate grossly at that time; his condition was diagnosed at one hospital, during this time period, as schizophrenia, catatonic type.

The second psychologist concluded, based on this analysis, that there was no evidence of psychosis at the time of the offenses which would be consistent with the behavior noted, but that the bizarre symptomatology manifested itself *following* the commission of the offenses and that therefore, under the law, the patient was criminally responsible though presently psychotic.

This example highlights the necessity for careful investigatory work in forensic evaluations to determine whether or not the behavior observed in the current examination is consistent with the behavior at the time of the offense. In this case, since the patient had been hospitalized, it was also noteworthy that none of the symptoms he manifested in the past were consistent with his criminal behavior. The case also points out the dangers of assuming that the current clinical impressions are consistent with the behavior at the time of the offense.

One of the issues which constantly plagues people attempting to perform criminal responsibility evaluations is the relationship of the behavior at the time of the offense to a particular mental disorder. Especially problematic are cases in which the patient is clearly mentally ill, but the mental illness appears to be unrelated to the offense. Frequently, the expert witness is under some pressure from an attorney to say that in a very broad sense, a person's mental disorder led him to a certain kind of predisposition which would in turn lead him to commit a certain kind of crime, and so on in endless progression. One of the most frequent examples of this is the individual who has so-called self-destructive behavior. Frequently, attorneys will attempt to relate such self-destructive tendencies to the fact that individuals commit crimes in order to be caught. While this is certainly a possibility, it does not approach the legal criteria for the utilization of the insanity defense. The expert should always remain close to the data available, close to the behavior observed at the time of the offense, and should not try to make large inferential leaps. One might certainly say, in many of these cases, that the person's apprehension, but not the crime itself, was related to his mental disorder. One might argue in response to this that a person could not be caught unless he committed a crime, but it is important to note that there are many ways of obtaining punishment, other than committing crimes.

It cannot be stressed too strongly that the facts should not be twisted, nor should theories be manipulated, if the evaluation and the criminal behavior do not yield consistent conclusions. On occasion this becomes very difficult, and at times the expert witness feels hampered by narrow legal standards.

EXAMPLE:

A man in his midthirties was charged with sexual molestation of his two teenage sons and, upon examination, indicated that what he was doing was performing a valuable service because he was teaching them about sexuality. In reviewing this statement, the examiner felt that the individual must have a gross defect in judgment, most likely of psychotic proportions, to really believe that he was assisting his children in learning about sexuality. However, the evaluation, including complete psychological testing, was completely negative regarding the presence of any thought disorder. It certainly pointed to the fact that the individual was suffering from a fairly severe anxiety neurosis, but there was no distortion of his thinking, no evidence of a psychotic process, and the report to the court stated that though he suffered from an anxiety neurosis, a diagnosable illness, it did not appear to have any relationship to the offense. His description of the offense clearly showed evidence of impaired judgment, but the judgment was not impaired to a psychotic degree. The report to the court did not attempt to determine the outcome of the case and the disposition of the individual. Certainly, however, the man was clearly in need of treatment, and this was stated in the report, without trying to manipulate the situation so that he would fall into the purview of an insanity defense.

Another difficult area often involves individuals who are charged with a variety of sexual offenses. Inevitably, when one examines such individuals, there is some disturbance in their sexual identity formation, but this is once again a far cry from saying that they possess a mental disease or defect which substantially impaired their understanding of the wrongfulness of their offense, or impaired their ability to conform their behavior to the law.

As a final example, a neurotic, insecure, late adolescent was involved in 18 armed robberies because he had a friend who was a "big gangster type," and he reveled in the identity of a big gangster, going along on all of the armed robberies with his friend. He even dressed the part, with black shirt, white tie, and pin-striped suit. He was, to be sure, getting "an ego trip" out of participating in the robberies, but again that did not approximate the legal criteria for substantial impairment of behavioral controls or of mental and emotional processes. The defendant was working through a severe adolescent identity crisis, and this was reported to the court; it was not the same, however, as insanity under the applicable legal standard.

Another area of difficulty frequently encountered is the diagnosis of a so-called latent condition. Often, one sees the latent mental disorder on the psychological testing, but it is not apparent in day-to-day behavior or in clinical interviews. One may be of the opinion that given certain kinds of stress, perhaps the stress the individual was under at the time of the offense, the psychosis may have been manifest, and that since the time of the offense, the individual has gone into a state of partial remission. How does one diagnose — and what does one say to the court — in such a case, since one cannot be sure of whether or not the underlying or latent psychosis was manifest?

If one has a fairly complete police report and witness statements, one can make an informed estimate of the degree of disturbance at the time of the offense. One should try to assess the probability, stating that "given this kind of stressful situation, it is conceivable (or likely, or highly likely) that his controls were much weakened." In other words, what appears to be a latent process at the present time was most likely far more manifest at the time of the offense, and the patient is currently in some degree of remission. This is not an evasion of the issue but rather a direct statement that "this is what we see now, and it appears to have been somewhat different at the time of the offense." Of course, not having been present at the offense, we cannot really tell, and we need to phrase our opinion in terms of probabilities.

Along these same lines, a particularly interesting problem arises with a specific diagnostic category, namely, manic-depressive psychosis. Frequently, when one sees a manic-depressive in between episodes, one may see virtually no signs of psychopathology. This is an extremely critical point because, in a cursory examination in which one does not carefully evaluate a person's history, one may not see any signs of psychopathology; thus one does not think about the fact that the person may well have been disturbed at some time in the past. A diagnosis may be made of "no mental disorder" based on the manner of self-presentation at the time of the examination. This may be doing the patient a terrible disservice. If one has evidence of something that sounds very bizarre in the past, and absolutely no evidence of any current psychopathology emerges, one needs to seriously consider the possibility of a manic-depressive illness. Certainly, one of the prime diagnostic indicators of this is a family history of affective disorder.

EXAMPLE:

A patient was screened for admission to the hospital in the jail; he looked bizarre and acutely psychotic. By the time that he was admitted to the hospital, he looked perfectly intact, and the examiner came to the conclusion, based on subsequent history, that the patient was a manic-depressive who was between episodes at the time of admission to the hospital. The patient went back to court, was released on bond, became acutely psychotic, and was readmitted; then one had the opportunity to see the patient's condition when he was "high." He was impulsive, euphoric, and hyperactive, and showed all of the symptomatology that one associates with an acute manic episode.

THE COMPLEXITY OF THE DELUSION

A case was described in an earlier chapter, regarding competency to stand trial, of an individual who, because of his mental illness, had refused to allow his lawyers and his doctors to interview his wife, with this refusal resulting in his incompetence to stand trial. The same case, however, illustrated a very critical point in reference to the issue of criminal responsibility, namely, the complexity of the delusional system and the change of a delusional system over time.

The crime itself, a murder, had actually occurred six years prior to the evaluation. The patient had never been apprehended because, following the offense, he had left the Washington, D.C., area and had gone to live in Philadelphia. He was involved in a traffic accident in Philadelphia, and when the officer who was taking the police report ran a routine computer check on him, it was found that there was an outstanding murder warrant for this individual. This happened, as already noted, approximately six years after the offense. Examiners were faced with the problem of evaluating criminal responsibility in an individual who had committed a crime six years earlier. When the patient was admitted, he was acutely psychotic, bizarre, and delusional, having elaborate, grandiose ideas about how he had developed a "hydro-compression machine" which was capable of artificially growing vast quantities of marijuana within a pressure chamber. Because of this, he felt that the Black Muslims wanted the machine so that they could peddle all of the marijuana he produced in the ghetto area of Washington, D.C. He had refused to sell the machine and thought therefore that the Black Muslims had been persecuting him. He also felt that the man that he killed was a "hit man" for the Muslims. That was his motivation for killing this man, because the Muslims wanted to take away his hydro-compression machine.

This case illustrates the difficulty in immediately leaping to a conclusion about the relevance of a contemporary delusional system to thinking at the time of the offense. Everyone in his family indicated that he had never expressed these delusional beliefs at the time of the offense, and indeed, the current talk about hydro-compression machines and Black Muslim conspiracies was a recent development. His belief that the Muslims wanted to take away his machine was his motivation for the murder. In short, based on the data gathered at the time, the patient had committed the offense and had reconstructed his motivations in a psychotic manner.

It was a very difficult task to tease out exactly when the delusional thinking began, when this individual appeared to deteriorate, and what (if any) kind of disorder was manifest at the time of the offense or prior to the offense. As noted, the patient was very guarded and evasive, and would not allow the hospital staff access to his wife or to any of the people who might help with his defense.

It became apparent, once access was granted to his wife, that this individual was indeed delusional at the time of the offense, but it had been a completely *different* delusional system. He had perceived a "down-and-out" alcoholic in the street and stated, "Here comes my father, I'm going to get him before he can get me"; then he shot the man several times. His history clearly revealed that his father had been an alcoholic, who frequently abused him both verbally and physically, and that many of the decedent's actions and behavior patterns while under the influence of alcohol unconsciously reminded the patient of his father.

What is critical to note in this case is that the entire delusional system which initially alerted the staff to the possibility of an insanity defense was not at all the same delusional system operating at the time of the offense. One needs to be exceedingly careful about what inferences one draws at any particular point in time.

THE IMPORTANCE OF PHYSICAL EVIDENCE

Very frequently, when the psychologist enters the forensic area, he/she is made quite uncomfortable by the need to consider carefully the physical evidence involved in the offense. That is, the expert, especially the novice, feels that his or her work should somehow go on in a more rarefied atmosphere than that in which a police investigation is carried on. In many cases, however, for an effective forensic evaluation to be done, the physical evidence must clearly be evaluated and considered before an opinion can be rendered.

EXAMPLE 1:

A person who had recently been released from jail was in a bar and allowed himself to be picked up by a homosexual, for money. They contracted that he would obtain some money if he would perform some homosexual act on that individual. Once back in the man's apartment, they apparently got into a fight, and during the course of the fight, the defendant grabbed the homosexual individual and threw him out of a three-story window; the man was killed in the fall. One of the pieces of physical evidence that was very striking was that there were bite marks all over the victim's body. During the course of examination, there was no evidence whatsoever of any mental disorder. The patient appeared to have a character disorder, most likely antisocial or passive/aggressive. At the time of trial, he presented a defense, through a defense psychiatrist, which he called "acute homosexual panic." In theory, acute homosexual panic occurs in individuals who have deeply repressed homosexual feelings and for whom the arousal of these feelings is so threatening that they act out in violent ways. In these cases, they lose behavioral controls and may be capable of exceedingly violent activity. The teeth marks noted were accounted for by the defendant, who stated that during the course of the fighting he had bitten the other individual a number of times. From the point of view of physical evidence, a forensic odontologist (dentist) had examined the teeth marks and offered the expert opinion on the witness stand that these marks represented passion bites, rather than aggressive bites that would have been sustained in the course of a fight.

Therefore, combining the physical evidence, the results of the evaluation, and the theory regarding the sort of personality that would experience homosexual panic led to the following determination: if the patient voluntarily engaged in a homosexual act, which he obviously did by contracting with the individual and by passionately biting him, it was clear that he could not have experienced a homosexual panic; his personality structure was inconsistent with that of a person subject to such panics. The man was regarded as responsible for his actions because he was voluntarily engaging in an act and was not in any panic state. His throwing the individual out of the window had nothing to do with any "panic."

EXAMPLE 2:

A rather difficult and involved case had to do with a patient charged with murder, who had had a history of epileptic seizures as well as a chronic history of alcoholism. He had been in another man's apartment and was charged with stabbing the man many times. The cause of death was listed as exsanguination. The defense was based on the fact that the man had some form of seizure activity precipitated by the alcohol, either a temporal lobe seizure in which he lost control and killed the individual or, consistent with some earlier medical records, an episode of postictal violence, that is, in the phase immediately following the seizure. It has been observed that if one tries to move a patient too rapidly before he emerges from the comatose, stuporous state following seizure activity, he may explode into rather violent and aggressive behavior of a diffuse variety. The defense was trying to establish this as the grounds for a lack of criminal responsibility. During a previous hospitalization, when the hospital staff had tried to move the patient too soon after his seizures, he had indeed gone "absolutely wild." There was documentation of this man's unusual strength: pushing the doctors aside, holding the nurses at bay, and throwing chairs and wastebaskets around the hospital room.

The physical evidence became very critical because there was a pattern to the stab wounds and to the location of the trail of blood in the apartment. The pattern of blood indicated that it was not at all the wild, random, purposeless, thrashing movement that someone experiencing a temporal lobe seizure might have had; rather, there was clear physical evidence that the defendant chased the man from room to room. Of course, in addition, there is the well-documented fact that violent behavior associated with seizure activity is exceedingly rare.

The interplay of knowledge of behavior typical of a temporal lobe seizure, or a postical state, with the physical evidence, and the inconsistency of the pattern of bloodstains with that expected if a seizure had occurred, were very critical in this case.

Another striking aspect of this case was that the police report contained a statement which the defendant made to the police very shortly after the stabbing. This statement was exceedingly coherent, and had the patient indeed been in a stuporous state following a seizure, he would not have been able to make such a coherent statement. Therefore, by process of elimination, the opinion was that most likely he was not having a seizure at that point in time. This was again one of those cases in which there was a documented history both of a seizure disorder and of severe alcoholism, but there was no apparent relationship of the mental defect (the seizure disorder) to the offense. It appeared that the patient's excessive consumption of alcohol, rather than any seizure activity, may well have been the precipitant of the stabbing.

THE PROBLEM OF DRUGS AND ALCOHOL

There is a great temptation, when dealing with an individual who appears to have had a long history of alcoholism and who speaks about heavy drinking at the time of the offense, to attribute the offense merely to the fact that the patient was intoxicated. This can pose difficulties itself if careful interview of witnesses is not also carried out.

EXAMPLE:

In a homicide case, an interview with the patient revealed the patient's perception that he was drinking heavily and that this was the precipitant for his killing the decedent. In interviewing the patient's sister who had been with him close to the time of the offense, it emerged that the patient had not been drinking at that time but had actually stopped drinking three or four days prior to the offense. His sister also reported a number of bizarre symptoms, including many visual and auditory hallucinations, which occurred following the termination of the drinking. Therefore, what initially appeared to be merely a case of alcoholism became an issue involving delirium tremens at the time of the offense. Indeed the ultimate opinion was changed: it was concluded that the man was in an acute psychotic state, delirium tremens, at the time of the offense and was actively hallucinating, rather than merely being intoxicated. This indicates that when one encounters an alcohol related crime, one should attempt to obtain secondary sources that can either substantiate or contradict the individual's own recognition and memory of what happened, especially since confabulation regarding time sequence frequently occurs in an alcoholic's reconstruction of events. One needs to ascertain when the alcohol was imbibed in relationship to the offense.

A somewhat related issue deals with the concept of a drug induced psychosis, a diagnosis which is becoming more and more prevalent these days, especially due to the proliferation of powerful hallucinogenic drugs. The law in most states, at the present time, does not allow for the raising of an insanity defense based solely on a psychosis induced by drugs. One must show that there was at least a potential for psychosis, an underlying mental disease or defect, which was brought to the surface by the drug or which was exacerbated by the drug. Some case law describes this as an illness that manifests itself even after the drug is out of the person's system. A psychosis that is created "out of whole cloth" by the drug is not regarded as grounds for an acquittal by reason of insanity. What this suggests is that when one does an evaluation on any case in which a drug induced psychosis is suspected, one must first wait for the acute psychotic symptoms to clear and then perform a careful evaluation, including neurological workup, and a complete battery of psychological and neuropsychological testing, so that one may state whether or not there was an underlying mental disease or defect which may have interacted with the drug. In the report to the court, if such a careful evaluation does not reveal the presence of an underlying mental disease or defect, one might state that while the patient was suffering from a drug induced psychosis at the time of the offense and behavioral controls were substantially impaired, there was no evidence of an underlying mental disease or defect. If, on the other hand, there is an underlying psychosis or underlying organic brain syndrome, one would indicate that the patient is diagnosed as having a drug induced psychosis and that this represents an underlying mental disease or defect, which in all likelihood was exacerbated by his ingestion of the drug. The ultimate issue is left up to the trier of fact, namely, the judge or the jury. The examiner indicates in the report the limits of expertise: namely, that there was an underlying mental disease or defect, if there was, and whether or not the behavioral controls were substantially impaired. It is up to the court to determine whether or not, in the legal sense, this combination in effect constitutes exculpability. The complete evaluation is performed and the facts are laid out for the court.

THE USE AND MISUSE OF NEUROLOGICAL DATA

The relationship of neurological dysfunction to various forms of violent behavior is, as we have noted, an area that is currently hotly debated. A growing body of literature suggests that violent behavior, especially when it is episodic, explosive, and out of all proportion to the provocation, can be a manifestation of what is currently called the episodic dyscontrol syndrome.[1] On the other hand, there have been attempts, roundly criticized by many neurologists, to link a variety of maladaptive, antisocial behaviors to various forms of brain dysfunction.

A recent case in which neurological and neuropsychological data came to be quite important is described:

EXAMPLE:

A young man had been charged with a rather brutal homicide. He strangled a woman, apparently following minimal provocation,

---

[1] Monroe, R. *Brain Dysfunction in Aggressive Criminals.* Cambridge: Lexington Books, 1978.

and while the woman was lying on the floor dying, he heard a gurgling sound coming from her throat. He perceived the gurgling sound as her laughing at him, proceeded to mutilate the body, and then jumped up and down on her until her rib cage was crushed.

At the time of the initial trial, the government psychiatrist, who had spent over 12 hours of clinical interview with the individual, concluded that the man was an explosive personality. The defense psychiatrists, feeling that the behavior was bizarre, diagnosed the patient as suffering from a gross stress reaction but were unable to specify the precipitating stress. A military jury convicted the patient.

Following a change in the standard for insanity from the McNaughten test to one approximating the ALI Model Penal Code, the case was reopened. The man was reexamined, and the rather bizarre aspects of the case were again taken into consideration. This, coupled with a history of head trauma, overresponse to minor provocation, and many verbal statements made by the individual, concerning strange bodily sensations and perceptual distortions, suggested the need for a full neurological workup. According to this workup, the patient did indeed have a central nervous system dysfunction consistent with episodic dyscontrol. The examination consisted, in addition to a neurological exam, of a series of base-line and activated electroencephalograms, a CAT scan, and complete neuropsychological testing.

In a subsequent trial, the evidence of all of the neurological dysfunction was presented, and in its deliberations, the jury returned a verdict of involuntary manslaughter, substantially less severe than the verdict of second degree murder which had been returned in the initial case.

While this was a case in which neurological workup and input were quite appropriate, there are frequent cases in which the neurological input is misused. An illustration of this involves an individual who had a long, documented history of brain damage. As a result of some prior injury, the patient had a Teflon plate in his head. He had been described as epileptic. However, the offense with which the individual was charged, was a well-planned, profit oriented offense.

The man was charged with armed robbery of a fast-food restaurant; after his escape from the restaurant, he led police officers on a high-speed chase down several streets. Eventually, he ran his car into a telephone pole, jumped out of the car, and proceeded to fire at several police officers. Witnesses described his shooting at the officers as highly accurate, not at all consistent with the impairment that one might expect from this degree of brain damage. An expert retained by the defense attributed the patient's behavior to a "complex partial seizure," and the patient was acquitted by reason of insanity. The reasoning of this expert was that the injury had been in the left temporal area of the brain, an area responsible for judgment. According to the expert, the patient manifested his illness by attempting an armed robbery in broad daylight, showing "poor judgment," and therefore the crime was felt to be causally related to the brain damage. Here again, as seen on so many previous occasions, there existed a critical need to evaluate the "fit" of the offense with the nature of the mental disease or defect. If the two do not coincide, then one should not try to "stretch" the facts of the offense to fit the disorder (as this expert did) or stretch the disorder to fit the facts. Rather, the expert witness will maintain his credibility most by stating that there is a mental disease or defect, but there does not appear to be any clear relationship of it to the particular offense.

THE PROBLEM OF MULTIPLE MOTIVATIONS

Another area that is sometimes problematic involves the individual who appears to have something genuinely "wrong," in the sense of suffering from a psychosis, with the psychosis being in some ways relevant to the offense, but who also has what appear to be other motivations, perhaps sociopathic in nature, perhaps oriented toward profit or self-gain. In performing the evaluation, the examiner sees both aspects of the diagnostic picture and is frequently in the position of needing to "tease out" the two of them: Was the crime related more to the sociopathy or to the psychosis? This situation frequently occurs with a patient who has had psychotic episodes but whose life-style, when in remission, appears to be that of a sociopathic individual. The question always arises, what was he like at the time of the offense? In reconstructing this, if the patient looks more sociopathic at the time one talks to him, does that mean that he was sociopathic at the time of the offense, or was he psychotic? If he looks psychotic at the present time (i.e., at the time of examination), can one be reasonably certain that he was psychotic at the time of the offense, or was he in remission at that time and acting in a sociopathic manner?

EXAMPLE:

A patient was charged with 27 counts of defrauding airlines under an assumed name. He would call up the airlines, order an airline ticket, type out an address label, and place it on a mailbox; the airline would send him the ticket in the mail. He would take the ticket, remove the address sticker from the mailbox, and leave the country. The patient went through about 30 different pseudonyms and flew all over the world.

On initial contact and after an initial reading of his police report, it appeared that this was an excellent "con game." The patient was able to fly all over the world, make substantial sums of money, and on occasion sell the tickets to other people for a price. On interview, the patient admitted to defrauding the airlines, but stated that it was all because a certain individual was pursuing him all over the world; indeed, the patient presented a fairly convincing picture, both on interview and on psychological testing, of a seriously disturbed individual. The patient honestly believed that someone was pursuing him all over the world. This man, according to the patient, had pursued him as far as Australia and had started influencing the owner of a television station in Australia so that the news announcer was "signifying" at him over television. The patient went to the television station, walked in while the television announcer was on the air, grabbed him around the neck, and threatened to slit his throat unless he stopped taking orders from this man who was pursuing him. The patient was charged with the offense, spent some time in jail, and was released. Following his release, he firebombed the producer's home. He was found not guilty by reason of insanity, once again because of the delusion of the individual pursuing him all over the world.

In summary, this appeared to be a valid delusional system and, at the same time, had a tremendous profit motive. One needs to ask whether the crime was a result of the mental illness or a result of the individual's sociopathic maneuvering. In looking at it from both points of view, the opinion reached was that the evidence was more on the side of the psychosis than on the side of the sociopathy, and the man was found not guilty by reason of insanity. Certainly, it could have been argued with equal validity from the opposite point of view.

What appeared most striking about this case is that several years after the acquittal by reason of insanity, the patient appeared to be in total remission and indicated, in his sociopathic way, that the entire story was a "con game" and that he never was mentally ill. He claimed that he had made up the story of his pursuer in order to "beat the rap." While one can take the new story at face value, it may also be necessary to ask whether or not this denial that he was ever mentally ill is indeed a valid statement. All too often, when a patient denies a previous mental illness, one leaps to the conclusion that the denial is a valid statement and that the mental illness never was. However, the denial itself can frequently be far from genuine.

Another case illustrates a similar difficulty.

EXAMPLE:

An individual robbed a bank, and one of his motives was a profit one. On the other hand, he had a variety of fantasies that he was doing the bank employees a favor. He stated, in support of this latter contention, that because there is so much confusion following a bank robbery, when the insurance money is later received it is very easy for the bank employees to embezzle the money with so many funds changing hands. He indicated that he felt, therefore, that he was doing a favor for the employees. He also indicated that since most of the tellers were women, they would get a "sexual charge" out of the bank robbery, because they would also think that he was interested in raping them and they would be titillated by this fantasy. Separating out which appeared to be the more dominant motive of his crime — whether it was the profit motive or the bizarre, somewhat delusional motive — became a difficult task.

THE REFUSAL OF A VALID INSANITY DEFENSE

As noted in the discussion of the recent Frendak decision (Chapter 2), there is more and more sensitivity on the part of the courts to the issue of a patient, for whatever reason, rejecting what would appear to be a valid insanity defense. The court has generally decided that an evidentiary hearing must be held, in which a patient's refusal of an insanity defense is examined to see whether or not it is based on rational or irrational beliefs. The expert witness may well wonder exactly what dimensions have to be considered in evaluating the question of rational or irrational. An example of an irrational belief would be the patient's insistence that he was indeed not mentally ill and that the entire attempt ·to discuss an insanity defense was a conspiracy against him. On the other hand, one might view a valid rejection of an insanity defense as grounded in the defendant's awareness that the period of commitment is indefinite (as opposed to the more definite term were he convicted) or that he would be stigmatized as mentally ill for the rest of his life. One needs to be increasingly aware of this dimension in the course of doing criminal responsibility evaluations, since more and more courts are asking for opinions on this matter. The court's question is frequently phrased in the language of the Frendak decision, namely, whether the individual can intelligently and rationally waive a defense of insanity if such a defense is appropriate. Frequently, one must distinguish the fact that a patient may be acutely psychotic, yet have valid and rational reasons for rejecting a defense of insanity. As discussed before, the fact that someone is mentally ill does not necessarily mean that the reason for rejecting an insanity defense is grounded in that mental illness. It is similar to the reasoning that if a person appears mentally ill at the time of the evaluation, this does not necessarily mean that he or she was mentally ill at the time of the offense.

When a patient raises a defense of not guilty by reason of insanity and is subsequently acquitted by reason of insanity, then the burden of proof in terms of release from the hospital is on him; that is, he must prove by a preponderance of evidence that he is no longer mentally ill, or a danger to himself or to others. On the other hand, when a defense of insanity is imposed *sua sponte* (on the judge's own initiative over the defendant's objections), then the burden of proof shifts to the hospital, and the criterion for keeping the person confined is far more stringent. That is, the hospital must prove beyond a reasonable doubt, a far more stringent standard than preponderance of evidence, that the patient is mentally ill and, by virtue of the mental illness, a danger to himself and others. When performing such an evaluation, the mental health expert must be aware of the more stringent standard and base a decision for continued treatment on demonstrable proof of dangerous behavior, rather than on a mere presumption of future acting out.

THE ROLE OF THE EXPERT WITNESS

As has been noted, there are many critics who feel that mental health practitioners have no business entering the legal system and that their analyses of criminal responsibility are no more accurate than those of a layman. It would be appropriate, at this point, to summarize some of the major situations in which opinions can and should, according to this author, be rendered, and then offer a conceptual scheme which may help increase the reliability of different experts.

The first criterion, as has been suggested, is that the patient appears able to reconstruct his mental and emotional experience at the time of the offense. When the patient is able to perform such a reconstruction, it can be of great benefit, as was noted in the case of the individual who was told by his therapist that rather than smoking cigarettes and drinking coffee, he should "get himself a woman." In reviewing this example, the reconstruction of the logic which the patient followed, in carrying out his criminal activity, was clearly related to his mental disorder.

The nature of this reconstruction, of course, should be tempered by an evaluation of the degree of retrospective falsification in the patient's presentation: namely, whether he is more or less disturbed at the time of the evaluation than at the time of the offense.

Another criterion involves the necessity of correlating long-term observations of a patient's behavior with his behavior at the time of the offense. This is most ideally achieved when one has the opportunity to observe a patient for a substantial period of time on an inpatient service. In the absence of this, one must have available to oneself at the time of examination, complete records of the patient's behavior while in the hospital or while incarcerated in a correctional setting. In such cases it becomes possible to state whether the typical behavior observed when the individual is psychotic is consistent or inconsistent with the kind of behavior exhibited at the time of the offense.

Somewhat correlated with the previous criterion is a situation in which the patient's responses to psychological testing provide a microcosmic description of his behavior in various situations of stress, which can in turn be correlated with his behavior at the time of the offense.

One also needs to have access, as noted earlier, to a comprehensive description from secondary sources of the defendant's behavior around the time of the offense.

Finally, a comprehensive description of the physical evidence and its "fit" or "lack of fit" with the particular mental disorder presented must be considered. If all of these criteria can be satisfied, then one has a reliable and valid basis for inferring a person's state of mind at the time of the offense, even if the offense occurred some time in the past. An important point is that if these criteria cannot be satisfied, then the expert witness should reserve the option of informing the court that not enough data are available to render an informed decision. Not only does this enhance the credibility of the expert witness, but it can serve to heighten reliability among the different experts involved in the evaluation and detract from the so-called battle of the experts.

With these underlying criteria met, one may then move to a conceptual scheme for the assessment of criminal responsibility, which can further heighten the reliability of the assessments made of an individual by different expert witnesses.

The basic assumption underlying the conceptual scheme is that the closer the mental illness is to the person's actual criminal behavior, the more likely the mental illness is to be producing the behavior. If, for example, a patient sees an individual walking towards him on the street and feels that the man is "after him" and that he, the patient, needs to kill the man in order to protect himself, this would be regarded in our conceptualization as a Stage One relationship, in other words, a direct link of the delusional system to the criminal behavior.

A Stage Two relationship would characterize the situation in which the delusional system impacts on the behavior but in a somewhat more indirect manner, or to rephrase it, there are more intervening variables.

EXAMPLE:

A young man examined several years ago felt that he had heard God's voice telling him that there were devils in the United States Senate and that what he needed to do was to proclaim the Kingdom of Heaven on earth. In order to do so, he decided to take a senator hostage and, with his machete, threaten to cut off the senator's head unless everyone in the Senate changed and listened to his proclamations. This would be regarded as a Stage Two relationship, in the sense that it is not quite as direct as a patient assaulting another individual because of a paranoid delusion. In this second example, the idea of using a machete was the patient's reconstruction of what God's voice instructed him to do. Nevertheless, the reconstruction itself was certainly grounded in the patient's mental disorder. While there is a correspondence, it is not quite as direct a correspondence as noted above.

A Stage Three relationship within this conceptual system involves somewhat more intervening variables and would probably become the point at which some individuals would feel that the patient was criminally responsible. Here there are many volitional elements in between the delusional system and the criminal act — many "choice points" — and these volitional elements appear to interface with the delusional elements. An example of this would be the case of the individual described previously who developed the delusional system that the Republican party had been persecuting him for the past ten years and had in fact developed a mind control machine which was implanting in his mind obsessive thoughts of self-destruction. This individual determined that he was going to expose the leaders of the Republican National Committee. He therefore robbed a bank, with the intention of using the money to obtain a lie detector machine to which he was going to hook up the leaders of the Republican National Committee. While his actions are certainly related to the delusion, he made a variety of choices regarding the manner of following through on the delusion.

Finally, a Stage Four conceptualization is one in which the mental disorder does not appear to bear any direct relationship to the offense but may be peripherally related to other behaviors at the time. This would encompass those examples, noted before, where an individual commits a crime in a manner which makes his apprehension quite easy. He could clearly be identified, and one could hypothesize an unconscious desire to be punished, but the relationship between the emotional problems and the crime (as opposed to the apprehension) is so distant that one cannot refer to this as a lack of criminal responsibility.

In summary, then, by utilizing the criteria discussed and the conceptual schemes proposed, it appears that expert witnesses could indeed perform valid and reliable assessments of criminal responsibility, maintain higher credibility in the courts, and render decisions on cases in which an insanity defense would be appropriate.

4
The Psychologist as Expert Witness

One of the most difficult tasks for the psychologist who becomes involved in forensic evaluations is to move from the relative safety of his own office, or hospital, into the rather unfamiliar and threatening territory of the witness stand. Here, his credentials are torn apart, his testimony and opinion subject to ridicule, and if he is not properly prepared, his ego shattered. The intent of this chapter is to provide the potential expert witness with some practical advice which will enable him or her to provide expert testimony to the courts in a manner that is effective and will not be subject to these kinds of attack.

The psychologist normally plays one of four roles in a courtroom situation. The first usually concerns the situation in which one has a therapy patient who becomes involved in some form of civil litigation. The therapist is asked to testify about the patient's treatment, diagnosis, and prognosis.

The second role is the one in which most people are likely to become involved: performing a pretrial examination of the patient, with issues involving competency or criminal responsibility in the criminal area; or doing evaluations involving child custody or issues of traumatic neurosis in the civil area.

The third role in which psychologists are sometimes involved, though to a lesser extent, is one in which no direct examination at all is performed. Here, one is asked to give an opinion on what constitutes "acceptable professional practice." This frequently occurs when there is a malpractice suit against another professional and one is asked to state whether or not a particular form of practice in which that professional was involved was appropriate professional practice.

A slight variation on this last role is one in which the psychologist is asked to review an evaluation prepared by another mental health professional and to critique that evaluation, in order to provide an attorney with some assistance in cross-examination. In this role, the psychologist is serving as a consultant to the legal system, rather than as a direct participant.

In what follows, a series of practical ideas, both for presenting data and for handling cross-examinations, will be presented.

PREPARE (AND ANTICIPATE) ATTACK

One cannot emphasize too much the importance of careful preparation. Attorneys are always taught to prepare their witnesses carefully, but one also needs to "put the shoe on the other foot." You must be able and willing to fully prepare the lawyer who has called you as a witness. No matter how strong an opinion is, it can appear in court to be an unmitigated disaster unless the attorney knows the kinds of questions to ask in order to best elicit that opinion. The expert should discuss with the attorney, for instance, aspects of the adversary process and the best way of presenting data.

The expert needs to anticipate in advance what some of the challenges to the opinion will be, making a frank assessment of the weakest parts of the evaluation and opinion. One must attempt to deal with these in direct examination, rather than creating the impression that one is surprised by these questions when they arise on cross-examination. A good example of the need for careful preparation is illustrated by the following case.

EXAMPLE:

A defense attorney was utilizing a defense based on the concept of an acute psychotic episode. The patient, while he was at the hospital, showed very little evidence of any disturbed behavior. He was perfectly well behaved, and of course, the issue that did come up at the trial, especially after a description of extensive inpatient observation of the defendant, was how one could state that the man was so disturbed at the time of the offense when there was no evidence of this disturbed behavior while the patient was on the ward.

Once this had been anticipated as grounds for cross-examination, it became critical to present in the course of the direct examination the fact of its being quite conceivable that a person could have an acute psychotic episode, that the psychosis could go into substantial remission, and that following the episode, there would be very few residual signs of the psychosis in day-to-day behavior. In this particular case, the residual signs of the psychosis were very clear on the patient's psychological testing, but not in terms of his behavior on the ward. On direct examination, the witness indicated that one must look for more subtle signs and for indications of the disorder in behavioral samples other than ward behavior. The questions on direct examination were phrased in terms of highlighting the distinction between a lack of disturbed behavior on the ward and the indices of psychosis on psychological testing. In short, by covering the material in direct examination, one can defuse the impact of an aggressive cross-examination on this point.

A closely related aspect of careful preparation is the need to review the entire case history, as well as the patient's clinical record, and to be aware of any factor that might provide the opposition with a basis for contradicting the testimony. Very often, a cursory reading of a record may result in the expert witness missing some items, which may substantially undercut an opinion in court. This occurs most frequently when an individual is recommending a conditional release or convalescent leave for some patient from the hospital, following an acquittal by reason of insanity or a civil commitment. The opposing side will usually examine the clinical record and will inevitably find various incidents of assault, violence, or otherwise inappropriate behavior. The question is invariably asked of the witness: How is it possible to reconcile a particular piece of violent or aggressive behavior with the recommendation that an individual should be released? One always needs to review the record carefully ahead of time, in order to see whether or not these incidents can be reconciled with the opinion which is being provided. If these incidents can be so reconciled, the apparent contradictions, and the manner in which the expert reconciles them with his or her opinion, should be presented *during direct examination*. This illustrates not only one's awareness of the issue but also the fact that one has carefully considered it, evaluated its significance, and incorporated it into one's decision making. If one does not think that the behavior is significant or thinks that it is somehow "out of context," then that too should be spelled out as support for the opinion. When the behavior appears inconsistent with an otherwise well-reasoned opinion, one may frequently find that the circumstances of the assault were somewhat unusual, that it represented the response to a provocation, that it occurred several years ago and the behavior has not been repeated since, that it was the result of some "situation specific" set of circumstances, or that the assault may have occurred prior to the patient's being placed on his or her present level of medication.

The necessity for being aware of, and capable of pointing out, the context in which a particular behavior occurred is critical. As noted, it may represent a response to a particular stress that may well exist only within the institution (i.e., close proximity with other individuals of the same sex, resulting either in homosexual behavior or in angry reactions to homosexual approaches).

The witness always appears in a weaker light to a jury when something appears to "catch him off guard" in cross-examination, whether or not in reality it does. One is, as has been noted, on much more "solid ground" when one anticipates as many areas of cross-examination as possible and deals with them in direct testimony.

Of course, one cannot consider all possible grounds of cross-examination, and often some material may be brought up in the cross-examination that one has not considered or with which one is unprepared to deal. Frequently, the question is phrased as follows: Doctor, would it change your opinion if you knew that . . . ?

One should never be led into the trap of either, on the one hand, acknowledging that such a statement would change one's opinion or, on the other hand, sounding rigid and inflexible by indicating that under no circumstances would it change one's opinion. One should indicate, rather, that the point is worthy of consideration, that one would need to evaluate it in order to place it in its proper context, and that one would need to reexamine the patient in the light of such information.

A point to be borne in mind, whenever one testifies in court, is that one should not consider oneself an advocate for the patient, for the defense, or for the government. One is an advocate only for one's own opinion. When the expert witness allows himself or herself to be drawn into a particular position because of a feeling that the patient needs treatment, that the patient should be incarcerated, or that society needs to be protected, the credibility and validity of one's testimony inevitably suffer. The jury of course is always going to assess the credibility of the expert witness's opinion and testimony.

One of the principles to which a lawyer attempts to adhere is never to ask a witness a question to which the lawyer does not already know the answer. Unfortunately, this is frequently not the practice. Oftentimes, when a lawyer is unprepared, he or she may ask questions of the witnesses which result in answers detrimental to the case. From the point of view of preparing the lawyer, then, the message is clear: discuss in advance the kinds of questions that will be asked, and make sure that no questions other than those are asked.

One of the subtle issues which this pretrial consultation engenders, however, is an occasional accusation by the opposing side that the lawyer influenced one's opinion — in other words, that one's opinion at the time of an examination was somehow different from one's opinion after consultation with the attorney. One can certainly emphasize, in a variety of ways, that in the course of pretrial consultation one's opinion was communicated to the lawyer, rather than stating something vague such as "yes, we discussed the case." Clearly, consultations with the attorney should be extremely limited prior to one's involvement in the case. Only after an opinion has been established should a consultation with the lawyer be made. Then, if the issue arises, one can indicate that an opinion was reached on a particular date and communicated to the lawyer on some subsequent date, rather than implying in any way that the lawyer influenced the opinion. The exact dates of examination, reaching one's opinion, and consulting with the attorney should be documented.

Among the most effective ways of defusing an attack like this is one that the witness can also use in many other situations, namely, rephrasing the question. A suggested approach, when asked such a hostile question, is to preface the answer with "now if what you are asking is . . ." and then rephrase the question to suit oneself.

While discussing influences on one's opinion, one needs to consider the issue of discussing the case with other witnesses, lay or expert.

As a rule of thumb, it is safest not to discuss the case with other witnesses, especially prior to one's testimony. When lay witnesses are testifying, an attorney will always ask the judge for a "rule on witnesses," meaning that everyone else testifying on that matter must be excluded from the courtroom. It is entirely within the judge's discretion whether the rule on witnesses is applied to expert testimony or not. Some attorneys feel that the expert has reached an opinion already and it should not make any difference what he or she hears the opposing expert stating in court. Other lawyers, who aggressively demand the "rule on witnesses," point out that allowing an expert to hear prior expert testimony provides an unfair advantage in that the expert can subtly rebut the previous opinion by the manner in which he or she testifies.

PRESENTATION OF SELF IN COURT

One of the most important aspects of one's testimony, aside from the substantive matters involved in one's opinion, is one's demeanor on the witness stand. Even in the Washington instruction (see Chapter 2), Judge Bazelon explained to the expert witness that the courtroom represents an adversary system and that lawyers feel they must attack the expert witness on the stand. There is a caution to the expert witness not to "take it personally" — that it is part of the attorney's job to try to discredit the opinion. The attorney will attempt to discredit one's testimony and one's credibility in many ways. However, no matter how many times one tells this to people in preparation for expert testimony, they still tend to get ruffled and upset when confronted with such attacks.

There are of course different methods of cross-examination. Some attorneys feel that they must attack the expert witness personally; others feel that if they attack the opposing expert too strongly, they will be undercutting the basis of their own expert's testimony. In other words, if they attack a given expert on the grounds that his conclusions are not valid scientifically, by inference that undercuts the scientific validity and credibility of their own rebuttal witness. Some attorneys then will be very selective in the areas in which they attempt to cross-examine the expert.

EXAMPLE:

A prosecuting attorney, cross-examining a psychologist retained by the defense, chose as an attack strategy a ridiculing of the inferences drawn from responses to various psychological tests. While the strategy was quite effective in some ways, it undercut the entire process of clinical inference from test data and rendered the attorney unable to utilize another psychologist as a rebuttal witness. He had already destroyed the basis on which his own witness would be basing conclusions.

The following rule of thumb can be kept in the back of one's mind during the course of being cross-examined; it may enable the expert witness to be less defensive and to avoid being "rattled." The first attack that a lawyer will attempt is on one's opinion. If the lawyer is unable to attack the opinion − if the opinion is solid − he will attack one's credentials. If one is unable to be attacked on the basis of credentials, a personal attack may follow. Therefore, if an attorney starts attacking the expert witness personally, making inferences such as, "How much are you getting paid for your testimony?" the witness can generally reassure himself or herself that credentials and opinion are on solid ground. The attorney then is pursuing the only avenue left. As an internal frame of reference, one can keep in mind the level at which the cross-examination is being aimed. This may provide some self-confidence; knowing what level the attorney is pursuing provides an index of just how strong one's case is.

EXAMPLE:

An expert witness recently was asked whether or not he had reviewed a patient's hospital record, and whether or not he was aware of the date on which the patient was first hospitalized. The witness responded that he had reviewed the records and that the patient had first been hospitalized in 1963. The attorney, upon cross-examination, then stated, "At that time, weren't you [the witness] still a green-behind-the-ears college sophomore?" Far from reacting defensively, the witness was able to assess this as being a personal attack, therefore indicating to him that both his opinion about the patient and his credentials were on solid ground.

With this perspective in mind, one is able to respond to this and future questions without "getting rattled."

Another important matter to keep in the back of one's mind when one is being aggressively cross-examined is that *you are the expert!* The expert knows the field better than the attorney, no matter how many books the attorney has read or how much he has prepared to cross-examine the expert in that given area. One should know one's own field thoroughly, including not only the basis for the examination but the relevant literature as well. Occasionally, an attorney may try to cross-examine by introducing literature that is irrelevant to the particular opinion. On such occasions, the expert should be well enough aware of the fact that the literature is irrelevant to indicate that such information was not taken into account because it was not regarded as relevant to the opinion. In short, one should have a comprehensive knowledge of the field in which one is testifying, and certainly the underlying caveat is that if one does not know the field that well, then one should not be taking the witness stand in reference to such issues.

A frequent line of attack regarding psychological testing, is for the attorney to ask a question such as, "Isn't it true that the test you gave is invalid?" Here, as noted above, a thorough knowledge of the field not only of clinical psychology but also of testing and assessment is critical. An example follows:

EXAMPLE:

In this particular interchange, the line of cross-examination dealt with the Minnesota Multiphasic Personality Inventory. The expert witness had rendered the opinion that, in part, his statement that the patient was malingering was based on the validity scales of the MMPI.

Attorney: Now then, doctor, hasn't research shown that the MMPI is invalid?

Expert: I really cannot answer that question; would you be able to define what you mean by validity?

Attorney: Come now, you're a doctor, don't you know what validity is?

Expert: Certainly, counselor, but there is predictive validity, construct validity, and face validity — to name only a few. You will have to define your terms more precisely before I can respond to the question.

Attorney: I withdraw the question.

This vignette serves as a good example of the fact that one's knowledge of the field should enable one to "throw back" such an attack to the attorney, by presenting him with aspects of the field of expertise with which he or she cannot cope.

Some psychologists and psychiatrists may believe that such an approach in responding to questions is somewhat argumentative and does beg the question being asked. This is to a certain extent a valid objection, but the level of sophistication of the judge and jury often determines whether or not a more involved response can be offered.

For example, when one is dealing with a fairly sophisticated judge or jury, a response to the questions in the example might be to point out the fact that most of the studies being cited are based on a research, as opposed to a clinical, methodology. That is, they take one variable, in isolation, from a series of others and attempt to predict another isolated variable at some point in the future (e.g., number of Rorschach color responses and violent behavior). This, of course, is not the nature of the clinical examination in which a wide variety of observations, tests, and impressions go into forming a particular opinion. Another way of dealing with such a line of attack when one has a more sophisticated judge or jury is to utilize responses to various tests, and one's interpretation of them, as a microcosm of the individual's behavior. One then demonstrates that his actual behavior during the time of the offense parallels the inferences drawn from the psychological testing. It goes without saying that in following such an approach, one must analyze the tests and the inferences from the tests in a relatively blind manner, without having the details of the criminal offense in mind.

EXAMPLE:

A patient's responses to a series of projective techniques were basically intact, with notable exceptions surrounding his perception of older men, authority figures, and "father figures." At such times, his thought processes became loose and illogical, and his reality testing was grossly impaired. In actuality, his mother had been murdered several years earlier, and the patient often felt that his father had been involved. The patient was charged with murdering a total stranger — an individual who was the same height, weight, and body build as his father — in a setting virtually identical to the father's place of business. The parallel between the inferences from the psychological testing and the facts of the offense was very striking, and led to the opinion that the patient had misperceived the victim as his father and had become acutely psychotic at the time of the shooting.

Another difficulty sometimes encountered by expert witnesses occurs when an attorney refers to a particularly obscure article and asks whether or not the expert is aware of it. If one is aware of the study, one should acknowledge it, and if the study reaches conclusions opposite to one's opinion, one should be prepared with other citations, or an analysis of the article in question, to demonstrate why it is not applicable or why one disagrees with it. Some of the statements given earlier, especially those regarding the differences between a clinical and a research approach, may be highly relevant.

A frequent example of this use of other literature to try to discredit the expert witness is, of course, citing any or all of the literature on the expert's inability to predict dangerousness. As noted earlier, the most effective means of rebutting such arguments is to explain that the reasons such studies fail to predict violent behavior is because of the primacy of social, rather than psychological factors, that is, factors over which the psychologist has no control in his or her predictive statements. An article by Jesse Rubin, M.D.,[1] regarding the prediction of dangerous behavior, cites this very difficulty and may provide valuable backup for one's explanation of the difficulty encountered in this area.

Another frequent line of cross-examination is to attack what the expert witness is doing as unscientific. In dealing with that question, one must indicate that one has never maintained that clinical psychology

---

[1] Rubin, J. Prediction of dangerousness in mentally ill criminals. *Archives of General Psychiatry* 27:397 (1972).

(or psychiatry) was a highly refined science. The judge will frequently ask the expert for an explanation. One can discuss the fact that this is a developing area which might be regarded as a highly refined craft, rather than a science. There are some scientific aspects to be sure, but clinical psychology is basically in the process of developing, and one is giving opinions based, hopefully, on the best available knowledge at that point in time.

If the opposing witness then tries to indicate that what he or she is saying is highly scientific, it is already in the record as a matter of opinion that such matters are not completely scientific at all. Frequently, attorneys will ask a witness to put a prediction into percentages; this, of course, is impossible. Such percentages do not mean anything, and the expert should not allow himself to be pushed beyond using terms such as probable, substantial probability, little probability, etc. Once again, these terms are essential because of parameters over which we have no control. If, for instance, in predicting dangerousness, one states that a particular individual is likely or highly probable to act out in an aggressive manner, one must specify the situation or parameters within which such activity is apt to occur. In a similar manner, one might state that given the following set of parameters (which one would describe), the acting out behavior would be very remote.

Above all, bear in mind that one's function on the witness stand is to give one's opinion — nothing more, nothing less. One is not giving a statement of facts, but is, rather giving a reasoned opinion based on the information which is available and which has been carefully analyzed. Once the witness starts feeling that he or she is on trial, then the testimony will inevitably fall apart.

One of the first aspects of testimony that is important is the manner in which the expert is qualified. Unless it is an uncontested trial in which one is being put on the stand to "make a record" and no one is contesting one's opinion, do not allow, or have the attorney allow, a stipulation to qualifications. If the opposing attorney offers to stipulate, the general interpretation is that he or she does not want the judge or jury to hear the extent of the witness's qualifications. One should instruct the lawyer that if the opposition tries to stipulate, the stipulation should not be accepted; the jury should hear the expert's qualifications.

Regarding qualifications, one should try to cite the aspects of one's experience relevant to the forensic area or to the particular case in which one is testifying. If one is testifying, for instance, in a case involving an insanity defense, it would be of little assistance for the attorney to ask how many patients one has psychoanalyzed, but it would be quite important to have on the record the number of defendants that one has examined for the purpose of assessing criminal responsibility. In addition, questions such as the number of times the witness has qualified in court in criminal cases, or the number of times the witness has testified for both the government and the defense (to indicate one's impartiality), would be quite crucial.

A frequent line of attack in cross-examination is for an attorney to state, "Well then, you are basing your opinion just on what this man told you." It is important to specify in testimony, in the report ahead of time, and in direct examination the fact that one's opinion is based on a variety of different sources, indicating which are the subjective sources, which are the more objective sources, and how the two of them fit together to form an opinion. It is critical — and this cannot be stressed strongly enough — that these matters be laid out in advance: in the report and in direct examination, so that the witness is not subject to attack on the charge of having based an opinion on "just what the individual told him."

When an expert witness feels unable to express an opinion on something, he should not allow himself to be backed into a corner but should simply state, "I am unable to answer the question." One does not have an opinion on some particular topic. State only what feels natural and consistent with the opinion given.

Frequently, an attorney will present a hypothetical question based on what he or she feels are conclusions from a report. If the witness is comfortable extending the conclusions to that hypothetical situation, *he may do so*. If, on the other hand, it is felt that the hypothetical situation is carrying the opinion too far from the data, it should be stated that such an inference is too far removed from the data. One should not try to express an expert opinion on a nonexpert observation. That is, do not allow the cloak of expertise to spread over judgments which are matters of "common sense." (This was also stressed by Judge Bazelon in the Washington decision discussed in Chapter 2.)

As noted in the discussion of attacks on the validity of one's observations, one needs to evaluate the general level of sophistication of the judge and jury, and the kinds of observations one should or should not make. One should have a general sense of the educational level of the jury and how attentive they are, and from that, determine the level at which an opinion is explained. In a rural county, for instance, issues may need to be discussed in far less technical terms than in a large metropolitan area. On the other hand, even in such a metropolitan area, the expert witness should not allow himself to fall into the trap of using extensive professional jargon. Under all circumstances, the opinion should be expressed in clear-cut straightforward language.

Visual aids can certainly be utilized as an adjunct to one's testimony (e.g., a blown up copy of an MMPI profile), provided that the results are carefully explained to the jury in lay language. In a recent case in which the insanity defense was asserted, the psychologist testifying as a rebuttal witness for the government presented an MMPI to the jury in which all the T scores were between 50 and 70, with validity scales in an acceptable range. This demonstrated rather graphically that at least in terms of serious mental disorders, the defendant endorsed items that a normal population generally did, and did not endorse any significantly deviant items.

As noted earlier, one of the most difficult legal traps to deal with is the "hypothetical question." Frequently, within the hypothetical question, an attorney will incorporate certain premises that are unacceptable to the expert witness. One must be alert to such a tactic and, in answering the question, indicate those aspects of the hypothetical situation with which one can agree, those aspects which are unacceptable, and in what way the hypothetical would need to be changed in order to render an opinion. One can point out, in the response, that the attorney is picking certain dimensions out of a total clinical perspective and that the question cannot be answered in the manner in which it is phrased. One often has to indicate that more background is needed, that more about the setting of the examination must be known, or that the statement is totally taken out of context and that it is impossible to answer it.

One of the problems frequently encountered in the use of hypothetical questions occurs either when there is an exclusion of the expert witness from the courtroom during the time of the factual basis of the trial or when the trial is bifurcated (split in two). In such cases, lay testimony often reflects or comments on certain pieces of the individual's behavior. In questioning the expert witness in another part of the trial, the attorney will frequently attempt to undercut the credibility of the opinion by citing actual behavior that was elicited from descriptions during an earlier proceeding. Of course, one of the best ways to deal with this is to have completely reviewed, as part of the preparation, all available police reports and witness statements. There are occasions, of course, in which one does not have access to all such information, and this can make the cross-examination with such hypothetical questions somewhat difficult to handle. As an example, in a recent rape case, the police report and the witness statement did not reveal any bizarre behavior whatsoever. During cross-examination by the defense attorney, the expert witness was asked whether, if he had seen evidence of some bizarre behavior at the time of the offense, his opinion would change. The answer given was as follows: "I am not aware from my review of the available documents of any bizarre behavior. Were you to present me with some indication of such bizarre behavior, I would be glad to reevaluate the case." The witness did not allow himself to be forced into giving an opinion based on a hypothetical question. The farthest out on a limb that the witness should go is to indicate, if it is felt that the material presented is legitimate, that one would be glad to reevaluate the case under those circumstances. Do not speculate on the stand; indicate that speculation is not the basis on which an opinion is reached, but rather that one operates on the basis of clinical and psychological examination, not forming opinions on the basis of hypothetical "what ifs."

In this case, significantly enough, the complaining witness had indeed indicated during cross-examination some bizarre behavior on the part of the defendant, information that was not presented in the police report or in her original statement. If one feels that one can respond to the hypothetical question with certain modifications, then one can always legitimately state, "I cannot answer the question as it is phrased." One can also try to rephrase the question by saying, "If what you are asking is . . ." and then rephrasing the question to suit oneself in a way that can be answered.

There are times, to be sure, when it becomes very difficult to rephrase a question in the manner in which one needs to. In these circumstances, the best tactic is merely to respond, "I cannot answer the question the way it is asked" or "May I be permitted to expand on or explain my answer in more detail?" Generally, this will suffice, but in the rare circumstances in which it does not, the attorney for whom one is testifying should use that as a cue to ask a similar question on redirect examination, in order to fully elicit the opinion which one was unable to give during the cross-examination.

There are many different schools of thought, in terms of expert testimony, regarding whether or not the expert witness should volunteer information. Some would indicate that one should answer only the question asked. Others feel that one should take any opportunity to explain one's position as fully as possible, not allowing oneself to be restricted by the scope of the questioning. The latter group of individuals will stress that the expert witness should insist on the opportunity, within bounds, to explain and expand as much as possible. Under any circumstances, if an attorney asks an expert witness an open-ended question, the expert witness should feel free to discuss it in as much detail as he or she sees fit. Any conceivable aspect of the situation that can be used to bolster or substantiate the opinion should be used.

Many attorneys are instructed in law schools never to ask a witness "why" anything. If a lawyer does ask a witness "why," the witness should feel free to take as much time as needed to explain something as fully as possible.

As best he can, the expert witness should learn to "talk off the top of his head" rather than continually referring to notes. In certain situations, there may be objections to reading from one's report. One should be familiar with the material that one wants to present and should utilize written notes as little as possible. Notes should be used only to refresh a recollection or to specify certain points such as dates and places, but they should not be used in the development of the overall opinion.

The expert witness should be aware that anything taken onto the witness stand can be marked as an exhibit. If there are aspects of the record that one does not want admitted into evidence, then by all means they should not be brought to the witness stand. One of the favorite ploys in cross-examination is for an attorney to say, "Now doctor, the notes that you have with you, are these all of the notes that you took during the examination?" Usually one has a final report, which is what is being referred to on the stand. The final report is generated as a result of notes that may have been saved or may have been thrown away. If they have been saved and the lawyer is intent on attacking the witness, he will insist on the witness getting copies of all the notes. The attorney can then say something to the effect that the witness has marked down things in his notes which he did not include in the report. In a highly accusatory fashion, the lawyer may then ask the witness to explain why that particular aspect was left out of the report or, if the notes were thrown away, why they were thrown away. One way of dealing with this, especially in an institutional setting, is never to make notes anywhere except in the medical record; then anytime one is asked about other notes, one can indicate that every note that has been made in this case is on the medical chart. Similarly, if there are questions as to whether the patient told one about a certain fact, and there is no record of this in the notes, one may indicate that only those findings which in one's opinion are clinically significant are included in the notes. If there is material in the notes that does not appear in the final written report, a similar response would be most appropriate.

A pitfall to be avoided at all costs is the attempt to extend a sound clinical or psychological judgment to an unfounded generalization. For example, through careful evaluation and testing, the psychologist has been able to reach a diagnosis; the documentation is clear as to why that diagnosis has been made; nevertheless, there is at times a misguided attempt to overgeneralize that diagnosis.

EXAMPLE:

According to the evidence, a patient charged with the first degree murder of an elderly man was found, following the murder, to have attempted to throw away his shoes which were bloodstained and also to give some of the money he had taken from the decedent to a friend of his, thereby implicating that friend in the offense. The patient was tested and, on the basis of his Wechsler Adult Intelligence Scale, was found to be mildly mentally retarded. One of the expert witnesses involved in the case stated that the patient could not possibly have committed the crime, since throwing away sneakers and trying to implicate someone else in the crime by giving them money were things which "someone who is that retarded would be incapable of doing." This clearly was an unsound generalization from the data.

A related issue concerns the question of generalizations being raised in cross-examination by an attorney. Questions such as, Isn't it possible that . . . ? or Isn't it conceivable that . . . ? are inevitably traps for the expert witness. One of the easiest ways of dealing with this, though it is also flippant and may well backfire on the witness, is to merely state, "Anything is possible." However, with very slight modification, the same impression can be created, but it can be phrased in a far more substantial manner. For example, when asked whether a particular outcome would be possible, the witness may answer, "While that is certainly possible, given the following data which I have collected, it is my opinion that it is highly unlikely." The witness then presents the documentation of a series of observations which would run counter to the impression which the cross-examiner is trying to create. When doing this, it goes without saying that, as noted before, the material should be presented in a straightforward manner, and professional jargon should be avoided wherever possible. If technical terminology has to be used, it should be defined carefully.

One important fact which expert witnesses frequently forget is that certain terms which have to be used in the course of testimony, especially diagnostic terms, have popularized meanings as well as clinical meanings. When talking about these terms, it is important to specify to the trier of fact (the judge or the jury) that one is discussing the clinical meaning of the terms, not the lay meaning, and when necessary, one should highlight the difference. Examples of some terms whose colloquial meanings are far different from their clinical meaning are "depression," "deterioration," "homosexual," and "paranoia."

As noted, when one does a complete psychological evaluation, one can respond quite adequately to the attack, "Well then, doctor, all you did was talk to him!" In response to such a question, it is also helpful, of course, to specify not only that a complete psychological evaluation was performed, but also that there is a significant difference between a clinical interview and "just talking." That is, aspects of the interaction in a clinical interview that are taken note of and recorded, such as coherence, pressure of speech, affective tone, looseness, tangentiality, etc., are all dimensions that are not typically taken into account when one merely "talks to someone."

A favorite technique on cross-examination is for a lawyer to equate the concept of negative, or "within normal limits," with the term "normal." It is important to distinguish among these terms and state that the term "normality" is meaningless when one is doing a diagnostic workup, that there is a continuum between mental health and mental illness, that one is always dealing with "shades of gray," and that a finding of an absence of a mental disorder significant enough, for instance, to raise an insanity defense, does not mean that the person is "normal."

EXAMPLE:

The psychologist had examined an individual who was charged with rape. During the course of the examination, from clinical interview, history taking, and psychological testing, it became clear that while the person did have a repetitive pattern of sexual acting out, and in fact had a variety of incestuous fantasies related to his sister, he was certainly not mentally ill in the sense of possessing any major impairment of mental or emotional processes, or behavioral controls. After this testimony had been presented on direct examination, the defense attorney in cross-examination asked, "Well then, doctor, are you saying that a man who has incestuous fantasies about his sister is normal?" The response was that the term normalcy or normality was not part of the evaluation at all, and that while there was certainly some distortion in the person's sexual identity formation, this was far different from his having a mental disease or defect under the applicable legal tests.

One needs to provide, in testimony, as clear and as comprehensive a description of the individual as possible. To some degree, an expert is dependent on the lawyer who retained him to ask questions that will elicit an opinion to its fullest extent. The lawyer should be instructed to ask, when an opinion is given, "Doctor, what are the grounds or the basis for your opinion?" That will then allow the expert to present everything on which the opinion was based. One is on shaky ground, at the time of cross-examination, if an opinion was given without the grounds for it having being presented. The cross-examiner may inquire of the witness how a particular conclusion was reached. When one tries at that point (that is, in cross-examination) to provide the basis for the opinion, the question may well be asked, in a rather demeaning fashion, why one had not said anything of this nature before. As much as possible then, as in many other situations already noted, the thrust of the opinion, as well as the total basis for the opinion, should be presented during direct examination.

Another favorite trick of cross-examination, with which the expert witness must be prepared to deal, is the attempt to pick out an isolated symptom rather than viewing human behavior as a totality. For instance, if the expert witness has been testifying about the daydreams or fantasies that the particular individual has, a question in cross-examination may be: "Don't normal people daydream, too, doctor?" The point of course, is that the daydreaming is not a symptom which means anything in isolation and that it cannot be isolated out of the total diagnostic picture which one is offering. When the symptom is isolated, it totally loses its clinical meaning and has no significance outside of the context.

A particularly effective way of guarding against such an attack is once again to fully utilize direct examination. That is, during the course of the direct examination, arrange to have the attorney ask *the basis* on which an expert opinion has been reached. In the course of discussing this, the expert should point out that one must take all symptoms as a totality and that no one symptom taken in isolation has any meaning whatsoever (e.g., one Rorschach response, one TAT story, or any particular response to any psychological test). Then, when the attack is made on cross-examination, the attorney is able to state an objection: the doctor has already testified during direct examination that no symptoms taken in isolation have any meaning whatsoever. This may rebut that entire line of cross-examination.

The expert witness must constantly be aware of, and alert for, certain words which are "heavily loaded" in terms of the law. Examples of such words are: "planning" and "knowing." Certainly, the issue behind the word "planning" addresses itself to the whole legal concept of premeditation. Not all crimes committed by a mentally ill individual are impulsive and poorly thought out. That is, planning something does not necessarily contraindicate the presence of a mental illness. In many cases, some of the most involved criminal activity can be based on careful plotting which, in turn, is rooted or grounded in an elaborate delusional system. Certainly, a fine historical example of this is Daniel McNaughten himself who, on the basis of the delusion that the government of Queen Victoria was conspiring against him, planned his activities over the course of an extensive period of time.

In a similar manner, the word "know" is frequently thrown at an expert witness as a way of attempting to discredit the witness's belief that the individual is mentally ill, since knowledge that something is wrong would render the person criminally responsible under, for instance, the McNaughten test. The approach to take when the term "knowledge" is used as part of cross-examination is to point out that the word "know" can be used in a variety of ways and that while a particular individual may cognitively understand that something is wrong, he may not possess the emotional understanding or appreciation of its wrongfulness.

On occasions, in cross-examination the attorney will attempt to contradict the testimony of the expert witness by drawing attention to certain events that occurred in the defendant's past life. Frequently, the attorney who is doing the cross-examination will make reference only to the events themselves, rather than to any more subtle behavior that is part of those events. One of the best ways to be prepared for this, of course, is to have fully researched the area so that one can respond by reference to various details of the events of which the lawyer is not aware, and which may further bolster one's opinion.

For instance, one may have diagnosed someone as progressively withdrawing from a series of interpersonal involvements as a prelude to a schizophrenic break. If the cross-examiner is able to list various activities in which the individual was involved, implying that he was indeed engaged in interactions with other people, it would be helpful for the expert to have interviewed some of those people to assess just what the *quality* of the patient's involvement had been. Was it indeed an active involvement or was the behavior characterized by much withdrawal as well?

As noted earlier, one of the favorite ploys in cross-examination is to indicate that "normal people" experience many of the same symptoms which the expert has attributed to the patient in question. An extremely effective way of handling this is to point out the continuity or continuum between mental health and mental illness. One very concrete example which a jury can understand is the dream state in which all of us are psychotic for a period of time every day. This enables the jury to picture vividly what an acute schizophrenic episode is like, and to comprehend that the schizophrenic is unable to distinguish between that dream state and reality.

One must remember that there is nothing in and of any particular diagnosis that makes a person competent or incompetent, criminally responsible or not responsible. Rather, it is the question of *how much* that condition, whatever it may be, actually impairs the individual. In evaluating many of the legal decisions which have been discussed, the term "substantial impairment" is very important. While this term has its own pitfalls to be sure, nevertheless attempting to define it is far more effective than saying, for instance, that an individual is schizophrenic and that his schizophrenia impairs his relationship with others. Rather, a particular aspect of the psychosis should be developed; for example, one can speak about the manner in which the individual's hallucinatory experiences keep him from being able to concentrate on his work and indicate that, therefore, he is impaired in that area. In a similar manner, one can speak about the distracting influences that a patient's auditory hallucinations may have on his ability to effectively interact with other people. The emphasis, in each case, is on how the illness, whatever it may be, interferes with or impairs the individual's functioning in a specific area.

A rather common technique, frequently resorted to by cross-examiners, is merely listing a variety of unrelated symptoms that have virtually nothing to do with the diagnosis being presented. They are presented to the jury as "a smoke screen." The jury will question the extent of the illness, since the patient suffers from none of the enumerated symptoms. There is very little that the expert witness can do in response to such an attack, except for alerting the attorney who retained him or her to ask on redirect, should such an attack occur, what if anything the symptoms listed could have to do with the diagnosis rendered. At that point, it can be made clear that what was presented was a list of isolated symptoms which have very little to do with the case being discussed.

Another technique which is common in cross-examination of a defense witness is to attempt to demonstrate the number of activities an individual was able to engage in on the day of the offense (or closely surrounding it) that did not bear the imprint of the illness at all. For instance, the cross-examiner may ask, "Doctor, was the man able to dress himself that morning?" "Was he able to prepare his own breakfast?" "Was he able to walk out of the house and take a bus?" The response to these, of course, is usually yes. The point of this line of attack is to indicate to the jury that the defendant was acting in a "nonimpaired" manner up until the time of the offense. Once again, the groundwork anticipating this line of attack needs to be laid in direct examination. It must be pointed out during the course of direct examination that very frequently any number of activities can be carried on, which, unless they "hit" the core of an individual's particular delusional system, may not bring forth the disturbed looking behavior at all. When such an attack occurs, of course, the expert witness can attempt to reiterate this point, but if he or she does not have the opportunity to do so, then the attorney will be able to return to it upon redirect examination. At such a time, the attorney would reiterate those aspects of the defendant's "nonimpaired" behavior and ask the expert witness why those pieces of behavior did not bear the imprint of the delusional thinking. At that point, the expert can respond that the patient is capable of performing many activities, as long as they do not interface with his distorted perception of the world.

MISCELLANEOUS CONSIDERATIONS

The expert witness should never, under any circumstances, accept a referral on a contingent fee basis. This can undermine the expert's credibility a great deal. Any questions about fee should be stated in terms of the fact that one is being paid for one's time, not for one's opinion or for one's testimony. Accepting a contingent fee makes the expert less an advocate of an opinion and more an advocate of a particular party to the litigation. In short, the stronger one presses one's opinion, the larger the settlement and the more money with which one walks away from the case. Obviously, this can greatly undermine the credibility of the witness and make it seem as if he or she is "a hired gun."

As a practical matter, one must bear in mind the actual impact that a particular crime or series of crimes will have on a jury, and how difficult, or how easy, it might be to present to a jury the evidence in that case supporting an insanity defense. While in a sense, it should not be the function of an expert witness to try to influence the court proceedings, one must be aware of the pitfalls of testifying in support of an insanity defense in certain circumstances. The expert witness should discuss with the attorney not only a finding of not guilty by reason of insanity but also, depending on the jurisdiction, the possibility of using the evidence which has been gained from the evaluation to support a defense of guilty but mentally ill or a plea of diminished capacity, as well as the possibility of having the defendant enter a guilty plea, with the material arrived at to be used at the time of sentencing.

This becomes an issue particularly when the individual perhaps had an isolated and encapsulated delusional system about the person whom he assaulted or attacked, but at the time of evaluation and at the time of trial, does not appear at all delusional. As a practical matter, therefore, one needs to evaluate what the impact of such statements would be on the members of a jury who will be looking at the individual in terms of their own "gut reaction" and not see any evidence whatsoever of a mental disorder.

If the expert witness represents a hospital or an institution of some sort, one of the questions that is frequently asked is to describe a typical evaluation procedure. Generally, the witness will then respond that the patient is oriented by the ward's staff; seen for an admission interview; referred for various workups (e.g., neurological and psychological); observed daily; given a complete social service history, with family members being interviewed; interviewed clinically; evaluated for medication; etc. The question is then asked whether or not this procedure was followed in this particular case. While on the surface this may seem like a meaningless question, it is important, from a legal point of view, to establish the fact that all aspects of the typical examination process were followed. The rationale behind this is that one of the grounds for malpractice is failure to follow the established procedures in any given institution. It goes without saying, therefore, that one must be familiar with the policies and procedures of whatever institution or clinic one is dealing with, and act strictly in accordance with those principles unless there are documented grounds for an exception. In other words, if the regulations of a particular institution mandate psychological testing on every individual and one chooses not to do such testing, then it must be clearly and precisely documented in the record why such testing was not done in this particular case.

In private practice, there is obviously no "policy and procedure manual." The standard to be followed is the level of accepted practice by "the reasonably prudent professional," a standard which is used in virtually all malpractice language. Such standards are found, for instance, in the *Standards for Providers of Psychological Services*[2] of the American Psychological Association and similar documents from other professional groups.

If one is working in an institution, it frequently needs to be pointed out that formal face-to-face examination is not the only part of a good clinical and psychological workup. Attorneys will often try to impugn a witness's testimony by detailing the exact number of hours that the witness spent with a particular patient, rather than dealing with the fact that much of the observation is done in an informal manner, in terms of observation on the ward and reports from the ward staff at various ward meetings.

One final area needs to be addressed in the preparation of expert testimony. In cases where there is a "battle of the experts," the attorney must be warned not to launch too broad-based an attack on the opposing witness (see example on p. 80). If the attorney, for instance, attacks the opposing expert and attempts to destroy the basis for any scientific credibility to his work, then the impression carries over that one's own testimony is no more scientific or no more to be trusted than that of the witness who has already been

---

[2] *Standards for Providers of Psychological Services,* Washington, D.C., American Psychological Association, 1974.

discredited. In such a case, in helping the attorney prepare to cross-examine the other witness, it is helpful to instruct the attorney to restrict himself to actual substantive areas of weakness in the other witness's testimony, rather than spending a great deal of time attacking the scientific basis of the other individual's opinion.

5
Family Law

The organization and emphasis of this chapter will be somewhat different from previous chapters. We will consider, at the outset, some practical guidelines which govern the conducting of evaluations, especially regarding custody. We will then consider the implications of a series of recent court decisions regarding the circumstances under which parental rights may be terminated. Many of the practical suggestions contained in Chapter 4, as well as the emphasis on careful and comprehensive preparation for testimony stressed in Chapters 1 through 3, of course, also apply.

One feature that is very distinctive to family law, especially in evaluation for child custody, is the fact that one is dealing with parties who are often in conflict, who have different perceptions of the same event or series of events, and who carry this difference in perspective over to their evaluations of their relationships with the children involved. This, therefore, gives rise to certain specific difficulties and issues in conducting child custody evaluations.

THE CONDUCT OF THE EVALUATION

First of all, in child custody evaluations, it becomes critical to involve as much of the family as possible, especially the disputing parties, in the evaluation process. That is, under no circumstances should a report on child custody be rendered to the court, based on the evaluation of only one party to the conflict. Certainly, as a practical matter, the opposing party will often refuse to submit to an examination. Under such circumstances, it must be made clear in the report to the court that the evaluation is a limited one, since it is restricted to work done only with one of the parents. In such cases, the thrust of the report is an evaluation of the fitness or mental status of *one* of the parents, *not* a recommendation for custody. This also becomes a problem, at times, since often when one is retained by an attorney for one side, the opposing attorney has hired an expert witness of his or her own choosing to evaluate the other party. While it is certainly no substitute for doing a comprehensive evaluation of the entire family, under such circumstances consultation with the other professional, and sharing observations and impressions, can be of some assistance. Hopefully, the other professional is equally interested in providing an impartial and objective opinion. Under any circumstances, if the entire family unit cannot be evaluated, then this must be carefully noted in the report to the court, and the limitations posed by that approach should be clearly spelled out. That is, one needs to make a statement in the report that one or the other party was unwilling (or unable) to participate in the examination and that, therefore, one is only able to assess the relationship of the child to a particular parent. Another danger of only evaluating one side is the possibility of identification with that party and, consequently, rendering a partisan decision by failing to see the needs of the family as a whole.

Of course, in interviewing and evaluating the child, certain inferences can be made about relationships with each parent but it must be stressed, and indeed indicated in the court report, that such impressions cannot be stated with the same degree of certainty or validity as would be the case if all parties involved themselves in the examination. Under ideal circumstances, the mental health professional should have the opportunity of examining the child alone, each parent alone, the parents together, the child in the company of each parent, and possibly, if the situation allows, the child in the setting with the parents together. Such multiple examinations are very helpful in arriving at an opinion about the child's interests and welfare, as he relates to each of the parents and as they relate to him. Frequently, individual intrapsychic factors are not the most important ones; rather, the critical factors are the dynamic interrelationships between members of the disrupted family. With younger children, it is helpful to utilize observations of the parents and children in a free play situation, to gain a sense of the nature of the interaction.

In examining the child or children alone, some important dimensions to consider are the overall level of cognitive and emotional development, the developmental history, the manner of coping with separation or loss, the child's subjective perception of each parent, and the extent of psychopathology.

When examining the parents individually, again the level of cognitive and emotional development is critical, but this must be interwoven with the manner in which these emotional and cognitive factors affect parenting capabilities. The parents' developmental history is also critical, especially their memories of their own childhood.

In examining the parents together, one needs to assess the nature of the interaction and, in consideration with the earlier evaluation of the children, hypothesize how the interaction might be translated into a custodial relation.

Finally, in evaluating the interaction of each parent with the child, one must consider the spontaneous response of the child to the parent (frequently by observing free play situations) and the degree of sensitivity of the parent to the child.[1]

Courts have often adopted the view of a number of developmental psychologists who stress the different needs of children for different sorts of environments at different ages. Within the first two years of life, the issue of mothering is regarded as critical, as basically a life-and-death issue. It should be stressed that what is being described is "the mothering function" not specifically the biological mother. According to the court, anyone who is able to fulfill the mothering function, or the person who can fulfill it most adequately, is the person who should gain custody from birth to 2 years of age. Here, if either or both of the parties have remarried, it is important to assess each *set* of parents for the adequacy of "mothering."

From 3 to 6 years of age, the court tends to stress the idea of "a whole family." That is, the ideal is the need of the child to see a male and female parental interaction. This again does not necessarily have to be the biological parents, but the courts stress the idea of the children's involvement in a whole stable family. An assessment here includes a comparison of the stability of the different family groups.

Between the ages of 6 and 12, the courts tend to use a "predictable environment" as the criterion, one in which there is a solid and estab-

---

[1] These criteria are discussed in more detail in Trunnell, T. L. Johnnie and Suzie don't cry: Mommy and Daddy aren't that way. *Bulletin of the American Academy of Psychiatry and Law* 4:120–126 (1976).

lished sense of trust, and one in which the child knows what is expected of him or her and what can be expected in return. Here, the sex of the parent matters much less than the home atmosphere. Again, the family assessment is crucial for evaluating the issue of how commitments and obligations are handled and followed through.

Finally, in adolescence, the custody issue tends to be seen in terms of the parent who is best able to provide constructive control over the many changes and upheavals in adolescence. Once again, the specific sex of the individual is seen to be of lesser importance, though one could argue the fact that an important issue is identification with an adequate role model of the same sex. Here, evaluation of the parents must include an assessment of how they might respond to, and deal with, the rebelliousness inherent in adolescence.

With this as a background, let us look for a few moments at the basis of some of the current thinking in the area of family law. The guiding force in current family law is a concept called "the best interests of the child." In part, it deals with the developmental idea just noted. In principle, both parents have equal custody rights. In practical terms, mothers still retain custody more frequently than fathers. However, fathers are awarded custody if an investigation of the "best interests of the child" reveals maternal unfitness or some kind of abandonment.

The phrase "best interests of the child" still remains quite vague. In an effort to clarify it, the legislature in the state of Michigan established standards upon which the decision of trial courts should be based, in attempting to assess the best interests of children.[2] This of course has no binding value in any other jurisdiction, but it does provide a good guideline for the manner in which some courts tend to put this concept into effect. The following are the ten factors considered:

1. the love, affection, and other emotional ties existing between the competing parties and the child;
2. the capacity and disposition of the competing parties to provide love, affection, guidance, continuation of education, and continued religious education, if the latter be deemed necessary;

---

[2] Michigan Child Custody Act of 1970.

3. the capacity and disposition of the competing parents to provide the children with what is regarded as "remedial care," that is, clothing and medical care (this dimension also refers to the provision of other material needs);

4. the length of time that a child has lived in a stable satisfactory environment and the desirability of maintaining continuity of that environment;

5. the permanence as a family unit of the existing or proposed custodial home;

6. the moral fitness of the competing parties (of interest is the fact that this, the only mention of "fitness," has nothing to do with parenting skills or the ability to rear a child);

7. the mental and physical health of the competing parties;

8. the home, school, and community records of the child;

9. the reasonable preference of the child if the court deems the child to be of sufficient age to express a preference;

10. any other issues considered by the court to be relevant to a particular child custody suit.

Spelling out these dimensions is particularly helpful to the mental health practitioner, for frequently, the individual doing child custody evaluations has tended to restrict his or her evaluation to the mental health of the competing parties. While from the point of view of many mental health professionals, this is of course an important dimension (as can be seen by a consideration of the other parameters), it remains only one of many on which the court bases its decision.

In a test proposed by the Uniform Marriage and Divorce Act,[3] many of these same dimensions are considered. It specifically adds one important point though: forbidding a trial court to consider conduct of a proposed custodian that does not "affect the relationship to the child." This may sound unnecessarily vague, but it refers to any life-style which individuals may find morally objectionable but which cannot be demonstrated to have any adverse effect on the child. For instance, utilizing this criterion, the court could *not* automatically deny custody to a homosexual mother. In limiting the

---

[3]National Conference of Commissioners on Uniform State Laws, Uniform Marriage and Divorce Act of 1970 (amended 1971, 1973).

scope of the inquiry into behavior, the drafters of the Uniform Marriage and Divorce Act stated that "there is no reason to encourage parties to spy on each other in order to discover marital, especially sexual, misconduct for use in a custody contest." In a similar manner, during the course of custody proceedings, various sexual deviations of one or the other party, noted during the marriage, may be introduced, but they cannot be utilized unless the litigant can carry the burden of showing how such sexual deviation affected or may affect the child. As an examiner, one must constantly be aware of one's own negative reactions to certain behaviors and not allow that to cloud the objectivity of the examination. A 1974 case in New York State ruled that a divorced mother could retain custody of her two children (aged 6 and 9) even though she was a "swinger." There was no evidence that the children were affected by her life-style.[4] Other criteria have included keeping siblings together and having both parents in the same state so that the child may have an ongoing relationship with both.

In the same manner, the greater financial security of one or the other competing parties does not necessarily justify placement in the more affluent home. The presence of a mental disorder does not in and of itself render a parent unqualified. A number of cases in fact show that a parent who has suffered and recovered from mental illness, and is otherwise known to be a "fit and proper person," may indeed retain preference for custody of minor children. Even with the likelihood that this individual might deteriorate in the future, custody may be awarded. When the court is faced with an issue regarding fitness for custody due to mental illness, the court must determine what the mental condition and health of the parent are at the time that the custody application is made, and must consider whether or not the disability is regarded as severe and potentially damaging to the child. If it is demonstrated to be so, by the burden of proof necessary ("clear and convincing"), then a child can be removed from the custody of that parent. Many states will allow a court, upon a writ of habeas corpus and a showing of good cause, to order an individual involved in a custody dispute to submit to a mental examination. On occasions, refusal to be examined can of itself result in the court's awarding custody to the competing party.

---

[4]Feldman vs. Feldman, 45 A.D.2d 320, 358. N.Y.S.2d 507 (2d Dept. 1974).

An excellent example of the parameters that have to be considered when one does a child custody evaluation is given in an article by Andrew Watson, M.D., a psychiatrist at the University of Michigan.[5] The dimensions outlined by Watson include the following:

1. The parents should be consulted in order that the examiner may receive permission from the parents to use confidential information such as school records.

2. Inform all parties involved of the manner in which the information and the diagnostic or therapeutic processes might be used, so that the people involved can choose what to reveal and what not to reveal. Nothing can be as damaging as something emerging at the time of trial, where a particular parent will indicate that he or she was deceived or "hoodwinked" by an examiner into revealing material which was then used against them in court.

3. A careful and comprehensive examination should include psychological testing. In addition, a good deal of time should be spent gathering background material, such as school records, and home observations.

4. The observations and conclusions should be organized in a manner such as to anticipate the questions that could possibly be raised in cross-examination. This of course is a dimension similar to the ones discussed earlier concerning preparation for testimony in a criminal trial.

When there is a separation or divorce, the visitation right of the noncustodial parent following the divorce is regarded as a fundamental right, and it cannot be restricted without a finding that the parent's activity severely impairs the physical or emotional health of the child.

EXAMPLE 1:

A psychologist was consulted by a woman who had custody of her 6-year-old son and was attempting to have the court bar her ex-husband from visiting her child. The woman contended that

---

[5] Watson, A. The children of Armageddon: problems of custody following divorce. *Syracuse Law Review* 55, 75 (1969).

her husband was a bisexual and was sexually interested in his son. The woman wanted the psychologist to write a letter in support of her position. What became very evident, in the course of dealing with the woman, was that she herself was a rather paranoid and unstable individual who had much delusional thinking regarding her husband. It was the delusional thinking that made her feel that her husband was unfit to see the child. The judge ruled, in light of the evaluation, that there were no grounds for denying visitation to the father and, in fact, made reference — in a rather lengthy and unusual opinion — to the emotional instability of the woman and her own need for further treatment.

EXAMPLE 2:

A psychologist was consulted by a couple who was concerned that the woman's ex-husband was sexually abusing the wife's 7-year-old daughter. There was no firm evidence of sexual abuse, but rather subtle behavior changes were noted in the girl following the visits. The psychologist told the parents that without seeing the natural father, no opinion on visitation could be rendered. Instead, it was agreed that the daughter would be seen for evaluation (and treatment, if necessary) to determine what her current emotional status was.

Evaluation revealed that the girl did indeed have diffuse anxiety regarding her relationship with her natural father. This was conveyed to the court, along with a recommendation that further evaluation would require the father's participation.

The court ruled that visitation would be restricted to four hours per week until such time as the father presented himself for evaluation. Once the results of such evaluation reached the court, further rulings were to be made.

As a practical matter, the mental health professional who is retained in such situations must be careful to do an objective evaluation, and must make it clear to the party retaining him or her that the evaluation will be objective and that the opinion will not necessarily sustain that particular party's contention. It should go without saying that payment arrangements must be clarified, preferably with payment in advance, regardless of the nature of the opinion forthcoming. Frequently, the attorney retaining a psychologist will present "affidavits" which outline the mental instability of the competing partner. This must all be taken into account and placed within the context of the distortions of the perceptions of all parties involved.

JOINT CUSTODY

Many courts in recent years have been awarding joint custody in which each party is a legal custodian, with both legal responsibilities and parental controls, in theory, being equally divided. Many mental health professionals counsel divorcing or divorced parents who regard this as a panacea; that is, the competing parties frequently believe, at times almost magically, that joint custody will solve all the problems. It can work, and work effectively, only if the parents can exclude the use of the children to fight their battles. Joint custody may be questioned on the grounds that constantly shuttling between parents may not be conducive to the child's sense of security or long-term development. Successful joint custody depends on the competing parties' ability to genuinely share decision making in the child rearing process.

THE FAMILY SYSTEMS APPROACH

Proponents of the family systems approach add an important concept to the "best interests of the child," namely, the solution which is "the least destructive to the entire family interaction." That is, several solutions may be in the best interests of the child, but the one causing the least disruption in terms of the child's interaction with *both* parents (and extended families when applicable) is to be preferred. Several parameters are proposed:

1. There should be continued contact among all individuals in the family over a substantial period of time.
2. Custody should be assigned to the parent more likely to provide access to the other parent and to other family members. Children need both parents for optimal psychological growth.
3. Mental illness does not, by itself, render the parent incapable of effective parenting.

4. Isolated behavioral factors (e.g., sexual deviations) *do not* necessarily affect the capacity for good parenting.

5. The child's opinion regarding custody is relevant, but should *not* be the exclusive determining factor.[6]

ADOPTION

In the United States, the first statutes regarding voluntary adoption are noted in approximately 1850. The concept of adoption without parental consent is a far more recent development, which is authorized by statute only in circumstances where there is clear and convincing proof of the unfitness of a parent or parents.

In the Uniform Adoption Act,[7] there must first be a termination of the parental rights of the natural parent, then a decree giving the adoptive parents custody, and a final decree of adoption based again on the concept of "best interests of the child." A requirement for parental consent usually exists unless the parents are incapable of giving the consent, have relinquished their rights through abandonment, or have had their rights terminated by order of a court.

The children of severely mentally disabled parents can generally be adopted without parental consent, with some exceptions which will be outlined in a later section. The reason these statutes allow adoption without consent is that people presumed to be or judged to be incompetent cannot give legally valid consent. Some recent decisions contain language indicating that a parent's consent is unnecessary for adoption if the parent has a documented history of mental illness extending more than three years into the past and if two qualified physicians (or psychologists, or one physician and one psychologist) selected by the court testify that the parent is unlikely to recover within the foreseeable future. That is, not only must there be a history of mental illness, but a professional estimate of the mental illness must indicate that the prognosis is poor.

---

[6] This approach is discussed extensively in: Group for the Advancement of Psychiatry, Committee on the Family. *New Trends in Child Custody Determinations.* New York: Harcourt, Brace, Jovanovich, 1980.

[7] Drafted by National Conference of Commissioners on Uniform State Laws, available in The Family Law Reporter (Bureau of National Affairs Inc.) reference file, Section 2 (1977).

Following the establishment of the fact that the parental rights of the natural parents have been severed, the determination needs to be made whether the proposed adoptive family can meet the physical and emotional needs of the child. Many of the factors to be taken into account are similar to those in the Michigan criteria for custody and the developmental criteria noted earlier, e.g., the age and health of the child being adopted, the age and health (mental and physical) of the prospective parents, the religious preferences, the stability of the family financially, the emotional climate, and the marital status.

Statute generally requires that an evaluation of the prospective home reveals the home to be suitable and that the child is not severely handicapped, mentally, emotionally, or physically. Once the adoption has been approved, it is regarded as permanent and can be changed only if the adoptive parents either fraudulently misrepresented the stability of their marriage or were unaware that the child was disabled.

Generally, adoption of a child by a couple is preferred to adoption by a single parent. It is somehow regarded as "more normal." On the other hand, with a very hard to place child, a single parent is preferred to an institution. The preference is normally for parents of normal child bearing age, rather than older couples. One of the very notable exceptions in the child custody literature is the case of Painter vs. Bannister.[8]

In this case, a father had voluntarily given up custody of a young child, feeling that he was unable to provide the care needed by the child because of his somewhat unstable career as a sort of "bohemian" artist. Custody was initially given to the grandparents. When the child was approximately 7 years of age, an attempt was made by the father to regain custody, and custody was indeed initially granted to the father on the grounds that the child should be with its natural biological parent. However, in a somewhat ground-breaking manner, the grandparents appealed the court ruling, stating that there was a stable long-term relationship established between them and the boy, and that the concept of a psychological parent as being more important than a biological parent needed to be considered. Indeed, final custody was awarded to the grandparents. This concept of the

---

[8]Painter vs. Bannister, 258 Iowa 1390, 140 N.W.2d 152 (1966).

importance of the "psychological" as opposed to the "biological" parent has gained much acceptance in the courts. This principle was recently reaffirmed (1981) in California.

In the case of Philip Becker, a child with Downs syndrome, a superior court in California awarded guardianship to the nonbiological parents. His biological parents placed him in a board and care facility when he was less than 6 days old, and he was then taken in by another family. The natural parents later attempted to regain custody. The court assessed: (1) the continuity of the relationship between the child and adult in terms of proximity and duration, (2) the love of the adult for the child, and (3) the affection and trust of the child toward the adult. The conclusion was that psychological parenting existed and that the biological parents were detrimental to the child.[9]

Courts will frequently try to place a child with parents of the same religious background when at all practical. If the natural parent is regarded as competent to make some statements along these lines, a stipulation frequently exists that the child should be brought up in a particular religion or background; at times, the court feels that if the child has been brought up in a particular manner, a change in religion could jeopardize the child's psychological welfare.

Having considered some of the practical aspects of these evaluations, we now are in a position to review and evaluate the related areas of child abuse, child neglect, and the legal rights of the mentally disabled regarding child custody.

CHILD ABUSE AND CHILD NEGLECT

Child abuse is regarded as a criminal offense in all states. Neglect is somewhat more ambiguous, but it generally refers to inadequate child care of a physical nature; in some states, it also includes psychological neglect. Statutes in most states prohibit cruel punishment, physical neglect, and sexual exploitation. Some states include language dealing with emotional abuse; currently, these are Arizona, California, Delaware, Idaho, Louisiana, Tennessee, Texas, and Maine. In Idaho, one of the most psychologically oriented negligence

---

[9]Guardianship of Becker, 1 Civ. 53419 (California Court of Appeals Oct. 19, 1981).

statutes has been organized. It gives the court jurisdiction over any child whose behavior indicates psychological maladjustment, in addition to those cases in which actual physical abuse occurs. Criminal negligence in several of these situations has been found even when there is no physical sign of abuse. Children may be removed from homes for many reasons, including chronic alcoholism of the parent (i.e., nonresponsive to treatment), sexual promiscuity, and mental incompetency. Nevertheless, despite the concept of psychological maladjustment, even severe mental disability of a parent does not constitute sufficient grounds for termination of custody if the parents have arranged for alternative care. Parents who are hospitalized in mental hospitals can retain custody if they make adequate arrangements for the children to be cared for while they are in the institution.

Following the termination of custody, the issue of the "best interests of the child" once again comes into play. Many of the same dimensions already enumerated are considered: for example, the age appropriateness of a child's behavior; the motives of the prospective caretakers; the pattern of reinforcements in the different environments; the sorts of role models, both peer and adult, the child would encounter; the child's manner of coping under stress and the way in which that particular coping mechanism fits or does not fit with the potential placement situation; and finally, the duration and potential stability of the setting into which the child may be placed.

Although the concept of emotional abuse is gaining acceptance, its wider recognition, of course, creates its own set of problems. It permits the state to promulgate standards of child rearing in private homes, when there is no evidence of physical injury and when the evidence of emotional abuse might be based on the opinion of a mental health professional. As discussed in previous chapters, the opinions of mental health professionals can (and frequently do) vary widely, and whether or not emotional abuse exists may become the subject of a "battle of the experts."

LEGAL RIGHTS OF THE MENTALLY DISABLED

In cases dealing with the rights of the mentally disabled, the criteria noted for the judicial determination of parental fitness have been summarized as follows:

1. the capacity of the parents to provide the child with nurturance;
2. the ability of the parents to maintain the home;
3. their capability of caring for the child's physical needs;
4. the ability to provide sufficient intellectual stimulation for the child.

Courts and social agencies have routinely concluded, in the past, that mentally retarded parents were incapable of meeting these standards and, therefore, have recommended removing the children from the home. Much research cited by advocates of the rights of the mentally disabled does not necessarily support the findings of these courts, which automatically terminated custody of mentally retarded and mentally disabled parents. Many studies have shown, for example, that women at some level of retardation are capable of exhibiting normal mothering abilities. Many of the advocates of the legal rights of the mentally disabled indicate that courts should use the same objective evidence with mentally disabled parents as in any other case for determining the fitness of parents.

In the following survey of recent court decisions regarding termination of the custodial rights of mentally disabled parents, while the inconsistencies across states will be noted, there will also be an outline of the specific issues underlying the thinking in these various jurisdictions.

The California Fifth District Court of Appeals affirmed a lower court judgment terminating a mentally ill mother's parental rights, pursuant to the civil code of the state of California. This permitted the termination of parental custody when the parent is mentally disabled, and cannot, by virtue of the disability, support or control the child. A challenge was made of the constitutionality of the statute, and the appeals court held that the statute was constitutional as long as the following two conditions could be demonstrated by *"clear and convincing proof"* (italics added):

1. The mental disability is established and will continue indefinitely regardless of medical treatment.
2. Immediate severence of the relationship is the least detrimental alternative for the child.[10]

---

[10] In re David B. 5 Fam. L. Rep. 2531 (California Fifth District Court of Appeals March 28, 1979).

Even though there was no indication of abuse, the court felt that the mother would be unable to care for her son in a proper manner. The appellate court needed to weigh the possible harm to the child against the parent's basic interest in raising the child. The usual presumption of the right of the parent to raise the child is reversed in these cases, and the agencies and courts presume that the retarded parents of the child are unfit solely by reason of their disability, even when there is no actual evidence of harm to the child of the sort required in other cases. Some further examples may clarify various parameters involved in such decision making.

In a case in Utah, in 1979, the court terminated the parental rights of a mentally retarded mother who gave birth to a physically handicapped child. Here, the court felt that because the handicapped child had special needs, the mother, in light of her limitations, was unable to provide the proper care.[11]

In Minnesota, in 1979, a mother's parental rights were terminated due to a finding that her mental condition, which had caused her to try to murder her child, would persist into the future.[12]

Several cases which supported the termination of parental rights also highlighted the inability of the parents to be treated successfully or to willingly involve themselves in treatment programs. In the case of Illinois vs. Brendendick,[13] the parents sought to regain custody of the children after the children had been in foster care, with no contact between them, for two years. The lower court had refused custody even though the mother was now discharged from a mental hospital and the father had obtained more stable employment. Nevertheless, they had done little to improve their parenting abilities. A social worker met with them and attempted to work out a plan for dealing with the emotional problems of the children, but the parents insisted that they could handle the situation if only they were given funds for "more milk and vegetables." An appellate court ruled that the parents were inadequately assisted by the social workers and that they could not, therefore, regain custody.

The importance of successful progress in rehabilitation in determining fitness of a mentally disabled parent is illustrated by the Young

---

[11] In re P.L.L., 597 P.2d 886 (Utah Supreme Court 1979).
[12] In re Baby Girl Suchy, 281 N.W.2d 723 (Minnesota Supreme Court 1979).
[13] Illinois vs. Brendendick, 393 N.E.2d 675 (Illinois Appellate Court 1979).

case in which the Washington Court of Appeals (1979) affirmed termination of parental rights on the basis of the court's finding that the mother's progress in her rehabilitation program was so slow that the children faced indefinite foster care.[14] In a similar case in Colorado (H.A.C. vs. D.C.C., 1979), parental rights were terminated because the mother was not following, or not successfully completing, the treatment plan, and it was felt that the passage of time was irrevocably injuring the children.[15]

As noted earlier, in cases in which the child presents specific problems, the court will look particularly carefully at the ability of the mentally disabled parent to provide "the special care needed." In a recent case in Idaho,[16] a mother was found unfit because of her mental retardation and the particular problems of the child. The child had a low frustration tolerance, tended to injure itself, and required constant attention. The court ruled that the mother, by virtue of her mental limitations, could neither understand nor accept the special needs posed by the child, especially since another child had been born, which "eroded" the mother's ability to cope with the situation. The court found that the best interests of the child directed it to terminate the relationship.

A court in Pennsylvania[17] ordered a 9-year-old girl to be placed in a home for crippled children until it could be determined if the placement would be effective. The child was a dwarf, and whenever she was not in her natural home, her growth rate improved dramatically. Each time she was placed in a stressful situation, her growth rate dropped below normal. It was felt by the court that speed was necessary to resolve the situation and that only if the placement was not effective could she be returned to her natural family, with the family then applying for counseling services.

In the state of Illinois, a premature baby girl was born without an anus, a condition which required surgery. Caring for the infant was unusually complicated, and both parents were mentally retarded. There was testimony offered that the parents were both enthusiastic

---

[14] In re Young 600 P.2d 1312 (Washington Court of Appeals 1979).

[15] Colorado ex rel H.A.C. vs. D.C.C. 599 P.2d 881 (Colorado Supreme Court 1979).

[16] In re Waggoner No. L-33123 (Idaho, Canyon County District Court Nov. 27, 1979).

[17] In re Pernishek, 408 A.2d 872 (Pennsylvania Superior Court 1979).

about their child, but that they frequently failed to follow feeding and bathing schedules set up by the nurses. The nurses also found small bruises on the child, but no broken bones. The father admitted that he spanked the baby when she was crying and at one time bit the baby on the nose because the crying made him nervous. The court found that this evidence sustained a lower court ruling that the child was neglected.[18]

The Supreme Court of the state of Kansas recently sustained a lower court decision to terminate the parental rights of a mentally disabled couple. Both were mentally retarded, but neither had been adjudicated mentally incompetent. Their daughter, as a result of being born microcephalic, was at high risk of being mentally retarded. The issue was a challenging one. Because of the microcephalic condition at birth, the daughter was regarded as having a high likelihood of developing neurological problems and mental retardation. She was adjudicated by a lower court to be a deprived child "not because she was abandoned, physically, mentally, or emotionally abused, neglected or sexually abused," but rather because she was without "proper parental care or controls, subsistence, education as required by law or other care and control necessary for the child's physical, mental or emotional health." In short, the court was stating that because the child itself had a high likelihood of developing neurological problems and mental retardation, it was deprived within the meaning of the law, since mentally retarded parents could not cope with the additional burden that such a condition would place on them.[19]

Of course, when it *can* be established that the parents' mental condition resulted in emotional disturbances to the child, parental rights are usually terminated.

Several other decisions, though admittedly far fewer in number, have ruled *against* the automatic termination of parental rights of the mentally disabled, absent a finding of abuse, neglect, or other major circumstances.

In a similar manner, a Massachusetts court ruled that the mere finding of a mental disorder was insufficient to terminate parental

[18] Illinois vs. Jackson, 400 N.E.2d 1087 (Illinois Court of Appeals 1980).

[19] In re Brooks 618 P.2d 814 (Kansas Supreme Court 1980).

rights. It stated that there must be specified symptoms or shortcomings which would endanger the well being of the child, in order to justify permanent removal from the parent.[20]

In the case of Williams vs. Mashburn,[21] the Oklahoma Supreme Court noted that both the mother and the father of baby girl Williams were mental hospital inpatients. Nevertheless, the court refused to terminate parental rights since the child was not suffering from willful neglect or harmful conduct, and a paternal aunt and uncle were caring well for the child. That is, the parents provided for other means of support while they were in the hospital. The court noted that mere confinement in a mental hospital does not constitute failure to give a child the necessary parental care or protection required for his mental or physical health in the purview of the termination statute. Some of the court rulings along these lines indicate that termination of parental rights solely on the grounds of mental illness or retardation violates the due process and equal protection clauses of the Fourteenth Amendment to the Constitution. It should be noted that the United States Supreme Court held that it was unconstitutional to punish conduct resulting from a disease. The court must first find the parents unfit before terminating parental rights.

Following this line of reasoning is a recent case in the state of Illinois. Here, the court ruled that an Illinois statute which allowed the children of mentally retarded parents to be placed for adoption without a showing that the parents were unfit was unconstitutional. The statute in question defined parental unfitness as acts harmful to the child such as abandonment, desertion, neglect, extreme or repeated cruelty, physical abuse, and habitual drunkenness or drug addiction. If a parent is adjudicated mentally ill or retarded, and two physicians testify that the parents will not recover from the condition in the foreseeable future, then no finding of unfitness need be made in order to terminate parental rights. In this case, the parents argued that this was a violation of due process and equal protection, because it created two classes of parents whose children could be placed for

---

[20] In re The Custody of a Minor, 393 N.E.2d 379 (Massachusetts Supreme Judicial Court 1979).

[21] Williams vs. Mashburn, 602 P.2d 1036 (Oklahoma Supreme Court 1979).

adoption: namely, those who have been found unfit and those who have been found disabled. The court agreed, stating that the statute implicitly created a presumption that all retarded parents were unfit, and added, "It cannot be argued that every retarded parent possesses one of the behavioral traits enumerated in the statute so as to be rendered unfit for parenthood."[22]

It is important to note that just within the past year, the tide has been turning in favor of the latter position, namely, that parental rights of the mentally disabled cannot be terminated automatically. In addition, the U.S. Supreme Court has ruled that the standard for determining whether a parent's mental disability is detrimental to the child must be "clear and convincing" evidence.[23]

Several recent parental termination cases (during 1981 and 1982) indicated that procedurally, the state must overcome significant burdens if it is to terminate custody based on mental disability. The petitioner must (1) prove the existence of a mental disability which is detrimental to the child by *clear and convincing evidence*; (2) prove that the detrimental situation is likely to continue indefinitely or, in the alternative, that the patient is nonresponsive to treatment; and (3) prove that state or local agencies have made all possible efforts to help the parent or parents remedy their problems. Courts have insisted that over and above the mental disability, there must be proof of neglect or serious danger of physical injury to the child as a result of the mental disability.

The implications for the mental health practitioner of this shift in emphasis are clear. The concept of "best interests of the child" in a case involving termination of parental rights due to mental disability must include a consideration and careful assessment not only of a parent's mental disorder and its impact on the child but also of (1) the likelihood that the illness will continue, (2) whether or not there may be substantial remission, (3) whether or not the parent is motivated for treatment, (4) what kind of treatment program he/she would be willing and able to follow, and (5) what their compliance with previous treatment programs has been.

---

[22] Helvey vs. Rednor, 408 N.E.2d 17 (Illinois Appellate Court 1980).

[23] Santosky vs. Kramer, 50 U.S.L.W. 4333 (1982). Also Matthews vs. Eldridge, 424 U.S. 319 (1976).

In deriving such practical guidelines from recent court decisions and using them to supplement the comprehensive, "multi-input" custody evaluation described, the mental health practitioner will be performing a valuable service to the courts and avoiding the criticism of being a party to the custody conflict.

6
Traumatic Neurosis

When the mental health professional becomes involved in the evaluation of "mental pain" in the area of civil litigation, many factors need to be considered before an opinion is rendered.

ABSENCE OR PRESENCE OF PHYSICAL INJURY

At the very outset, one must be aware of the different parameters involved when (a) the "psychic injury" is secondary to or derived from a physical injury and (b) the psychological distress appears to exist independently of any physical injury.

In the former case, the demonstration of how the psychological problems derived from the physical injury or assault is of paramount importance. All too often, this connection is "taken for granted" when a report is prepared, and the inability to carefully establish a link significantly weakens the subsequent testimony in court.

EXAMPLE:

The patient was a 38-year-old woman who, throughout her life, had demonstrated a mildly compulsive attitude, feeling a need to be in control of all her actions, emotions, and thoughts; however, she never found this disabling to any extent. She was driving a van for her church and was carrying five children of various ages in the van. She was hit, head on, by a car driven by an individual who was quite intoxicated and "high" on various drugs. The impact made her swerve off the road and drive "out of control" for a period of several seconds, eventually stopping in a ditch. She recalled a feeling of intense panic and "losing control" over the lives of the children "whose care was entrusted to me." Following her medical treatment for her injuries, she developed a chronic fear that she was always losing control, consequently heaping such additional obsessive-compulsive mechanisms on her life-style that her life came to a virtual shutdown. She was encouraged by her lawyer to seek psychotherapy, which she did.

In preparing the case for trial, the lawyer was concerned that a claim of "traumatic neurosis" would be countered by the position that the woman had *always* been compulsive, that compulsive individuals are in need of treatment, and that the expenses resulting from her treatment were not compensable. It was explained to her lawyer that while she had a preexisting condition, it was essentially an ego-syntonic character style. The accident so shattered the compulsive defenses that she continually felt *out of control* and was in treatment to restore her to a level of functioning in which she felt comfortable with her chosen life-style. She would not have sought treatment had it not been for the psychic distress caused by the accident and the feeling of "loss of control." The concept of "loss of control" became the key link between the accident and the psychic distress. In other words, it was not the preexisting character structure that caused psychic pain; rather, the accident and its psychological sequelae had rendered that former level of adjustment inadequate to cope with the current anxieties, depressions, or other symptomatologies.

In the case in which there is no injury, one has, at times, an even more demanding task, in that there is no clearly defined inception or starting point of the emotional or mental problem.

EXAMPLE:

A woman who was six months pregnant was awakened one night by a pounding on her door. When she opened the door, several policemen rushed into her apartment, ordered her to sit still, and would not allow her to obtain a robe. She indicated that she was extremely embarrassed and had no idea why the police were in her apartment. The police had apparently entered the wrong apartment with a search warrant. Following the incident, the woman developed symptoms of severe anxiety, including shaking, repetitive nightmares, a hypersensitivity to stimulation in her environment, and a fear of being in her apartment alone. While she had indeed suffered from a rather deprived and rootless childhood, the specific nature of the symptoms clearly linked them to the incident. The attorney was advised not to attempt a "cover-up" of the woman's early experiences of deprivation, but to acknowledge them and indicate that the present symptoms were the sequelae of the incident in question rather than of her early experiences.

An additional factor of extreme importance involves the need of the mental health professional to clearly understand the nature of the symptom picture presented.

THE NATURE OF SYMPTOMS

The true traumatic neurosis is one that appears in a previously mentally intact individual who has no predisposition to mental illness. Following a particular accident, this individual may manifest tremulousness, sweating, palpitations, crying, and disturbing dreams, with the inception of all of these symptoms at the time of the accident. The disturbing dreams may be regarded as the sine qua non of the traumatic neurosis and are often useful in diagnosing such a condition. Other frequently associated symptoms are muscle tension, increased irritability, difficulties in concentrating, sexual dysfunction, and withdrawal from interpersonal situations.[1]

The second kind of disorder is referred to as a triggered or compensation neurosis. This neurosis does not differ markedly from the neurosis of a nontraumatized individual. However, it generally does not have the nightmares as a part of the symptom picture. The compensation or triggered neurosis is the overt expression of a latent disease process. The triggered neurosis seizes on the occurrence of the trauma as an "excuse" for certain regressive behavior or for the overt manifestation of a disease process that has been latent for some time. It only *appears* to have its inception at the time of the accident, but careful investigative work will often point out the precursors, in the patient's past life, of the condition which now appears on the surface. Such investigative work is always necessary to establish

---

[1] Modlin, H. C. The post-accident anxiety syndrome, psychosocial aspects. *American Journal of Psychiatry* 123:1008 (1967).

whether the symptom picture represents a traumatic neurosis (no significant indications of previous similar symptoms) or a compensation neurosis (history of similar, dynamically equivalent, or related symptoms). In the triggered neurosis, the individual is latently emotionally or mentally ill, and decompensates because of a stress that would not be bothersome to an average individual. In the true traumatic neurosis, by distinction, a basically well-integrated individual suffers emotional distress as the result of an extremely stressful situation.

The third area of which the mental health professional needs to be aware is of course malingering, in which one finds a conscious simulation of illness in order to evade work or responsibility, or to gain something else. Many of the same techniques previously utilized to detect the faking of mental illness in the criminal justice system are applicable here as well. These would include careful use of the MMPI, including validity scales and subtle-obvious dichotomy, and analysis of the nature of the symptoms presented (and what, if any, relationship they bear to the accident or injury).

WORKMEN'S COMPENSATION

The one exception to the distinction between a true traumatic neurosis and a triggered neurosis is the whole area of workmen's compensation. Many companies offer workmen's compensation insurance, and in such cases, compensation is usually awarded whether the injury is regarded as a true traumatic neurosis or as a triggered neurosis. The landmark case in the history of workmen's compensation was a lawsuit against General Motors', in which an employee was compensated for a psychiatric breakdown which was not associated with a physical injury, accident, specific event, or unusual stress or incident. He was diagnosed as paranoid schizophrenic; the specific causation of the mental illness appeared to be the stress of working on the assembly line; the patient had decompensated due to stresses that were "inconsequential to the average individual."

In actual practice, workmen's compensation laws vary dramatically from state to state in terms of the extent of compensation that may

---

[2] Carter vs. General Motors Co., 361 Mich. 577, 106 N.W.2d 105 (1961).

be awarded to someone with a "preexisting" condition. The mental health professional is well advised to review carefully the laws of the state in which he/she is practicing to determine the broadness or restrictiveness of the specific compensation laws.

For example, a recent ruling in the state of Michigan adopts an extremely liberal view of compensability. In a case entitled Dezio vs. Difko Laboratories,[3] the state supreme court ruled that a connection between an industrial injury and a given mental or emotional disorder is compensable if the claimant has an honest (even if mistaken) subjective perception that they are indeed related. Here, any preexisting illness is regarded as totally irrelevant, as long as the worker perceives a causal link between the illness and the injury. This case certainly ignores the whole concept of unconscious secondary gain. The expert's role, in such an evaluation, would be primarily to evaluate the "integrity" of the claimant's perception of the causal link.

A variation suggested by some legal scholars is to utilize the time-honored "reasonable man" test: i.e., Is it reasonable to assume that a particular mental or emotional illness is causally related to some industrial accident? Here, the role of the mental health professional would be similar to that outlined initially, namely, determining the likely course of a particular illness or injury and whether or not it corresponds to the presenting symptoms.

On the more conservative extreme, for example, is the workmen's compensation statute in the state of Maryland. Here, the Workmen's Compensation Code defines occupational disease as an "ailment, disorder or illness which is the expectable result of working under conditions naturally inherent in the employment and inseparable therefrom, and which is ordinarily slow and insidious in its approach. Where an occupational disease is aggravated by any other disease or infirmity, not itself compensable or where disability or death from any other cause not itself compensable is aggravated, prolonged, accelerated or in anyway contributes to a finding of occupational disease, the percentage of such contribution is to be determined by the Medical Board as hereinafter created. *The compensation payable shall be reduced and limited to such portion only of the compensation*

---

[3] Deziel vs. Difco Laboratories, 268 N.W.2d (Michigan Supreme Court 1978).

that will be payable if the occupational disease was the sole cause of the death. Such disease acts as a causative factor and bears to all causes of disability and death." (italics added)

In other words, in a state with a more conservatively oriented statute, such as Maryland, it is critical for the mental health professional not only to perform a current mental status examination and psychological testing, and be able to relate the findings to the instant injury, but also to take a careful history to investigate the possible contribution to the current condition of "preexisting causes." This would include interviews with family and friends who have known the claimant both prior to *and* after the accident, as well as a review of previous medical and/or psychiatric records. The professional must then determine the extent of the involvement of the preexisting condition, and assign a percentage to it and to the precipitating injury. The current emotional illness will then be compensable only for the portion attributable to the industrial accident or occupational injury, not to that portion attributable to the preexisting condition.

EXAMPLE:

A woman who was employed as an art therapist at a state mental institution was evaluated for workmen's compensation after having suffered an acute psychotic episode during the course of her employment. Current mental status examination and psychological testing revealed a young woman in a rather unstable remission from the aforementioned psychotic episode. During the course of the evaluation, she mentioned several previous involvements in psychotherapy, some of which preexisted the psychotic episode. When questioned about this, she indicated that at those times she had not been in psychic distress but was in therapy for reasons of "personal growth"; an opinion on degree of compensability was deferred until these previous psychiatric records were made available.

Several recent cases highlight the variations across states regarding the liberality or conservatism of various workmen's compensation laws. On the conservative end, for example, are two recent cases, one from Minnesota and the other from Rhode Island.

In the case of Lockwood vs. Independent School District No. 877 (Minnesota Supreme Court, December 4, 1981),[4] a high school principal who suffered a disabling mental injury caused by work-related mental stress was not entitled to workmen's compensation *unless he suffered physical trauma.*

In the case of Seitz vs. L. & R. Industries,[5] an office manager for a firm that made a disruptive interstate move was unsuccessful in claiming that the stressful nature of the new office aggravated her rigid personality characteristics into a disabling obsessive-compulsive disorder.

On the liberal end of the spectrum, we find several more cases. For example, in the case of James vs. Oregon State Accident Insurance Fund, the plaintiff's neurosis was so exacerbated by her supervisor's criticism that she became unable to work and was compensated for her injury.[6]

In Fayne vs. Fieldcrest Mills, Inc. (North Carolina Court of Appeals, 1981),[7] an employee who injured her back as a result of a work-related accident was entitled to compensation for mental problems she suffered after the injury. The testimony of a psychiatrist was sufficient to establish a causal connection between the accident and the resulting severe neurotic depressive reaction which made the woman unable to work.

In the case of Franz vs. Comet Construction Co. (New York Supreme Court, Appellate Division, 1981),[8] a construction worker who claimed his mental illness resulted from an on-the-job leg injury that later required amputation was entitled to have his repeated hospitalizations and psychiatric treatments covered by worker's compensation. The court upheld an administrative law judge's findings that the employee's earlier psychiatric hospitalizations were causally related to the accident and that an award for an additional extensive healing period should be made.

[4] Lockwood vs. Independent School District No. 887, 50 U.S.L.W. 2368 (Minnesota Supreme Court December 4, 1981).

[5] Seitz vs. L. & R. Industries, 437 A.2d 1345 (Rhode Island Supreme Court 1981).

[6] James vs. Oregon State Accident Fund, 624 P.2d 565 (Oregon Supreme Court 1981).

[7] Fayne vs. Fieldcrest Mills Inc., 282 S.E.2d 539 (North Carolina Court of Appeals 1981).

[8] Franz vs. Comet Construction Corp. 444 N.Y.S.2d 271 (New York Appellate Division 1981).

In Lopucki vs. Ford Motor Co.,[9] the Michigan Court of Appeals ruled in 1981 that the widow of an employee who committed suicide may be awarded worker's compensation benefits if the deceased's employment "aggravated or contributed to a self-destructive state of mind."

The Oregon Court of Appeals in 1981 ruled in the case of State Accident Insurance Fund vs. Gygi[10] that expert testimony stating that the stresses of a job aggravated a preexisting mental illness was sufficient to make the mental illness a "compensable occupational disease."

Some states (e.g., Maine) indicate that "gradual" mental injury may be compensable under workmen's compensation. However, testimony must demonstrate that greater than usual everyday stresses and tensions common to all employees were involved or that the "usual and ordinary work-related pressures" were the predominant factor in producing the injury.[11]

MENTAL HEALTH PROFESSIONALS AND LAWYERS — PROBLEMS IN COMMUNICATION

Mental health professionals frequently complain that they are unable to communicate with attorneys effectively in personal injury cases, because of apparent differences in emphasis. Indeed, there are some very marked philosophical differences between the legal and the psychological approach to causation, and these need to be spelled out so that mental health professionals can gain a firm grasp of the reasons they feel in conflict with the legal profession and determine how they might deal with these differences.

Psychologists tend to be concerned with *all* possible causes of a patient's current condition, whereas legal practitioners in personal injury cases focus on some event that aggravates a particular aspect of a condition to the extent that the event in question is, in the language of the law, the proximate cause of an injurious result. This concept of "proximate cause" is one that is often inadequately

---

[9] Lopucki vs. Ford Motor Co. 311 N.W.2d 338 (Michigan Court of Appeals 1981).

[10] State Accident Insurance Fund vs. Gygi, 639 P.2d 655 (Oregon Court of Appeals 1982).

[11] Workers' Compensation Act, Me. Rev. Stat. Ann. Tit. 39 §§ 1 et req. Townsend vs. Maine Bureau of Public Safety, 404 A.2d 1014 (Maine Supreme Judicial Court 1979).

understood by psychologists. The law is not asking the psychologist to state that the illness is the result solely of the accident, but that the accident was the most important factor or the most recent in time, in terms of its relationship to the mental or emotional condition.

In cases in which such causation questions arise, the law will frequently ask whether or not an identifiable event, such as an accident, a physical or emotional trauma, stress, or a particular treatment or lack of treatment, was "the proximate cause" of personal injury: Did the event create a new disorder or did it aggravate an underlying disorder, which resulted in impairment *sooner than would have ordinarily been the case in the natural progression of the preexisting condition*? This of course is a very important distinction which psychologists frequently overlook. In many cases, the psychologist notes that there is a preexisting condition and that the condition being attributed to the accident or trauma would eventually have occurred under any circumstances. In such cases, psychologists frequently feel very uneasy about testifying. They need not feel so uneasy. A careful reading of the laws indicates that the only thing which has to be established is that the injury or stress either *exacerbated* the underlying mental disorder or hastened its movement towards a particular disability. In other words, the preexisting condition is not excluded, but compensability is based only on the treatment related to the sequelae of the specific injury. This sometimes becomes very difficult to spell out and can be a practical pitfall for the mental health expert involved in such cases. However, if careful investigative work is performed, one can establish what the prior level of adjustment was, the extent to which there was a preexisting condition, and what its nature was. Then a comparison and contrast can be made of the differences in the person's life since the accident. One is able to assess, in a far more concrete manner, the actual impact of the accident, trauma, treatment, or lack of treatment. What very frequently becomes essential is an establishment of what form of character structure the person most likely had prior to the incident, what the disruption in that life-style was, and whether the life-style was adaptive or maladaptive at the outset.

When dealing with such an issue in terms of personal injury litigation, the psychologist needs to make clear just what the premorbid level of adjustment was and in what specific ways that differs from the condition attributable to the accident or injury. Psychotherapy in such cases can be compensable to the extent to which it restores the person to the premorbid level of functioning, *regardless of whether or not the mental health professional judges that premorbid level of functioning to have been a healthy or optimal one.*

As a practical matter, insurance companies will frequently be "looking for an excuse" to deny compensation in some personal injury cases. They will cite the preexisting condition as grounds for rejecting the claim. This puts the psychologist in somewhat of a bind. On the one hand, when one sees a patient in distress, one attempts to assist them in obtaining the help they need. On the other hand, under the American Psychological Association's code of ethics, one must render a complete, accurate, objective report, neither making unwarranted inferences from the data nor deleting material unfavorable to the legal resolution being sought.

Some mental health professionals unfortunately (and sometimes unwittingly) border on such an ethical violation when they stress material related to the accident and downplay or delete material related to a preexisting condition.

EXAMPLE:

A mental health professional rated a patient as "100% psychiatrically disabled" as a result of severe anxiety and depression, relating the anxiety and depression to the automobile accident in which the patient was involved. The history that was taken revealed that the patient's wife had a terminal illness which caused the patient significant distress as well. However, in a misguided attempt to assist the patient in securing compensation for psychotherapy, the professional attributed all the anxiety to the accident, deleting any mention of the wife's illness.

Not only are such inaccurate reports misleading and bordering on the unethical, but they also present the mental health professional as a "hired gun," a reputation highly damaging to the credibility of all mental health witnesses in court.

A more constructive manner of handling such situations is to acknowledge frankly the preexisting situation, how the patient had adapted to that situation, and how the accident or injury altered that adaptation.

EXAMPLE:

The patient was a 33-year-old married woman who had been the victim of a traffic accident which resulted in severe emotional disability. She had changed from a vivacious outgoing person to an individual unable to leave her home, go shopping, do housework, cook, or socialize in any way without experiencing severe anxiety, confusion, and fainting spells. She was asked, during the evaluation, to describe symptoms she had previously experienced and those which appeared to have occurred since the accident.

She noted that she had been diagnosed as dyslexic as a child and had learned to control it, but had suffered a loss of control since the accident. She described her early home life as "awful," with her mother committing suicide and there being substantial discord when her father remarried. Prior to the accident, she had been able to suppress her memories of these traumatic situations, but since the accident, she found them continually intruding into consciousness. She had also gained control over a variety of other symptoms and "worked through" many feelings of rejection, hurt, and anger prior to the accident, but found herself flooded with the feelings since the accident.

She also reported a number of new symptoms since the accident, including sexual dysfunction, headaches, insomnia, and nightmares.

History taking and psychological testing confirmed the presence of a severe anxiety neurosis, with no evidence whatsoever of malingering. The conclusion of the report read as follows:

In summary, then, Ms. B. appears to be a young woman who had had a series of exceedingly traumatic experiences in her childhood, with which she learned to cope with a variety of defense mechanisms, and indeed she was performing at an exceedingly high level. The accident shattered her defensive structures, and threw her back to a series of more primitive defense mechanisms and a far more regressed manner of dealing with the environment around her. She appears to have made substantial progress in psychotherapy up to this point, but given the degree of disorganization, anxiety, and depression at present, it is my opinion that she will need to be involved in psychotherapy for a substantial period of time before she is able to regain the level of coping and adjustment which she had prior to the accident. In my opinion, intensive psychotherapy, for a period of three to four more years, would be an absolute minimum to restore Ms. B. to her previous level of functioning.

In contrast to the previous example, it can be seen that here the preexisting condition was acknowledged openly, with the stress being on how the patient adapted to that condition and how the accident altered, in a regressive manner, the level of mature adaptation and coping.

THERAPIST OR EXAMINER

One final practical pitfall in personal injury litigation should be discussed. On occasion, an individual will be in psychotherapy prior to a trauma or an accident, or the person will consult the therapist for treatment as a result of the accident but prior to any notice to the mental health professional that he/she is going to pursue litigation. The therapist establishes a treatment contract with the patient. When the "gears are shifted" and litigation ensues, the therapist should generally not become the patient's advocate in the litigation. Clearly, doing a comprehensive psychological evaluation in reference to any case, civil or criminal, involves many investigative dimensions which are quite distinct from the therapeutic or helping orientation that one has in psychotherapy. As noted earlier, when accepting a patient into therapy, one generally does not consider issues such as malingering, secondary gain from the symptoms, or whether similar symptoms were present prior to the trauma or accident.

Disastrous results can ensue if a psychologist enters court merely on the basis of his therapeutic interaction with a patient, and tries to render valid opinions in a particular case based on this therapeutic insight, without doing the investigative work necessary in any forensic case.

EXAMPLE:

A therapist was consulted by a patient who complained of anxiety and depression subsequent to his being arrested and questioned by the security force in a large metropolitan department store. The therapist, six months later, wrote an "evaluation" of the patient in support of the lawsuit against the department store. Regarding himself as an advocate of the patient, he stated that the incident in the department store precipitated not only the anxiety and depression, but also the patient's subsequent arrest on another charge. The therapist did not take any history, maintaining that histories were irrelevant to the ongoing dynamics of therapy. History, however, did reveal a pattern of filing grievances against institutions, some evidence of paranoia, and a "shopping around" for a therapist who would unquestioningly accept his position.

In many ways, therefore, the comprehensive forensic evaluation in civil litigation must closely parallel that described in criminal matters for competency and criminal responsibility. One must not only evaluate the surface presentation of symptoms but also look for issues of malingering, "retrospective falsification," secondary gain, and the nature of the symptoms present. Clinical interview is *never* sufficient; interview must be supplemented by careful review of records, history taking, and interviews with family, friends, or employees. Hospital records must be consulted, and counsel should be consulted for his or her appraisal of the patient's symptoms. Psychological testing, frequently including neuropsychological evaluation, is essential, as is the utilization of tests such as EEGs and CAT scans, and their interpretation by a skilled neurologist. In preparing testimony, consultation with counsel is again important to determine both the strengths *and* the weaknesses in any given case, the issues to be presented, and the questions to be anticipated in cross-examination.

CONCLUSION

This chapter has outlined some of the parameters which must be evaluated and considered in working on personal injury cases. It has stressed the need to carefully investigate the symptom picture, to determine the role of "preexisting causes," and to avoid mixing the roles of therapist and examiner.

7
Professional Liability

PRIVILEGED COMMUNICATION

Many aspects of professional liability interface closely with issues of confidentiality and privileged communication, critical issues for the mental health professional. On the one hand, confidentiality is regarded as perhaps the most essential aspect of the therapeutic relationship. On the other hand, many recent court decisions have challenged the absolute right to confidentiality. Initially, the American Psychological Association Code of Professional Ethics regarded confidentiality as an absolute. More recently, in revisions of the code of ethics, perhaps in light of the thinking engendered by these decisions, it has been modified to allow psychotherapists to breach the confidentiality of a therapeutic relationship when there is an identifiable threat to harm or injure a third party. Still, there are many who oppose the loosening of the confidentiality aspect of the code of ethics, most notably Dr. Max Siegel, current president of the American Psychological Association. Dr. Siegel has stated in writing on many occasions his belief that the confidential nature of the therapeutic relationship should under no circumstances be breached.[1]

Within the law, the applicable language is found in statutes on privileged communications. Perhaps the most comprehensive treatment of the issue of privileged communication can be found in the writings of Dean Wigmore, who stated four conditions for privileged communication: (1) the communication must originate in a confidence that it will not be disclosed, (2) confidentiality must be essential to the satisfactory maintenance of the relationship, (3) the community must believe that this relationship should be fostered, and (4) the injury to the relationship from disclosure of the communi-

---

[1] President's Message, *The Clinical Psychologist,* Vol. 31, Number 2, Winter 1978.

cation must be greater than the benefit that would be gained from the correct disposition of the litigation.[2]

Dr. Ralph Slovenko, of the law school of Wayne State University in Detroit, has applied Dean Wigmore's arguments to the area of psychotherapy in the following manner: (1) the communications in psychotherapy are confidential, (2) a patient will not communicate to his therapist if he knows that his communication can be revealed, (3) the community believes that a psychotherapeutic relationship is one that should be fostered, and (4) the information gained in psychotherapy would be less beneficial to justice than it would be to the continuance of therapy. That is, one may interpret the last statement as indicating that breaching the confidentiality would be of less benefit to the proper disposition of certain litigations than the maintenance of confidentiality would be to the preservation of the therapeutic relationship.[3] Dr. Slovenko argues rather compellingly that the benefit to justice in allowing confidential testimony is outweighed by the injury to the psychotherapeutic relationship where parties, fearing later exposure, would not make full and honest disclosure in therapy.

Several landmark cases, however, regard the issue of privileged communication somewhat differently. In the Lifshutz decision in 1970, the California Supreme Court indicated that psychotherapists do not have an absolute right of privacy, but there is permitted "limited intrusion into the psychotherapist/patient privilege when it is properly justified."[4] In an appellate decision from the California Courts of Appeals, the decision was basically sustained. When limited within certain parameters, the statute in question — which concerned waiver of privilege — did not constitute an impermissible invasion of privacy.

The situation dealt with a patient who requested that a therapist disclose information which the patient felt would be beneficial to the pursuance of certain litigation. The therapist refused, claiming that the therapeutic communications were privileged. The Lifshutz decision required disclosure *only of the information directly pertinent*

---

[2] Quoted in Slovenko, R. *Psychiatry and Law.* Boston: Little, Brown, 1973, pp. 61–74.
[3] Ibid., pp. 61–74.
[4] In re Lifshutz, 2 Cal. 3d 415, 467 P.2d 557, 85 Cal. Rptr. 829 (1970).

to issues raised by the patient in the litigation. In both the Lifshutz decision and a subsequent decision (Caesar vs. Montanos),[5] the constitutionality of the California statute which waived the psychotherapist/patient privilege when a litigating patient put his or her mental or emotional condition into issue was discussed. In the latter case, the psychiatrist in question, Dr. Caesar, challenged the statute and was found to be in contempt of the California court for refusing to answer questions relating to a former patient's mental and emotional condition. Dr. Caesar had treated the patient for emotional distress and depression following two automobile accidents for which the former patient was seeking damages. The patient had at one point authorized Dr. Caesar to testify, but he refused to do anything more than reveal his diagnosis. Specifically, he refused to answer a series of questions concerning the relationship of his patient's emotional condition to the accident. These questions were found by the court of appeals to be clearly relevant to the issue of the patient's emotional condition which the patient herself had raised. The statute in question stated that there was no psychotherapist/patient privilege when the patient placed his or her emotional condition in issue by claiming damages for mental and emotional distress.

An important point should be added in the aftermath of both of these decisions. The burden is on the patient, once the "Pandora's box" of psychotherapy notes has been opened, to prove that other material is unrelated. As stated earlier, these decisions spoke about the necessity of disclosure *only* of the information directly pertinent to issues raised in the lawsuit. However, the defendant in such a suit could insist that the therapist's entire file was relevant, and the burden would remain on the plaintiff to show that the information was unrelated. The plaintiff or patient has the burden of making a showing that a given confidential communication is not directly related to the issue that the patient is bringing before the court. The patient's own action, in other words, initiates the exposure; thus the intrusion into the patient's privacy remains, according to the court, under the patient's control.

---

[5] Caesar vs. Montanos, 542 F.2d 1064 (Ninth Circuit 1976).

EXAMPLE:

The therapist has been treating an individual who, in the course of psychotherapy, requests disclosure of therapeutic notes regarding the emotional sequelae of an automobile accident in which he was involved — specifically, anxiety and depression. The patient, in addition, has been discussing extensively with the therapist the fact that he has recently manifested symptoms of impotence, but he does not want that aspect of treatment revealed. Now that the patient has effectively waived the privilege to that confidential information, the burden would be on the patient to show that discussions with the therapist regarding the impotence were *not* part of the issues directly related to the investigation.

MALPRACTICE

The concept of what is and is not privileged communication leads us into the area of professional liability, which interfaces quite closely with many aspects of the preceding discussion.

Psychologists who read a variety of professional journals have, in recent years, seen the following type of ad by various carriers of malpractice insurance:

One Dissatisfied Client Could Send You into Bankruptcy!

The case is somewhat overstated, for there is in reality rather limited litigation against psychotherapists. The reason for the limited litigation in this area, of course, is that patients are generally reluctant to reveal all of their psychopathology in front of a court and, perhaps more important in terms of the law itself, there is considerable difficulty in establishing the elements of malpractice.

Forms Of Relief

The forms of relief that one is able to obtain in a trial court in a malpractice action are generally broken down into three areas. The first is an *injunction,* in which the trial court orders a therapist to do or not do something. The therapist is told that certain practices in which he or she is engaging are not to be followed any further, that the conduct is not in keeping with the standards set by other practicing professionals, or that there are certain aspects of the behavior as a therapist which must be changed. The second form of relief is called a *declaratory judgment.* Frequently, the therapist or practitioner will initiate proceedings on his or her own which result in a declaratory judgment from the court. For example, the individual therapist, wanting to know whether a given law is unconstitutional, will approach the court and ask for an opinion on the constitutionality of a specific issue, for example, whether aversive therapy with mentally retarded patients violates due process. The response that one gets from the court is referred to as a declaratory judgment. The final form of relief is called *damages,* which in turn can be broken down into nominal, compensatory, and punitive.

Nominal damages represent the mildest of the three. Here, there is evidence of wrongdoing on the part of the professional, but no evidence that any real injury resulted from the wrongful behavior. The court issues in such cases, an admonition which tells the therapist or practitioner that his or her behavior was improper. Compensatory damages are those which are generally recovered in malpractice actions; they are viewed as compensation for a loss. Compensatory damages most frequently refer to the impairment of future earnings (a loss of earnings that would be a result of the injury itself), medical or other expenses necessary to restore the patient to optimal functioning, or compensation for a vague and elusive concept called "pain and suffering." Especially in the description of various "psychological injuries," the concept of pain and suffering can be very difficult to define. Punitive, or exemplary, damages are the most extreme of all. Here, the behavior is so egregious that over and above the compensatory damages, an additional monetary award is made.

The Concept of a Tort

A tort is basically a civil (as opposed to a criminal) wrong by one private individual against another. Torts may be broken down into three kinds of wrongs. An *intentional wrong,* by definition, is knowingly or purposefully done. In a *reckless wrong,* one finds a conscious disregard of a known risk. The third form of wrong is known as *negligence,* the occurrence of some event which is harmful because the person does not know something that he or she should have known. Negligence, therefore, is a wrong that is not committed deliberately. It is the easiest of the three forms of wrong to prove. That is, in trying to prove intentional wrongs, there must be proof, by a preponderance of evidence, that the perpetrator of the wrong deliberately, knowingly, and purposefully engaged in the action which resulted in the wrong. In attempting to prove recklessness, there are again great difficulties. The plaintiff must prove that the individual practitioner was aware of the risk involved, and consciously and knowingly disregarded it.

EXAMPLE:

Much of the recent litigation involving the long-term effects of psychotropic medication (resulting in such irreversible conditions as tardive dyskinesia) has attempted to prove that the prescribing of these drugs was a reckless wrong. However, the courts have noted that at the time these medications were prescribed, the state of the art was such that the research regarding tardive dyskinesia was not solid; therefore, the practitioners who prescribed the drugs could not have been consciously disregarding a known risk.

The concept of malpractice comes under negligence since it is regarded as some action, conducted or performed by a professional, in which the professional acts unreasonably or shows a lack of skill in professional duties. In malpractice actions, one must evaluate the gravity of the harm, the likelihood that the harm would have occurred even in the absence of the practitioner's actions, and the various benefits that might have occurred as a result of the actions. These benefits must be weighed against the likelihood of the harm. In malpractice litigation, the burden of proof is always initially on the plaintiff, that is, the party initiating the litigation. As noted earlier the elements of malpractice must be proved by the preponderance of evidence: i.e., it must be slightly more likely than not that the injury was related to the actions or inaction of the practitioner.

The burden of proof being on the plaintiff is referred to as the *per-suasion burden.* The plaintiff must commence the litigation by producing documentation that proves, by a preponderance of evidence, four elements of malpractice. The defendant, at the termination of the plaintiff's case, can move for summary dismissal which indicates that no case for malpractice has been made. At this point, the judge may agree that the four elements of malpractice have not been proved by a preponderance of evidence, and grant the summary dismissal. If, on the other hand, the judge feels that the four elements have been met, then the motion for a summary dismissal is not honored, and the burden for production of evidence shifts to the defendant.

The first element of malpractice which must be proved in order for the case not to be summarily dismissed is the existence of a duty to the client, defined in terms of the skill and care exercised by the average practitioner. What is critical here is the establishment of a professional relationship; the standard of care follows from the nature of that relationship. It is in such cases that documents like the American Psychological Association's *Standards for Providers of Psychological Services*[6] become critical; this document defines what the service is and what sort of behavior is expected of the professional engaged in providing such service. The concept of *relationship* is a crucial one, since a number of malpractice suits have been summarily dismissed because there was no professional relationship involved. The second element of malpractice that must be proved by a preponderance of the evidence is that the existing duty was breached; the third, that an injury was sustained by the client. Finally, it must be proved that the breach of the duty was the *proximate* cause of the injury; that is, there was a clear connection between the injury and the breach of the duty by the professional: *but for* the breach of duty, the injury would not have occurred.

The Causes of Malpractice Actions

There are a number of different bases for malpractice actions. The first is faulty diagnosis. This refers to a diagnosis that results in misclassification, which misdiagnosis or misclassification was the proxi-

---

[6]Standards for Providers of Psychological Services, Washington D.C. A.P.A., 1974.

mate cause of a specific injury. In such cases, it must be established that if the correct diagnosis had been made, some correct treatment would have been undertaken and, therefore, the injury which did occur would not have. Before mental health professionals become overly concerned about the possibility that anyone can misdiagnose a patient, it should be pointed out that the cause for malpractice under this heading is not merely the issue of misdiagnosis. There is no malpractice if other well-trained mental health professionals could have made the same error. Rather, such actions come about when there is evidence that in reaching the diagnosis, the practitioner ignored or overlooked aspects of the situation which a well-trained professional should not overlook, and that overlooking those aspects resulted in a treatment or lack of treatment which was the proximate cause of the injury.

EXAMPLE:

A patient is referred to a psychologist by a psychiatrist who has been unable to determine the etiology of the patient's headaches. The psychologist administers a standard battery of psychological tests, but fails to do any neuropsychological evaluation or to refer the patient for neuropsychological or neurological workup, if neuropsychology is not one of his or her areas of expertise. Evidence of anxiety is found on the tests, and the headaches are diagnosed as being of psychosomatic origin, with no one paying attention to the possible organic basis of the illness. Were the patient to become seriously ill, or die, as a result of a diagnosable brain injury (perhaps diagnosed upon autopsy), then both the psychiatrist and the psychologist could be held liable, on the grounds of faulty diagnosis.

A second reason for malpractice is known as wrongful commitment. This has become particularly relevant in recent years, since psychologists in many states now have the authority to sign papers for the involuntary commitment of individuals. Here, clearly, the issue would be whether or not there was a breach of professional duty in declaring someone to be dangerous, or in need of hospitalization, who really was not. The particularly critical aspect of this is highlighted in the Donaldson decision,[7] handed down by the U.S. Supreme Court in 1975. In this decision, both the institution in which Donaldson was confined and his personal physician were held liable. Wrongful commitment is one of the few grounds for malpractice in which an individual employed by an institution can be held personally liable.

The third ground for a malpractice action is the concept of wrongful release, in a sense the exact opposite of the prior one. Here, an individual or a hospital can be held liable for releasing someone who does not meet the criteria for release; that is, the "reasonably prudent professional" would feel that this individual was not ready for release, that he or she remained a danger to self or others, and that some injury could well result from that wrongful or premature release. The courts' language under this criterion generally refers to liability if the premature release resulted in someone committing a dangerous act and if it should have been reasonably assumed that the dangerous act would be committed in the foreseeable future.

The fourth cause of malpractice actions is failure to take precautions against suicide. Mental health professionals can be held liable for self-inflicted injuries sustained by a patient. However, the failure to detect suicidal tendencies is not regarded as malpractice in and of itself for, in the language of the court, there is no malpractice if there is no proof that generally accepted standards require a conclusion that the patient is likely to commit suicide. If, on the other hand, the patient gives notice that he is planning to harm himself, and if from history it is reasonably predictable that he will do so, the therapist's failure to take reasonable precautions to prevent this could render him or her liable. Improper attention to the patient's history is in this circumstance part of the grounds for liability. If the professional is working in an institution and there is good indication that a given patient will attempt suicide, a failure to give appropriate orders to the staff concerned, or the staff's failure to carry out orders that are written, can also be grounds for this liability or negligence. However, some recent court decisions, especially in the case of Bellah vs. Greenson (1977),[8] indicate that if a therapist feels that a patient may be suicidal, adequate precautions do not necessarily include

---

[7] O'Connor vs. Donaldson, 422 U.S. 563 (1975).

[8] Bellah vs. Greenson, 1 Civ, No. 39770 (Cal. Oct. 5, 1977).

warning the family of that patient. Under any circumstances, the necessity for extensive and careful documentation of a patient's history, suicidal or otherwise, is critical. Further, any attempts that the therapist tries to make to have the patient hospitalized or, if the patient refuses, any attempts to have the patient involuntarily committed must be carefully and completely documented in the therapist's notes. Similarly, if the therapist is unsure of certain aspects and consults with colleagues on the matter, then once again it is critical that all this material be carefully documented.

The fifth basis for malpractice actions is the breach of confidentiality and privacy, when there are no compelling reasons for such a breach of confidentiality or privacy.

A sixth area deals with defamation of character. In order to be sued for malpractice on these grounds, there must be a communication to a third party. There must be evidence that the plaintiff has been subjected to hate or ridicule because of some publication, or manifestation, of certain statements in a public place.

The seventh cause for malpractice involves sexual contact with the patient. Here, of course, there is very little debate. Most reasonably prudent professionals agree that sexual contact with a patient constitutes totally unprofessional behavior.

The eighth basis for malpractice actions can be injuries resulting from a physical aspect of nontraditional therapy. The landmark case in this was a malpractice action against Dr. John Rosen. Dr. Rosen was sued by a patient who stated that in the course of "direct analytic therapy" with him, Dr. Rosen had physically beaten him.[9]

A ninth area of potential liability for the mental health professional is the failure to obtain informed consent to treatment. Of course, the lack of informed consent must be shown to be proximately related to the injury sustained. One would need expert witnesses to testify to the facts that it was the treatment which resulted in the injury, and that the patient was not informed of the potential risks of the treatment. One of the difficulties that arises in cases of informed consent is the occurrence of emergency situations, in which lifesaving measures must be taken and informed consent cannot be obtained. Of course, the definition of what constitutes an emergency

---

[9] Hammer vs. Rosen, 198 N.Y.S. 2d 803, 165 N.E. 2d 756 (New York Court of Appeals 1960).

will differ from one professional to the next, but expert testimony would have to establish the fact that failure to obtain informed consent in this particular case was a departure from accepted professional practice.

A very important area of potential liability is failure to warn, in which the protection of a third party is involved. A number of recent cases highlight the so-called duty to warn and indicate that the breach of this duty can constitute grounds for malpractice. The failure to warn emerges when the therapist is involved with a patient who threatens to do bodily harm to another individual: Should the therapist breach the confidentiality of the therapy relationship and warn the intended victim? Should the patient be warned ahead of time that all communications are not necessarily privileged? This may lead to overprediction of dangerousness (i.e., false positives), and a great deal of damage may be done to confidentiality and to the whole therapeutic enterprise. A related question is whether a therapist knows when a patient is talking about a real threat and when it remains on a purely fantasy basis. Another issue involved the distinction between a purely verbal threat and a threat which the individual really intends to carry out.

The final basis for malpractice is abandonment, which generally arises when a therapist stops seeing a patient, or refuses to see a patient further, and no satisfactory arrangements have been made for follow-up care.

Duty and the Breach of Duty

Duty is established first by statute and secondly by the rules of professional practice, e.g., a code of professional ethics or the standards for providers discussed earlier. A standard of care exists and is established in court by an expert witness, who testifies to the level of skill of the average psychologist or average practitioner who is exercising reasonable care. The test of the breach of duty always falls back on "what would have been done by the reasonably prudent practitioner." The breach of duty is always judged in terms of foreseeability of injury by a reasonably prudent practitioner.

For instance, in a case where someone commits suicide, suicidal thoughts in the past do not necessarily result in current liability.

Rather, there must be strong recent evidence, usually a recent overt suicide attempt, to support a finding of negligence and malpractice.

Defenses in Malpractice Actions

Recently, St. Elizabeth's Hospital in Washington, D.C., was held not liable for a patient's participation in a bank robbery or for a homicide committed during the course of that robbery.[10] The suit was brought by the surviving spouse of the bank teller, who stated that the hospital and its staff should have reasonably foreseen that the patient was dangerous. The patient had failed to return from a motion picture he attended with other patients, and his whereabouts were not known until after the robbery, which took place a week later. He had originally been committed in 1965 as not guilty by reason of insanity. In 1971, he was placed on conditional release, enabling him to seek employment in the city during the day and reside at the hospital at night. The court relied on a standard that required a hospital to exercise the same degree of care that a reasonably prudent professional would have under the same or similar circumstances. The court ruled that it was *not* foreseeable that the patient would be a danger to himself or others (the clinical record did not document any assaultive behavior), and consequently there was no duty of the hospital to seek revocation of conditional release status in court after the patient failed to return from the movies. In an opinion rather sensitive to the vagaries of prediction in the field of mental health, the court stressed that if it held the hospital liable for damages under this statute, it would be holding the hospital responsible for performing a prediction which, in the words of the court, "the state of the art in the field of psychiatry and mental health really does not allow it to perform." In addition, the court acknowledged the hospital's contention that a need exists to take calculated risks in a patient's treatment program so that the hospital is indeed treating, rather than merely jailing, individuals who have been found not guilty by reason of insanity.

Courts have rarely held mental health professionals liable for failures to predict dangerousness which resulted in injuries to third parties by

---

[10] Davis vs. United States (Civil Action #75-0843 — oral opinion of the court — United States District Court for the District of Columbia, unpublished).

patients or former patients. If the court can find support in the patient's clinical record for a release decision by the staff, there is no finding of liability. On the other hand, if there has been recent aggressive or violent behavior by a patient, or threats directed to identifiable third parties, courts expect mental health professionals to be aware of such incidents and to demonstrate that there was strong countervailing evidence to justify the decision to release the patient. When liability does occur for the mental health professional under these circumstances, it often reflects what courts view as "unambiguous warning signals" which should have warned mental health professionals as to the inappropriate nature of their release decision or of the conditions attached to that release. Courts have rather consistently imposed liability when release decisions contradicted or ignored important information contained in case histories. Courts have also indicated that they expect release recommendations to be supported by clinical data of sufficient detail to enable a judge or jury, if necessary, to evaluate the appropriateness of the release decision.

One of the problems often encountered, and frequently exaggerated by the media, is the release into the community of a patient considered dangerous but not mentally ill. Frequently people like this have been committed to the hospital inappropriately, and the hospital is in the position of having to affirm that these individuals are dangerous, perhaps by virtue of a character disorder, but that they are not mentally ill and, therefore, cannot be confined in a mental hospital.

In a decision similar to the one involving St. Elizabeth's Hospital, the U.S. Fourth Circuit Court of Appeals in 1969 affirmed a trial court decision that there was no responsibility as a result of negligence on the part of Veterans Administration doctors for injuries sustained by the wife of a patient who attacked her while on a 15-day home trial visit.[11] The courts once again spoke about the basic premise of release and recognized that release decisions involve some measure of risk. The court reiterated the view that calculated risks are involved in pursuing a policy in which patients are gradually reintegrated into the community, but it felt that the necessity for treatment justified the release.

---

[11] Eanes vs. United States, 407 F.2d 823 (Fourth Circuit, 1969).

Courts will impose liability, however, for release decisions which violate prior orders or attempt to circumvent the required participation of the court. Courts will clearly impose liability on mental health professionals for noncompliance with their directives regarding changes in treatment status. Perhaps the best illustration of this aspect of malpractice is a case decided in 1976 involving the Psychiatric Institute of Washington, D.C.[12] Pursuant to a psychiatric recommendation, a patient named John Steven Gilreath was not felt to be a danger to himself or others as long as he was within a supervised, structured way of life such as that at the Psychiatric Institute. He had been given a 20-year suspended sentence for abducting a young girl, with the condition that he enter the Psychiatric Institute for treatment. The critical aspect of the court's ruling was that any change in Mr. Gilreath's status was to be approved by the court. A year and a half later, Gilreath's doctor recommended, and the judge approved, his transfer status to day care patient: he would remain at the Psychiatric Institute from 8 A.M. to 5 P.M., with parental supervision on nights and weekends. Several months later, the psychiatrist *without* the court's approval transferred Gilreath's program from day care to participation in a therapy group that met only twice weekly. This arrangement lacked the close supervision that the court had insisted upon, and also allowed Gilreath to move out of his parents' home and live alone. Six weeks after the unauthorized modification in the treatment program, Gilreath killed a young woman, whose family then sued for damages. The trial court held that the psychiatrist, the probation officer, and the Psychiatric Institute were negligent, and liable for the wrongful death of the plaintiff's daughter, because the Psychiatric Institute had not received the court's approval for release. The court indicated that it wanted to take an active role in judging whether Gilreath's release would be in the best interests of the community. The defense contended that transfer from day care to out-patient status was simply a normal progression of treatment requiring no additional judicial approval. The court rejected this reasoning, stating that while Gilreath was in the hospital or on day care status, medication could be carefully monitored, his condition could be observed, and most important, there would be backup should

---

[12] Semler vs. Psychiatric Institute of Washington, D.C., 538 F.2d 121 (Fourth Circuit 1976).

he start deteriorating. While he was on outpatient status, he lived alone and attended only two outpatient psychotherapy sessions weekly; there was no supervision of his compliance with medication. The court insisted that the mental health professional be held account-able for failure to follow court orders regarding release or change in treatment status when a court conditions such modifications on its prior evaluation and approval.

Courts have frequently insisted that they have a complete case history which they may review prior to determining the validity of the release recommendation. A recent case, once again decided against St. Elizabeth's Hospital in Washington, D.C., pointed to the fact that courts will impose liability upon mental health professionals for failing to provide a complete case history.[13]

The plaintiff asserted that the fatal shooting of a woman by her husband who had recently been released by a mental institution was proximately caused by the negligence of the institution in releasing him. The patient had had a history of alcoholism, disorderly conduct, and assault, and on one occasion was arrested after he threatened to kill his wife. The hospital report concluded that the man was com-petent to stand trial, but the court rejected the finding and found him incompetent. After four months of treatment, the hospital again reported that he was competent. The critical aspect was that the letter to the court said nothing about social service reports which recommended that his family *not be used* as a community resource and documented the destructive relationship between the patient and his wife. In addition, the report to the court made no reference to psychological test findings which indicated that the patient had a serious propensity for assaultive acting out.

While in the hospital, during a visit from his family shortly before his release, the patient again became agitated and threatened to kill his wife, blaming her for his commitment. Again, the details of that encounter were not made known to the court. When the patient came to the family home after his release on bond, his wife told him that he could not stay, and he shot and killed her.

He was found not guilty by reason of insanity on the murder charge. The court found negligence on the part of the hospital, not

---

[13] Hicks vs. United States, 511 F.2d 407 (D.C. Circuit 1975).

because there was an erroneous diagnosis but rather because the report to the court "was not a complete reflection of the patient's existing psychological profile." The report gave no indication, according to the court finding, of any uncertainty about the patient's condition or of the danger to his wife should he be released. The court ruled that the hospital had a duty to make a full report and that the superintendent's brief, conclusory letter violated the duty if knowledge of an underlying chronic condition existed. The court rejected the hospital's contention that only an opinion on competency was rendered because that was all the court order requested. It cited an earlier finding of the same court that the report of a court-ordered pretrial mental examination should be made in substantial detail, including both what was done to arrive at the facts concerning the accused's mental condition and what those facts are, not merely the conclusions that mental health professionals have drawn from the facts. (The language of this is very similar to the language of several of the opinions noted by Judge Bazelon, especially in the case of Washington vs. U.S.; see Chapter 2.) The concurring opinion added that a hospital owes a duty to the courts to disclose information in its possession which would undermine or cast doubt on its diagnosis, as well as divulging facts consistent and consonant with the diagnosis.

The Hicks decision suggests that courts required by statute or order to review a release recommendation expect to be involved in interpreting the significance of the psychiatric or psychological evaluation and in weighing the risks involved; this reasoning is very similar to that seen in the Semler case. In both cases, liability is imposed not for an error in diagnosis, but rather for not allowing the court to make informed judgments on the advisability of release or of changing treatment strategy.

As noted in earlier discussions, such decisions can pose some difficulties. For example, if a court asks for an opinion on competency or criminal responsibility and for a diagnosis, and the mental health professional or the hospital provides some gratuitous opinion to the court that the individual is dangerous, there could potentially be a lawsuit for violation of confidentiality or, conceivably, for wrongful commitment if the recommendation led to the individual's being involuntarily confined.

Another important area in terms of liability for malpractice involves the failure to follow prescribed procedures. In order for a mental health professional, an institution, or a state to be held liable, something more must be present than an error in professional judgment. For instance, if a given hospital has an established procedure for reviewing cases of violent patients by what is often called a violence committee, and an individual who was regarded as seriously assaultive or disturbed is not referred to that violence committee as required in the hospital regulations, there can be grounds for liability if that patient subsequently acts out. Certainly, in private practice, the procedures are less clearly delineated, but again one does have, as noted earlier, a code of ethics and the standards for providers.

Release decisions and programs must be based on a thorough review of the patient's case history. In a case entitled Merchants National Bank and Trust Co. of Fargo, North Dakota vs. United States,[14] liability was imposed because psychiatrists had provided insufficient information about the patient to his employer during a leave period. The employer was told that the patient had had a mental disturbance and breakdown, but was not told what might constitute unusual behavior on the patient's part, to provide an indication to the employer of when the man's condition might be deteriorating or when he might, consequently, become assaultive. The employer, not being aware of the signs of decompensation, did not notify the hospital, and subsequently the patient did indeed murder his wife. Where authorities have knowledge of prior behavioral problems and fail to take reasonable precautions, then the probability of a finding of liability increases.

THE DUTY TO WARN

Perhaps the impetus for the recent decisions regarding the duty to warn third parties began with the case of Tarasoff vs. The Regents of the University of California.[15] In brief, a psychologist in the health

---

[14] Merchants National Bank and Trust Co. of Fargo, N.D. vs. United States, 272 F. Supp. 409 (D.N.D. 1967).

[15] Tarasoff vs. The Regents of the University of California, 17 Cal. 3d 425, 551 P.2d 334, 131 Cal. Rptr. 14, 83 Ad. L.3d 1166, 1976.

services of the University of California at Berkeley was treating a patient who in the course of therapy informed him that he was planning to kill a girl named Tatiana Tarasoff. The therapist made the decision to notify the campus police, in an attempt to have the student detained for involuntary commitment. The police, however, felt that there were not sufficient grounds for the student to be detained. Subsequently, the patient did indeed murder the intended victim. There were a number of internal disputes within the health service over the appropriate action to be taken, but apparently no one considered the need to warn the intended victim.

The Tarasoff family then sued the Regents of the University of California. The suit was upheld; the court stated that a psychotherapist who knows or "should know" that a patient might harm someone has a legal obligation to use reasonable care to protect the intended victim against such a danger. The Tarasoff opinion said that the duty to warn third parties arises when the defendant bears a special relationship either to the dangerous person or to the potential victim. In this case, of course, the special relationship is that of therapist and patient. In such a case, said the court, "When the therapist determines, or pursuant to the standards of his profession *should* determine, that his patient presents a serious danger of violence to another, he incurs an obligation to use reasonable care to protect the intended victim from such danger." Even this responsibility to a third party, the court noted, does not create a rigid standard that "ignores the necessity of professional discretion." The court stated this as follows:

> In the broad range of reasonable practice and treatment in which professional opinion and judgment may differ, the therapist is free to exercise his or her own best judgment without liability. Proof aided by hindsight that he or she judged wrongly is insufficient to establish negligence.

The Tarasoff ruling does not mean that psychotherapists will be held to a higher degree of accuracy in the attempt to predict or determine dangerousness. In fact, a number of people have misinterpreted the Tarasoff case as one in which liability was imposed because of a failure to predict dangerousness. This is not the case at all. Here, the determination was already made that the patient was dangerous, and the liability resided in the fact that the subsequent actions were not deemed to be sufficient to protect the intended victim.

Psychiatrists or psychologists may be wrong without being negligent. In cases in which there are reasonable bases for concluding that a patient poses no threat or in which a threat is unforeseeable, courts will not impose liability. An excellent example of this point was another suit against St. Elizabeth's Hospital in Washington, D.C., for the negligent release of a young man who, 15 months after his release, committed several homicides in his family and then ultimately committed suicide. There was, in the court's review of the hospital record, insufficient indication that the patient was an imminent danger to his family, and in fact, there was difficulty in predicting dangerousness that far into the future. The court basically ruled that the homicide against the family was unforeseeable and, therefore, there was no negligence on the part of the hospital.[16]

The majority ruling in Tarasoff stated that liability could be based on two grounds: (1) a failure to warn after a determination was made that a third party may be in serious danger or harm, and (2) a failure to warn when that determination was not made but *should have been made*. The phrase "should have been made" is a very ominous sounding one because, again, one may speak about the inability to predict dangerousness, and a multitude of mental health professionals may say that a decision *should have been made* on certain grounds, while others say that it should not have. Once more the issue is that the majority opinion would at most hold the therapist to the current generally accepted standard of professional practice, which certainly amply documents the problems in predicting dangerousness.

A recent article in the *Stanford Law Review* (November 1978) attempted to assess the impact of the Tarasoff decision.[17] A questionnaire was mailed to over 3500 mental health professionals. The survey revealed that the issue of dangerousness had indeed received considerable attention from therapists, both inside and outside therapeutic

---

[16]Watts vs. United States, No. 77-1428 (U.S. Court of Appeals for the District of Columbia Circuit 1977, (unpublished).

[17]Stanford Law Review, Vol. 31:165, Nov. 1978.

sessions, after they became aware of the Tarasoff case. Most had heard of the case, and a large majority believed that the decision impacted on their practice. Many therapists noted that they were currently paying attention to threatening comments and had generally "lowered the threshold" for considering a client dangerous. Therapists also found themselves more careful in their attempt to predict violence and were more likely to consult with other mental health professionals when encountering potentially dangerous clients.

Unfortunately, it was noted that there were some detrimental effects on psychotherapeutic practice as well. The increased time and attention devoted to a client's propensity towards violence were often unwarranted, and thus detracted from more pressing therapeutic issues. The therapist-client relationship might be damaged, not only by the fact that patients may lose trust in their therapists but also by the therapists' uneasiness. The most pervasive change noted, in fact, was the heightened anxiety that therapists felt in any clinical situation in which the potential violence of the patient was an issue or in which the duty to warn arose. Some therapists even reported that they were turning away people from treatment who they felt had homicidal tendencies. Some therapists noted that there was a tendency to label an increasing number of people as dangerous, which was leading to an increasing number of involuntary commitments.

A New Jersey court, relying upon the Tarasoff decision, has ruled that a psychotherapist who determines, or in accordance with the standards of his profession should have determined, that the patient presents a probable danger to a third party, assumes a duty to take reasonable steps to protect the potential victim.[18] In 1973, Dr. Milano began treating Lee Morgenstein, a 15-year-old youth involved with drugs. Morgenstein related fantasies of using a knife to threaten people, and told of his sexual experiences and emotional involvement with a woman five years his senior. Among other events, Morgenstein confided to his therapist that he had fired a BB gun at this woman while she was in her car, when he was high on drugs. During a therapy session on the day of the tragedy, the patient stole a prescription form and attempted to obtain 30 tablets of Seconal, a drug he had abused in the past. The pharmacist became suspicious and

---

[18] McIntosh vs. Milano, 403 A.2d 500 (N.J. Superior Court 1979).

contacted the doctor who advised him to send the patient home. Later the doctor unsuccessfully attempted to reach Morgenstein by phone, but by that time Morgenstein had already shot the woman.

In this case, the plaintiff submitted a report by a psychiatric expert who expressed the opinion that the defendant, Dr. Milano, had "committed a gross deviation from acceptable medical practice by failing to warn the decedent, her parents, or the appropriate authorities." The critical factor in this psychiatrist's report was that the patient's dangerousness was not a prediction but a known fact, based on his previous violent activities, namely, firing the BB gun. The defendant, in turn, argued that the Tarasoff principle would impose an unworkable duty based on an unreliable prediction of dangerousness, that it would interfere with effective treatment by compromising the patient's confidentiality, that it would deter therapists from treating potentially dangerous patients, and finally, that it would result in increased involuntary commitments.

One other important aspect of the case of McIntosh vs. Milano involves an issue which we have already noted. Morgenstein did indeed fire a BB gun at the decedent while she was in her car on previous occasions but she was never injured. Violent activities, such as stabbing people, were exclusively in the realm of fantasy. One of the issues was whether or not the fantasied violence was grounds enough for the therapist to believe that real violence would occur.

Basically, the court rejected Dr. Milano's arguments, saying that some type of duty to warn exists, unless therapists state that they have no ability to predict dangerousness whatsoever. The court reiterated a point of view noted several times before that confidentiality was not absolute and that the community must come first where the duty to disclose is compelled by law.

It would certainly seem that the direction being followed by the courts these days is in support of Tarasoff-like reasoning. However, in 1980, in a case entitled Shaw vs. Glickman,[19] a Maryland court handed down a decision which appears to be a total reversal of the reasoning followed in Tarasoff and McIntosh vs. Milano.

Shaw vs. Glickman differed a good deal from the prior cases in that it involved the shooting of a man who was having an affair with

---

[19] Shaw vs. Glickman, 415 A.2d 625 (Maryland Court of Special Appeals 1980).

the estranged wife of another man, with the cuckolded husband's violent tendencies being known to the psychiatrist who was treating the couple. However, there was no direct threat made against the intended victim. The important part of the decision in Shaw vs. Glickman did not involve the specifics of the case as much as its implications. As noted, there was no specific statement of intention to harm the victim as there was in the Tarasoff case, or history of violence against the party as there was in the McIntosh case; the primary issue in Shaw vs. Glickman was the fact that had the confidence been violated, it would have been a violation of the psychotherapist-patient privilege statute in the state of Maryland. The Maryland Courts and Judicial Proceedings Code Annotated[20] indicated that "a patient or his authorized representative has the privilege to refuse to disclose and to prevent a witness from disclosing communications relating to diagnosis or treatment of a patient's mental or emotional disorder." There are exceptions, but none of the exceptions speaks to the issue of dangerousness. Exclusion of privilege exists if the disclosure is necessary for the purpose of commitment; if the communications are made during a pretrial examination in which the issue of a mental or emotional disorder is raised; if the patient introduces his mental condition as an element of litigation, as noted in previous decisions; or if there is a claim for malpractice. To quote the Maryland Court of Special Appeals, "The lips of the psychologist and psychiatrist are statutorily sealed, subject solely to being unsealed by the patient or the patient's authorized representative." The court concluded that under current Maryland law, it would have been a violation of the statute for the doctor or any member of the psychiatric team to disclose to the victim any violent propensity on the part of the assailant.

Several recent cases, along the lines of Tarasoff and McIntosh vs. Milano, have dealt with the need for a readily identifiable victim. For example, in a case filed by a family named Lipari against Sears Roebuck, the issue of "readily identifiable third party" was noted.[21]

A patient named Ulysses Cribbs, who was in a psychiatric day care program at a Veterans Administration hospital, had purchased a shot-

---

[20] Maryland Courts and Judicial Proceedings Code Annotated § 9–109(b).

[21] Lipari vs. Sears Roebuck, No. 77-0-458 (D. Neb. July 17, 1980). (unpublished)

gun from Sears Roebuck and subsequently fired the shotgun into a crowded dining room in a restaurant, killing Dennis Lipari and seriously wounding his wife. The suit was initially against Sears for selling the gun and subsequently against the government for failing to give proper care and treatment to the patient, Mr. Cribbs, and for failing to predict the danger. The government contended, and the court agreed, that the recognition of a duty to warn does not make the psychotherapist liable for *any* harm caused by his patient; he is liable only when the negligent treatment of the patient caused the injury in question, that is, the danger was foreseeable and no precautions were taken. Also, the duty to warn was limited to a *readily identifiable potential victim.*

The practical difficulty, of course, that emerges from such a decision is how readily identifiable the victim must be. The court did not state this or, in its opinion, provide any parameters or guidelines for determining this matter.

EXAMPLE:

A patient, previously discussed in the context of being evaluated for civil commitment, indicated that he felt the Catholic church to be responsible for all of his ills, and that as soon as he left the hospital, he was going to bomb and destroy Catholic churches, and kill Catholic priests before they were able to kill him.

In such an actual example, does the fact that the "victim" has been identified as the Catholic church and its priests render the hospital potentially liable, in terms of having to warn all priests? Or does the hospital need only to warn priests and churches in the immediate area, or must a warning be made at all?

Nevertheless, even when a victim is not readily identifiable, a hospital may be held liabile if the patient has a general history of violent activities. The Minnesota Supreme Court recently upheld a jury verdict finding the state hospital liable for $75,000 worth of damages to a lumber yard caused by an escaped mental patient's arson.[22] The patient in question had been mentally ill for some time and had involved himself in a variety of violent acts, necessitating

---

[22] Rum River Lumber Co. vs. Minnesota, 282 N.W.2d 882 (Minnesota Supreme Court 1979).

confinement in a maximum security ward. He had managed to escape by taking a passkey from an unlocked supervisor's office and, during his escape, had set the fire. The hospital contended that the arson was not foreseeable because no previous acts of arson had occurred. The court held that this contention was erroneous because the patient did have a history of previous violence even though that activity was not confined to arson. The critical issue was whether a causal connection could be established between the injury and the activities, or lack of activity, on the part of the hospital or therapist.

For instance, in a recent decision, a Veterans Administration hospital was absolved of all liability in a case in which a patient was released from the hospital in the custody of his mother and then hurled his daughter to death approximately a month later after failing to return from a pass. In the review of the documents, the court ruled that the hospital had followed generally accepted medical and psychiatric standards, practices, and procedures, and that there was no causal connection between granting the pass and the girl's death. Proper care had been used by the physician in charge, and the court felt that a reasonable person could not believe otherwise.[23]

A federal district court recently found no Civil Rights violation by Illinois officials for releasing and failing to supervise a patient who committed a knife murder a year after his release. The district court found the victim's death *too remote* a consequence of the state official's action to hold the state officials responsible under the Civil Rights Act.[24]

THE NEED FOR DOCUMENTATION

A number of the cases discussed here very clearly point to the critical need for careful documentation in medical, psychiatric, and psychological records. Perhaps this has been illustrated most clearly by a very recent case, Abille vs. United States.[25]

A patient by the name of Abille was admitted to a U.S. Air Force hospital for treatment of depression. No orders within the medical

---

[23] Ellis vs. United States, 484 F. Supp. 4 (D.S.C. 1978).

[24] Bowers vs. DeVito, 486 F. Supp. 742 (N.D. Ill. 1980).

[25] Abille vs. United States, 482 F. Supp. 703 (N.D. Cal. 1980).

records were left for the patient to leave the ward, but by the fourth day of his hospitalization, the nurses had begun to let him go various places in the hospital unescorted. On the fifth day, he went to breakfast by himself and was found dead soon thereafter below the window of an unsupervised seventh floor lounge. Following his death, a note was added to the patient's chart indicating that two days earlier the doctor's orders had been changed to permit him to leave the ward unescorted. The doctor testified that he had in fact authorized such a change in status, but the court would not regard the inserted note as a valid medical order. The court also found that even if the doctor did change the patient's status, the hospital would still be liable because the manner of changing the order was improper medical procedure. The doctor's failure to maintain contemporary notes or other records fell below the applicable standard of care — once again, the standard of care exercised by the reasonably prudent practitioner. In the absence of any record reflecting the thinking of the doctor, the plaintiff had no way to prove whether the reclassifying order was negligently made, assuming that it had been made at all.

Finally, a recent article (1981) in the *New Jersey Psychologist* by Leon Wilson, general counsel to the New Jersey Psychological Association, established some very concrete guidelines for the therapist concerned with issues surrounding the duty to warn.[26]   Mr. Wilson points out that the therapist's principal duty is always to the patient. Only in the most extraordinary circumstances can the duty to warn be invoked. However, if it is felt that these extraordinary circumstances are present, then the duty clearly exists, but one should first attempt to dissuade a patient from the threatened violence. If one is convinced of the genuineness of the threat, one should not hesitate to warn a victim or family, even if there is fear of legal reprisal by the patient. Colleagues should always be consulted in these cases.

Records must be clearly kept, and various characterizations of the patient's statements must be documented in detail. The nature and extent of the confidentiality should be discussed with the patient, preferably in advance of treatment. In this context, one can assure the patient that a therapist needs to act in the patient's best interest, even to the point of preventing him from committing a crime.

---

[26] Reprinted in The Clinical Psychologist Volume 34, Number 3, Spring 1981.

8
Civil Commitment, Right to Treatment, Right to Refuse Treatment

One of the concepts that must be understood when one talks about civil commitment is, of course, the concept of dangerousness, since it is central both to the commitment and to the criteria for release.

THE PREDICTION OF DANGEROUSNESS

It has been well established that dangerousness is a very difficult factor to predict. One of the problems involved is that the base rates for serious assaults by psychiatric patients are very low. No more than 10% of hospitalized mentally ill patients tend to be assaultive. The base rates, in fact, of violent behavior among mental patients frequently are no different from those of the general population. Violent behavior is seen as a function of the social context as much as of the individual's personality. When psychological testing is called upon to predict dangerous behavior, it poses a problem, because most studies show that such testing cannot predict. The most important variable in the prediction of future dangerous behavior is past criminal conduct; however, this is frequently ruled irrelevant by many statutes, mental health commissions, and courts.

While one can obtain a fairly accurate assessment of an individual's personality, one very often has little idea into what social context the person might be returning. It appears that much of the difficulty in predicting dangerousness results from the fact that one cannot predict this social context and, therefore, whatever predictions the mental health professional does make can actually fall short. In other words, the instruments and skills relied upon by a mental health professional are not deficient; rather, they can be accurate, but only for predicting behavior within certain well-defined parameters.

It is suggested, based on many cases, that the psychologist needs to educate the court to abandon the vague and elusive term of "dangerous," and rather restrict himself to a description of the patient's personality and of the kinds of situations in which that personality structure may deteriorate or result in assaultive behavior. This statement should be based not only on the psychological testing, but also on a careful history taking and an understanding of the manner in which the individual's personality structure meshes with various pressures and various social contexts.

EXAMPLE:

A patient was being evaluated for release, following an acquittal, by reason of insanity, of a homicide. It appeared, both from the patient's psychological testing (which clearly indicated some highly ambivalent feelings about maternal figures) and from his history (he had married, and severely assaulted, a number of older women) that the parameter which demanded attention was this individual's attraction to domineering older women. Clearly, the psychologist was not able to control the social context that this individual would never be involved with an domineering older woman. On the other hand, he could — in presenting this material to the court — indicate that according to both history and psychological evaluation, this was the *only* situation in which the individual tended to act out. This would enable the court to impose (as indeed it did), as a condition of release, intensive psychotherapeutic follow-up on an outpatient basis, with materials being provided to the therapist which would alert him to the possibility of this individual being attracted to situations such as those described.

In short, rather than utilizing a vague statement of dangerousness, the expert should limit himself to a statement that, within a range of given probability, there is a likelihood that this individual will act out in a particular manner under this particular set of circumstances.

In Dr. Alan Stone's volume, *Mental Health and the Law,*[1] a compelling argument is made that using dangerousness as a criterion for

---

[1] Stone, A. *Mental Health and the Law: A System in Transition.* New York: Jason Aronson, 1976, pp. 43–82.

civil commitment is "false and misleading" and is not at all progressive, a position espoused by many mental health advocates. It is in fact noted that the definition of dangerousness is so fluid that different individuals can define it in different ways. What some individuals regard as dangerous behavior, others may recognize only as an annoyance. An example given is that as eminent a jurist as Chief Justice Burger, who at the time of the opinion was a trial judge, wrote that an individual who writes a bad check is dangerous to himself because the person who is defrauded may become angry and attack the check writer.

Dr. Stone proposes that the concept of dangerousness as a criterion for involuntary commitment be totally discarded and suggests in its place, the following series of criteria:

1. There should be a reliable diagnosis of severe mental illness.
2. The immediate prognosis involves major distress.
3. Treatment for the illness is available.
4. The illness impairs the person's ability to accept such treatment voluntarily.
5. A reasonable man would not reject such treatment.

Given this model, according to Dr. Stone, one can indicate the patient's current mental state and the likely course of the patient's illness. Since one cannot control the social context, one cannot really predict dangerousness and should not rely on it alone as a criterion for commitment or release.

One of the problems that occurs when one attempts to "tighten up" civil commitment procedures is that police charge the individual with criminal offenses. Studies in California, Utah, and the District of Columbia substantiate this. Various acts designed to protect the mentally ill from involuntary civil commitment indeed do not protect these individuals; rather, the correctional system absorbs the overflow from the mental health system. An individual police officer, frustrated in his attempts to have someone committed involuntarily on an "emergency hold," will charge a person with a relatively minor criminal offense; the patient then is processed through the criminal justice system, eventually deteriorates psychologically in a correctional setting, is taken to a forensic facility, and spends more time in the forensic facility, and in the criminal justice system, than he would had he initially been involuntarily confined for a shorter period of time, treated, and released to outpatient status.

Several misperceptions frequently exist in the court's understanding of mental disorders; once again, the informed mental health professional can frequently be of service to the court in clearing away these misconceptions.

First, a frequent misconception is that certain mental illnesses are in and of themselves dangerous. A judge on more than one occasion has asked, "Do you expect me to let a schizophrenic out on the streets?" Clearly, the nature of schizophrenia and the general fact that there is no distinct correlation between schizophrenia and assaultiveness must be brought to the court's attention.

A second misconception, perhaps more subtle but nevertheless critically important, is that courts frequently regard impulse and ideation as interchangeable. Frequently, as many studies on aggression demonstrate, having a discharge in fantasy is precisely what prevents the person from acting on the impulse.

EXAMPLE:

Perhaps one of the best illustrations of this is the opinion of a highly sophisticated court. In this case, the individual had been charged with a brutal mutilation and murder in 1967, and was being recommended for a conditional release in 1975. The psychologist involved had performed a complete psychological evaluation and had noted in the course of his report that there appeared to be a consistent increase in the patient's ability to bind his aggressive impulses by use of his fantasy life. That is, in the early reports it was noted that much of the aggression was unbound; however, there appeared to be a subsequent development of the capacity to discharge many of these elements in fantasy, coupled with an actual decrease in the amount of the patient's sexual and aggressive acting out over the course of the seven years in question. Nevertheless, the court rejected the recommendation for conditional release, citing as one of its reasons the fact that the doctor's report and testimony showed that the patient still had sexual and aggressive fantasies.[2]

---

[2]United States vs. Ecker, Appeal from the U.S. District Court for the District of Columbia, No. 1481-67 (1967).

LEVEL OF PROOF FOR CIVIL COMMITMENT

Until quite recently (1979), the standards — that is, the level of proof required for civil commitment — varied from state to state. Depending on the state, the degree of proof needed could be regarded as preponderance of evidence (slightly more certain than not), clear and convincing, or beyond a reasonable doubt. A case which reached the U.S. Supreme Court (Addington vs. Texas)[3], had the following history.

The trial judge had initially instructed the jury that the state's burden was to prove each of the required standards for civil commitment by clear and convincing evidence. On appeal, an intermediate appellate court reversed this, stating that the proper standard was "beyond a reasonable doubt." When presented to the Texas Supreme Court, however, the court issued an opinion which required a standard of preponderance of evidence, a lower standard than either of the other two. The matter was then appealed to the Supreme Court of the United States which, in April of 1979, ruled that the proper standard for civil commitment was "clear and convincing evidence." The patient in question, Addington, had complained that his commitment to the Austin State Hospital violated due process because the jury had been instructed to use not the standard of beyond a reasonable doubt, but rather the standard of clear and convincing evidence. The appellate court, as noted above, agreed with Addington that "beyond a reasonable doubt" should have been used, but the Texas Supreme Court reversed this, stating that the lower standard of preponderance of evidence was sufficient.

Finally, the U.S. Supreme Court ruled that the proper standard should be clear and convincing evidence — basically a "middle ground between the two extremes" — and, in fact, a decision that was in line with the initial trial court recommendation. What makes this decision particularly important is that it represents the first time that the Supreme Court of the United States considered any aspect of the civil commitment process.

A very important collateral issue was raised by the American Psychiatric Association (APA) in an amicus curiae brief, which argued that the level of due process protection should be measured

---

[3] Addington vs. Texas, 47 U.S.L.W. 4473 (1979).

by the "state's purpose in confinement." That is, since the purpose of confinement for civil commitment should be treatment and not punishment, the APA argued that there ought to be a less demanding standard than in criminal trials. The Supreme Court's argument, as noted above, is basically a compromise, taking a middle level of burden of proof, and striking "a fair balance" between individual rights and the concerns of the state. The Supreme Court rejected the argument of the American Psychiatric Association that commitment to a mental institution deserves less due process protection than other types of confinement. The Court concluded that commitment for *any purpose* constituted a significant deprivation of liberty which required due process protection.

Other recent court decisions also point to some of the difficulties involved in using the concept of dangerousness as a criterion for involuntary commitment and propose a variety of ways of dealing with it. In the case of Aaron Nelson which was handed down by the District of Columbia Court of Appeals in 1979,[4] the court made it clear that it had no intention of utilizing "recent overt acts" as the criterion for dangerousness, but rather that it must consider the nature of the mental illness and the pattern of associated behavior. One is able to use the patient's prior criminal history, as it relates to the mental disorder, in determining the criteria for commitment. That is, if the mental illness which the individual suffers from is by history associated with particular kinds of antisocial acting out, then the prior criminal history can indeed be used to justify involuntary commitment. This represents a significant departure from earlier thinking which embraced a rather narrow definition of dangerousness as "recent overt acts."

In several other recent cases, patients have been denied motions for discharge from hospitals on the grounds that a record of prior criminal activity indicated a high probability of return to a life of violent crime. That is, the likelihood of injury to others in the future *was based on the patient's past criminal activity.*

Some related issues dealt with situations in which individuals threatened to behave dangerously, or threatened to place themselves in situations that could lead to personal injury, though no overt acting

---

[4]In re Nelson, 408 A.2d 1233 (D.C. Court of Appeals 1979).

out may have occurred. These recent cases, in summary, indicate that when there is a clear showing of mental illness, the courts are far more likely to rule that a threat to oneself or to another person constitutes an overt dangerous act. The courts found dangerous behavior in several cases in which the actions placed the person in a vulnerable position. The courts tended to draw a line of demarcation, however, at the point where the evidence merely *suggested* a remote possibility of harm or where there was no mental illness involved, but rather a series of eccentricities.

Other recent cases have dealt with situations in which a patient's delusional system made the individual feel persecuted; a finding of dangerousness was warranted because of the possibility that the patient would act out in misguided self-defense. Once again, the courts have reasoned that a number of factors had to be balanced, including how likely it was that the individual would come in contact with situations that would stimulate the paranoid system. This is, of course, a statement very similar to the concept already noted in our discussion of dangerousness of attempting to define just what the parameters of future behavior may be.

A recent case (also described briefly in Chapter 1) involved a rather striking example of the misuse of the concept of dangerousness and of psychiatric assessments of dangerousness. In the case of Estelle vs. Smith,[5] the American Psychiatric Association filed an amicus curiae brief in a murder case before the U.S. Supreme Court. The APA asserted that psychiatrists' predictions of future dangerousness are unreliable and should not be taken into consideration in sentencing a defendant to capital punishment. The individual in question was indicted for murder after participating in a robbery in which a victim was fatally shot by the man's accomplice. A competency examination was conducted by a court-qualified psychiatrist who concluded that the patient was competent to stand trial. The client's competency was not contested, and he was found guilty of murder in the first phase of a bifurcated trial. The second trial was the penalty proceeding to determine if the death sentence should be imposed. The critical question was whether the defendant would commit further violent acts and thus pose a continuing threat to

---

[5] Estelle vs. Smith, cert. granted 48 U.S.L.W. 3602 (March 17, 1980).

society. *Without any prior notice to the defendant,* the psychiatrist who had performed the competency examination was called as the prosecution's only witness. The doctor testified, based on his competency examination, that the patient was an antisocial personality; according to DSM III,[6] criteria, he was certain to commit further acts of violence; he would therefore pose a threat to society. The criterion previously noted of the only reliable prediction of future dangerousness being past dangerous behavior was overlooked by the psychiatrist. The defendant had no prior history of violent acting out; his previous criminal history consisted of a single conviction for possession of marijuana. Nevertheless, based on the psychiatric testimony, the jury returned a verdict mandating the death penalty. The death sentence was set aside by a district court based on the fact that the state failed to give prior notice of the psychiatric testimony. The Fifth Circuit Court confirmed that a defendant could not be compelled under the Fifth Amendment to talk to a psychiatrist when his statements could later be used against him at the sentencing stage of a trial for a capital crime.

The American Psychiatric Association in its amicus curiae brief to the U.S. Supreme Court supported the earlier opinion of the circuit court. It argued that psychiatric assessments of the probability of future dangerousness are unreliable, especially in the absence of a prior history of violent activities, and that such a prior history must serve as a base rate for prediction. The brief contended that if psychiatric testimony is ruled admissible, the defendant must be guaranteed an opportunity to challenge and rebut such testimony.

The general reasoning behind this decision has led many attorneys to question even the use of an expert witness retained by the government to assess an issue of criminal responsibility. Much of the impetus for this line of attack stems from the case of United States vs. Byers.[7] Billy Byers was an individual who was charged, in the District of Columbia, with murdering his girl friend with a sawed-off shotgun. Psychological and psychiatric evaluation at St. Elizabeth's Hospital resulted in an opinion to the court that Byers had suffered

---

[6]Diagnostic & Statistical Manual of Mental Disorders (3rd ed). Washington, D.C.: American Psychiatric Association, 1980.

[7]United States vs. Byers, No. 78–1451 (D.C. Circuit Dec. 24, 1980). (unpublished)

an acute psychotic episode at the time of the offense and should therefore not be held legally responsible for the shooting. The specific delusional system concerned the decedent's having cast spells on him through the use of "roots," as well as having the power to control *his* mind through *her* menstrual cycles.

The U.S. Attorney's Office sought a second opinion from the Federal Psychiatric Center at Springfield, Missouri. This psychiatric staff found not only that the patient showed no evidence of mental illness, but that the talk about "roots" was malingering. The critical aspect to the government's case was that when Byers was interviewed at Springfield and asked why he had shot his girl friend, he replied that he did not know (i.e., he did not mention roots, menstrual cycles, or mind control). When asked about roots, Byers indicated that he and his wife had talked about that possibility *while he was* a patient at St. Elizabeth's. The doctors at Springfield concluded from this that Byers and his wife had "concocted" the roots delusion after the offense was committed, that it had nothing to do with the shooting, and that, in fact, telling it to the St. Elizabeth's doctors was a deliberate attempt to feign mental illness. However, the opinion about malingering was not contained in the letter sent by the Springfield doctors to the court. Rather, it was "sprung" on the defense at the time of trial, which clearly gave the defense no opportunity to rebut this line of reasoning. (The doctors at Springfield *did* have the complete record from St. Elizabeth's.)

Byers was convicted, largely on the strength of the government's presentation of the theory that he was malingering. The prosecutor, in his closing argument, described the defense's position as having come "crashing down," and the trial judge described the government's evidence as "devastating" to the defense.

The case was appealed, based largely on reasoning analogous to the case of Estelle vs. Smith in which, as noted, the defendant was not informed that his statements could be used against him in a capital sentencing phase of the trial. Byers, it was argued, had his statements taken out of context and interpreted as malingering; the court was not informed of this in advance of the trial, and the opinion was not rendered until the defense's case was being rebutted.

The United States Court of Appeals rejected this argument, but in a strongly worded dissent, Judge David Bazelon agreed with the appeal and cited violations of both the Fifth and the Sixth Amendments when a defendant is ordered to submit to a "government compelled psychiatric examination." Judge Bazelon spoke of the fact that the Springfield staff had "transmogrified" Byers' comments and, in effect, used his own words to testify against him. Judge Bazelon noted that while such violations occur rarely, there is the potential for widespread abuse of examinations conducted by "government doctors." He suggested, as possible safeguards, either the presence of defense counsel at the examination or a tape recording (video or audio) of the examination. There would then be an opportunity, at a pretrial evidentiary hearing, for the "government doctor" to present his opinion and be questioned on its congruence or lack of congruence with the material contained on the tape or in the lawyer's notes.

Amicus curiae briefs were submitted by both the American Psychological Association and the American Psychiatric Association. The brief of the American Psychological Association basically supported Judge Bazelon's position that there is potential for widespread abuse, and that there must be procedures to prevent violations of Fifth and Sixth Amendment rights. The brief filed by the American Psychiatric Association essentially held that there was *not* any constitutional need for the presence of counsel or the provision of other safeguards in "government sanity examinations."

Both briefs, as well as Judge Bazelon's dissent, eloquently dealt with a variety of complex legal issues. However, they all overlooked some rather important clinical considerations. First of all, the actions of the "government doctors" in the Byers case are a poor example on which to base legal precedent. It is clear that because of their interpretation of an ambiguous statement as clear evidence of malingering, their ignoring of many other clinical details suggesting a bona fide mental disorder, and their failure to fully inform the court of their opinion or the bases for that opinion, they had lost any objectivity and were becoming advocates for the government, rather than for their own opinion.

In addition, as discussed extensively in Chapter 4, the expert witness must remain objective in order to maintain his/her credibility. Complete examinations must be performed in order to render an accurate opinion, whether or not it comports with the position of the side by whom the expert was retained. Therefore, when one is truly functioning as a forensic expert, the term "government doctor" (or for that matter, "defense doctor") is a misnomer and is totally irrelevant. One's opinion should be open and objective in court; one is therefore an advocate *only for one's opinion,* not for the government or for the defense. Thus since there is no "government doctor" who will automatically be a prosecution witness, the concern over possible violations of Fifth and Sixth Amendment rights becomes moot. That is, the expert is presenting an opinion based on the available data, is impartial, is not tainted by association with one side or the other, and is therefore not violating any of the defendant's constitutional rights.

Finally, the U.S. Supreme Court has recently ruled on a number of issues involving commitment of juveniles. The Court upheld the rights of parents to commit their children to mental institutions without court approval. This reversed rulings of lower courts that required due process safeguards to determine the suitability of a child's commitment by parents to a mental hospital. Treatment professionals viewed the recent ruling as giving them freedom from extensive involvement in adversarial proceedings, but of course many view it as a setback to the civil rights movement.

The Parham case,[8] filed in 1975 against the Georgia Department of Mental Health, and the case of Bartley vs. Kremens,[9] in the state of Pennsylvania, both elaborated on the need for due process protection for juveniles. The decisions in both cases indicated that juveniles had personal rights separate from their parents' interests and were entitled to protection of counsel at hearings in order to guarantee that their involuntary confinement was in their best interests. The decision was challenged by a number of the states involved, and many professionals in the various institutions felt that the conflicts between parent and child were worsened by the due process hearings. In addition, these professionals were in court so often that they complained they could not provide adequate treatment for the juveniles concerned.

The U.S. Supreme Court held that such adversary hearings were not constitutionally necessary because the concern of the parents for

---

[8] Parham vs. J. L., 412 F. Supp. 112 (M.D. Ga. 1976).
[9] Bartley vs. Kremens, 402 F. Supp. 1039 (E.D. Pa. 1975).

the child's welfare, combined with what was described as "the unbiased discretion of the admitting physician," afforded sufficient safeguards to protect the child's civil liberties. Indeed, the Supreme Court found that the child's interests were the *same as* those of its parents and presumed that the parent always acted in the best interests of the child, except where there was a well-established pattern of abuse and neglect. The Court held that the juvenile's protection against his/her parents trying to use the institution for unjustifiable reasons can be provided by the "neutral medical authority." The Court agreed with the opinion of many of the states that the hearings would further aggravate the existing tensions between parent and child, and would interfere with later efforts on the part of the parents to assist the child.[10]

Of course, many civil rights advocates point to a number of weaknesses in this decision, especially the fact that the Supreme Court does not balance against the supposed harms noted, the harmful consequences to the child of an erroneous commitment. Criticism also pointed to the Court's unrealistic view of public mental health facilities ("neutral medical authorities") and its equally unrealistic view of families seeking to hospitalize children as being conflict-free units, sensitive to — and able to assess accurately — the needs of their children.

RIGHT TO TREATMENT

The history of right to treatment litigation points to a gradual development of some of the major ideas. The issue of right to treatment was raised initially as a constitutional issue: if one confines an individual involuntarily, without providing the person the means by which he may leave the institution — namely, treatment — this constitutes a deprivation of due process.

The first case of note is Rouse vs. Cameron.[11] This suit against St. Elizabeth's Hospital in Washington, D.C., was the first opinion of a court that the right to treatment is a constitutional right. Failure to

---

[10] Parham vs. J. L. 47 U.S.L.W. 4740 (1979). Also Secretary of Public Welfare of Pennsylvania vs. Institutionalized Juveniles 47 U.S.L.W. 4754 (1974).

[11] Rouse vs. Cameron, 373 F.2d 451 (D.C. Cir. 1966).

provide treatment could not be justified by the lack of resources. However, while the right to treatment was stated as a constitutional right in this case, *no guidelines were provided for the treatment.* Rather, there only had to be what was defined as a *bona fide effort at treatment* and a provision of the treatment programs with periodic reviews.

The next major case was Wyatt vs. Stickney in the state of Alabama.[12] The decision was written by Judge Frank Johnson and went so far as to actually spell out the standards of adequate treatment in terms of staff/patient ratios, what constituted a therapeutic environment, and what was deemed appropriate treatment by a reputable segment of the professional community.

Finally, the most recent case is O'Connor vs. Donaldson,[13] which involved an individual named Kenneth Donaldson who was committed for 20 years to the Chattahoochee State Hospital in the state of Florida, without ever having committed what could be considered a dangerous, violent, or assaultive act. The court's decision in the Donaldson case stated that it was unconstitutional to confine a nondangerous individual without providing treatment. It was further noted that Donaldson's physician was personally liable for improper confinement in addition to the institution as a whole being liable.

The whole issue of court-ordered treatment presents a number of "theoretical issues as well as practical dilemmas."[14] The first theoretical issue deals with the actual definition of "treatment." When a court commits a person for treatment, the court often makes the implicit assumption that the definition of "treatment" is a consistent one shared among a variety of mental health professionals. Of course, nothing could be further from the truth. Treatment can range all the way from providing a somewhat less stressful environment to procedures as invasive as psychosurgery, aversive therapy, or drug treatment with all its concomitant side effects.

Closely related is another theoretical issue, namely, defining the adequacy of treatment. Generally, adequacy is defined in terms of

---

[12] Wyatt vs. Stickney, 325 F. Supp. 781 (M.D. Ala. 1971).

[13] O'Connor vs. Donaldson, 422 U.S. 563 (1975).

[14] Jackson, N. Court-ordered treatment: theoretical issues and practical dilemmas. Paper presented at annual meeting of American Psychological Association, 1970.

accepted levels of practice in the same general community at the same time. One would hope that the courts would examine the issue of adequacy of treatment before committing the individual to a particular institution, rather than waiting for the individual to file a writ of habeas corpus stating that no treatment is being rendered. The question of what "the same general community" refers to is also ambiguous. For example, are treatment methods used by private practitioners on voluntary patients also applicable to involuntary patients?

Another critically important theoretical issue is whether the disorder is treatable. For instance, the treatment of sexual psychopaths poses many problems. Most forms of therapy with this group have proved to be ineffective, for the very reason that there is so much gratification in the behavior. As much motivation as there is for treatment, there is an equally strong motivation to avoid treatment. In such cases, the person might conceivably be detained without the possibility of recovery at all. Certainly, the patient would spend a longer period of time in a state mental institution than he would had he been sentenced to prison in a straightforward manner for the same offense. A related issue, of course, is whether or not some of the more radical treatments for these conditions which are untreatable by more conventional means can be justified, for example, aversive therapy or antiandrogen ("chemical castration") treatment. This involves issues of assault, the concept of the intrusiveness of the treatment, and informed consent.

Another important theoretical issue concerns who the client or patient really is. The therapist always experiences conflicts in treating the forensic patient with the same aura of confidentiality and trust that one creates with a private patient. Does the therapist owe the state, the government, or the institution the obligation of disclosing certain information? For instance, if, in the course of psychotherapy, a patient who has been acquitted by reason of insanity incriminates himself in another offense, is the therapist expected to reveal that information to someone else? If the therapist feels he must give a patient a Miranda warning prior to initiating psychotherapy, then the likelihood of developing a meaningful treatment relationship is threatened.

There are a number of practical issues that also emerge. Measuring change after treatment is generally done in a very impressionistic, subjective manner. There are few objective measures for "success" of treatment. Who is actually responsible for carrying out the treatment is another practical matter, since the people doing the actual treatment in large institutions are usually the ward staff; they are not the individuals who testify in court. Most of the treatment consists of group psychotherapy involving patients and ward staff, frequently not including professional staff. Also, special treatment programs may be available for certain kinds of disorders, but these are usually not available in the large institutions that normally provide the treatment.

Another issue involves the absence of personal motivation to receive help. When a patient is ordered to receive treatment, the motivation is an extrinsic one. Even if the patient appears motivated for treatment, one often sees a resistance to the acceptance of personal responsibility for one's own behavior. As discussed in Chapter 2, if a person is told *at the time* of trial that he/she is *not* responsible for criminal activity because of a mental illness, it becomes difficult to later insist in treatment that the patient take responsibility for his/her actions. There is also, of course, a stigma attached to people ordered by the court to participate in treatment; these individuals will eventually have to cope with people's negative responses, both socially and in terms of employment.

Finally, it remains a truism that patients charged with criminal offenses are generally treated differently from other patients. They are usually in the most secure building or most secure ward in the hospital; there is very often an unspoken resistance on the staff's part to becoming intensely involved with them. When one adds the occasional assault on a staff member by a patient in a maximum security setting, one is frequently faced with a highly untenable treatment situation.

Recently a patient at St. Elizabeth's Hospital smuggled a gun onto his ward and shot to death a nursing assistant with whom he had had a disagreement. Both during pretrial confinement and after an acquittal by reason of insanity, many staff members expressed serious reservations to the court about their ability to treat the patient considering the fact that he had murdered a colleague with whom they had worked closely.

Courts have recently ruled that dangerous mental patients, even those committed through the criminal justice system, are constitutionally entitled to treatment "minimally adequate to provide them with a reasonable opportunity to improve their condition."[15] The defendants (the state of Missouri) in this case denied the allegations against them and argued that there was *no constitutional right* to treatment for patients committed under police power due to their dangerousness. The court carefully distinguished optimal treatment from minimally adequate treatment and did insist that seven aspects of the treatment be adhered to, namely: (1) adequacy of physical environment, (2) adequate staff/patient ratio, (3) individualized treatment planning, (4) treatment in the least restrictive alternative, (5) right to visitation, (6) telephone and mail privileges, and (7) specific guidelines regarding seclusion and restraint.

In some ways, this decision regarding forensic facilities parallels the decision in Rouse vs. Cameron, described earlier: it speaks of a right to treatment but does not concern itself in any detail with implementing such treatment. Given the resistance, noted earlier, on the part of many staff to involvement with forensic patients, a decision parallel to Wyatt vs. Stickney is needed in the forensic area. This would address not only adequacy of a physical environment but also the specific ways of maintaining a humane environment without compromising needed security. Staff/patient ratio would include not only numbers, but types of training and supervision necessary to deal with specific problems in maximum security settings. Treatment planning would also need to be highly individualized, with specific attention paid to the *meaning* of the pattern of criminal activity and to ways of altering the behavior. Guidelines for seclusion and restraint have to specify the exact therapeutic need for seclusion or restraint and for periodic observations, in behavioral terms, to establish when that goal is achieved; not only will such specificity ultimately benefit the patient, but it will assist staff in developing the requisite skills for effectively dealing with this admittedly difficult population.

RIGHT TO REFUSE TREATMENT

In looking at the issue of the right to refuse treatment, perhaps the most important point is whether the patient is competent to decide

---

[15] Eckerhart vs. Hensley, 475 F. Supp. 908 (W.D. Mo. 1979).

whether or not to undergo treatment. This, of course, leads to the issue of how one determines such competency. It is a far different kind of competence than competency to stand trial, competency to execute a will, competency to make a contract, etc. On occasion, individuals will refuse treatment on religious grounds, and while these are at times legitimate, a practical issue frequently arises in terms of weighing a person's religious beliefs against the fact that they may also be seriously psychotic and in need of treatment.

EXAMPLE:

A patient who had had a prior history in the same hospital of being acutely psychotic and responding well to psychotropic medication was admitted for a second time. On this second occasion, he insisted that he had embraced the Christian Science religion and refused medication repeatedly. The patient was seriously assaultive, and on several occasions, assaulted and hurt two staff members. In light of his refusal of medication, the staff felt that there was no alternative, especially since his belief was grounded at least partially in religion, to placing him in seclusion so that he would not be able to harm other people; he also remained unmedicated. The issue was posed to the court, and the court ruled that because of the patient's assaultive behavior, there was a "legitimate state interest" in providing treatment against the patient's objections, even if they were partially grounded in a religious belief. It appeared that the critical issue here was the fact that the patient was assaultive. Had he been psychotic, but not assaultive, most likely the court would not have ruled that the hospital could override his objections to treatment.

The nature of informed consent is central to acceptance or rejection of treatment, and is an exceedingly fluid and difficult issue on which to obtain precision. One of the landmark cases dealing with the refusal of treatment, as it relates to the issue of informed consent, is the case of John Doe vs. Michigan Department of Mental Health, or as it is sometimes called, Kaimowitz (John Doe's attorney) vs. Michigan Department of Mental Health.[16] This case involved a patient

---

[16] Kaimowitz vs. Michigan Department of Mental Health, No. 73-19434-AW (Michigan Circuit Court, Wayne County 1973).

who had been subject to periods of violent behavior and had been confined in a mental institution for many years as incompetent to stand trial. The patient became aware of innovative psychosurgery procedures which showed some promise of reducing or eliminating such violent outbursts. The patient volunteered for such treatment, but the American Civil Liberties Union entered the case as an amicus curiae and argued that when an individual is involuntarily confined, there is in essence no such thing as informed consent to treatment. The opinion expressed in the amicus curiae brief indicated that there is coercion, albeit subtle, any time an individual is confined within any institutional setting, and that this was further heightened by the fact that, in this case, the patient was mentally incompetent.

A related issue involves possible professional liability or malpractice in situations in which the staff either administers or withholds certain involuntary treatments of various kinds. Under a variety of malpractice decisions, it is striking that there appears to be a great deal of inconsistency, with liability being found on some occasions in cases where medication was forced on an unwilling patient and on other occasions in cases where the court felt that medication should have been given but was not.

While there are frequently refusals of treatment based on some kind of delusion, for example, that the medication is poisoning a patient, one occasionally encounters precisely the opposite problem. Here one questions whether the consent to the procedure is truly informed, because the desire for the procedure is borne out of some masochistic need for punishment or the seeking out of highly intrusive kinds of treatments.

EXAMPLE:

A patient who had been in the hospital following an acquittal by reason of insanity continually insisted to his therapist, for the first year and a half of intensive psychotherapy, that he wanted to have psychosurgery performed on him. It took considerable time to work through this issue in therapy before it became apparent that the need was a neurotic one, and was involved in some fantasies of needing to be punished for past activities. Had the patient's wish been acceded to, serious questions of informed *consent* could also have been raised here.

One of the questions that frequently arises is, If a patient refuses an effective somatic or physical treatment (e.g., medication, ECT), can the therapist or the hospital employee be forced to provide a less intrusive treatment such as psychotherapy? This has never been definitively answered by the court, but certainly in understaffed public institutions, such a directive could create serious problems.

Informed consent according to most laws can be overridden when there is an emergency situation, but of course the problem of defining exactly what "emergency" means is a very difficult one. The time spent in trying to obtain an informed freedom of choice often creates obstacles to effective clinical practice. Certain regulations can prevent lifesaving measures.

In assessing a patient's competency to give informed consent, one must recall, as previously noted, that it is competency only as it relates to that particular issue. That is, if a patient is able to make a reasonable assessment of a need for treatment and a reasonable statement as to whether or not he wants to accept the treatment, providing some reasons for nonacceptance, then the patient may be regarded as competent, regardless of the fact that he may indeed be incompetent to stand trial, incompetent to execute a contract or will, etc.

EXAMPLE:

A patient described earlier indicated that he had assaulted an individual because that person was a paid assassin from the Catholic church with a "contract" out on his life. This delusional system persisted and was impervious to any psychotherapeutic intervention. The patient remained incompetent to stand trial. The delusional system was well encapsulated, and the patient experienced virtually no anxiety. In a sense, the delusion "did its job well"; it bound all possible anxiety. The patient refused medication, indicating that he was not anxious, he knew for a certainty that the Catholic church was his only problem, and further, no medication would "make me change my mind." He also was aware of a variety of possible side effects from the medication. He was felt to be competent to refuse medication but, at the same time, incompetent to stand trial. His refusal of medication was rational and was honored.

In trying to define more precisely what informed consent is, one is required to provide the patient with adequate information, available alternatives, and the possible risks of the treatment. Again, a practical issue arises: What risks must one discuss? If all of the possible risks were mentioned, it might prevent the patient from accepting the treatment at all. For instance, while a physician may feel that it is clinically justifiable to prescribe a powerful psychotropic medication for an individual, is the physician compelled to tell the patient that a possible side effect of the drug is tardive dyskinesia, an organic brain syndrome which some research suggests is irreversible?

Some statutes in certain states require a patient's consent to specific modalities of treatment, while other modalities do not require such consent. These are generally referred to as the intrusive and nonintrusive treatments, although exactly what constitutes intrusive treatment varies from state to state.

Some broadly related issues are concerned with whether or not the mentally ill patient must give consent in the same manner as any other patient; whether a mentally ill individual can fully understand all the procedures and risks; and whether such an individual even has the authority to give his own consent or whether, alternatively, the consent should be given by people better able to understand the implications of the procedure.

Other arguments are advanced for restricting the right to refuse treatment. If a voluntary patient refuses recommended treatment, he or she should be discharged and referred elsewhere. If such patients are deemed dangerous without treatment, they should be converted to involuntary status. It is argued, sometimes rather compellingly, that the right to refuse treatment requires a seriously mentally ill individual, who is under additional stress because of involuntary hospitalization, to make a major decision in a relatively short period of time. The decision is of course a major one, because a refusal of treatment will likely have an impact on a person's life for several months or even years. Generally, even psychiatrists who are accustomed to making such decisions routinely admit difficulties in accurately identifying patients truly in need of treatment. Therefore, to ask a patient who has never made such a decision before to do so, while struggling with a mental illness, is simply demanding too much.

Opponents of the right to refuse treatment also feel that *most* refusals of treatment are not likely to be based on rational or reasonable grounds, though this of course is one of the issues to be decided in each individual case. One of the unfortunate pieces of "fallout" of right to refuse treatment suits is that many patients will be hospitalized without being treated. These are the patients who are severely mentally ill, who are too dangerous to be discharged, and yet who continually refuse treatment.

A short-term benefit of medication, especially antipsychotic medication, is the ability to calm agitated, potentially violent individuals, consequently raising staff morale. When patients are adequately medicated, staff feel less anxious and more willing to interact closely with the patients; this interaction itself can lead to important therapeutic gains. Additionally, without medication, the length of a patient's illness could be much longer than in a treatment program with adjunctive medication.

Advocates of the right to refuse treatment point out that involuntary treatment is generally much less effective than the same treatment voluntarily received. Patients can "fight" the effects of a medication, much as they can resist psychotherapy. The question as always is, Are the potential benefits worth the risks? The concept of the least restrictive alternative, which has been applied in issue of choice of custodial setting, has been extended to the choice of treatment in recent court decisions. Alternative, less intrusive treatment methods must be tried before more intrusive techniques can be justified. The question of exactly what is or is not intrusive is of course subject to much debate. Generally, psychotherapy is regarded as a less intrusive type of treatment, but one has to consider various forms of behavior modification as potentially intrusive as well. There have been some constitutional challenges, for instance, to aversive therapy. Even if psychotherapy may be a less intrusive form of treatment, how can one perform psychotherapy effectively with a protesting patient? If a patient insists that there is nothing wrong with him, no therapeutic alliance can be formed and the treatment is doomed to fail. Many of the court decisions point out that the most effective treatment involves both medication and psychotherapy, and that medication cannot be used as a substitute for therapy. Medication can be successful only within the framework of a good treatment plan; only in the context of a trust relationship achieved through psychotherapy can medicine be employed in a manner beneficial to the patient. While medication may calm some patients, this fact cannot be used as a rationale to drug all patients. Individualization and individual treatment plans must be central issues.

Two recent cases dealing with the right to refuse treatment are particularly important. In the case of Renee vs. Klein,[17] five state hospitals in New Jersey were involved. This case dealt with the prohibition against forcible medication in nonemergency situations. It was described as a right to privacy (of one's own body), with that right being qualified by the following dimensions: (1) the extent to which the person poses a danger to others, (2) the extent to which the person is capable of making a treatment decision, (3) the extent to which a less restrictive treatment is available, and (4) the extent of possible side effects.

Renee vs. Klein was phrased in terms of both the right to privacy and due process. The efficacy of high dosages of medication was questioned, especially with respect to the side effects involved which might deprive an individual of the social skills necessary for a transition into the community. Psychotropic medication is frequently used to control behavior and is often a substitute for, rather than *part* of, a treatment program. The conclusions of the court were as follows: (1) there is a constitutional right to refuse treatment; (2) there is a right of privacy to one's body; (3) the right to privacy is qualified by the four factors previously noted; and (4) there must be a procedure for due process. No damages were involved in this case, the relief granted being injunctive.

The due process provisions were: (1) there must be a written informed consent that medication can be given, with the patient being told that he can refuse the medication; (2) if the medication is refused, there must be a due process review presided over by an independent evaluator (someone outside the hospital system), and the patient must be given advance notice of this procedure; (3) a patient advocate system must be implemented when the patient is incapable of making a treatment decision; and (4) the medication can

---

[17]Renee vs. Klein, 462 F. Supp. 1131 (D.N.J. 1978).

be administered over the patient's objections only in an emergency situation; emergency is defined as "a sudden significant change in the patient's condition that results in harm to himself or others." An emergency, by definition, can last only 72 hours, at which time it must be reevaluated. If an individual is incompetent to make a treatment decision, a guardian can be appointed.

A second related case is Rogers vs. Okin,[18] decided in Massachusetts in 1979. The patients argued here that their constitutional rights had been violated and spoke of their right to refuse treatment except in emergencies. The Rogers decision prohibited the nonemergency use of medication on any patient who refused treatment. The defendant (the state of Massachusetts) argued that *all* patients were incompetent to make treatment decisions, and no patient had a right to refuse treatment. The state defined emergencies in very broad terms, including bizarre behavior, unforeseeable changes in condition, and virtually every kind of psychiatric disorder. The court rejected the state's argument and made the following findings. When a patient is competent to make a treatment decision (able to appreciate the risks and benefits of the treatment), the patient *can* refuse the treatment except in an emergency situation. Emergency was defined as a substantial likelihood of personal injury. If the patient is incompetent, then the hospital must seek the appointment of a guardian, much as in the Renee decision. The guardian should meet with the patient and the hospital staff to work out an agreement; this is to be followed by a formal adjudication by the court regarding the medication agreement. The only "state interest" involved is to protect the other patients on the ward from harm.

As in the Renee vs. Klein decision, no monetary damages were awarded because: (1) the plaintiffs were unable to show that any injuries had been caused by the deprivation of the rights, and (2) the defendants were immune based on "good faith" at the time that the suit was filed.

The defendants in this case appealed the trial court decision, and the First Circuit Court of Appeals recently handed down a decision placing considerably more discretion in the hands of the treating

---

[18] Rogers vs. Okin, 478 F. Supp. 1342 (D. Mass.) 1979.

physician than was evident in the district court decision.[19] The appellate court included only antipsychotic medication in the area of treatment that could be refused, leaving other medication in a "gray area" awaiting further litigation. The court differentiated between involuntary and voluntary patients, which the initial decision had not done. It agreed with the defendants that a person who was admitted voluntarily may be forced to choose between accepting a prescribed treatment or leaving the hospital. The appellate court ruled that there must be a competency determination before a decision-making role is removed from the patient. The district court had ruled that the guardian would make all decisions, but the appellate court divided the decision-making role between the guardian and the physician, with the physician's decision being accorded more weight.

Finally, the appellate court broadened the definition of emergency to include situations in which a delay could result in a "substantial likelihood of significant deterioration in the condition of the patient's mental health." The court defined the term "substantial likelihood" as "preponderance of evidence." The court insisted that such a likelihood be measured along with the likely effects of a particular drug on a particular patient. The emergency is defined as the reasonable likelihood, weighed with certain medical considerations, either that the individual will cause serious bodily injury to self or others, or that there will be a significant deterioration in his mental health.

The Supreme Court of the United States decided to review this case but, rather than making definitive statements on the right of involuntary mental patients to refuse antipsychotic medication in non-emergency situations, returned the case to the trial court for further consideration of certain specific issues. The issues are complex and involved, and any unilateral approach (i.e., totally for or totally against) vis-à-vis a right to refuse treatment ignores these complications.

---

[19] Rogers vs. Okin Nos. 79-1648 and 79-1649 (1st Cir. Nov. 25, 1980). (unpublished)

9
Preparation of a Comprehensive Forensic Evaluation

Mental health practitioners who are involved in large numbers of forensic evaluations eventually become aware of the fact that preparing a comprehensive forensic report is an enterprise very distinct from preparing a traditional clinical evaluation. Many of the standard clinical devices need to be adapted, in light of the specific population with which one is dealing; perhaps even more important is the fact that many dimensions must be considered which are not considered in traditional clinical work. Several general issues, expanding on this concept, will be presented in this chapter, along with more specific recommendations for the organization and preparation of a comprehensive evaluation.

Initially, it must be noted that there are particular dimensions that have to be assessed in any forensic evaluation, which are not traditionally part of the clinical enterprise. For example, malingering is a dimension which must be taken into account in virtually every forensic assessment. That is, within a criminal setting, if a patient can successfully convince the clinician that his mental illness is so extreme that he should be adjudicated incompetent to stand trial, it is conceivable that the patient may ultimately be released from the hospital and never have to stand trial. Similarly, if a patient wants to convince an examiner that he was mentally ill at the time of the commission of a criminal offense, when indeed such an illness did not exist, the patient could conceivably be adjudicated not guilty by reason of insanity and, since there is no actual mental illness, be released within a month or two following the acquittal because there are no grounds to retain him within a mental hospital.

In evaluating claims in civil litigation, the same issue must be considered, for if a claimant demonstrates to a clinician's satisfaction that he or she is disabled (when indeed he or she is not), or can appear to be more disabled than he/she really is, this can result in substantially higher monetary rewards.

In the traditional clinical setting, on the other hand, the clinician more or less takes at face value the symptoms presented by the patient. Therefore, specific techniques for the assessment of malingering must be part of the comprehensive forensic evaluation.[1] In a similar manner, other dimensions essential to the forensic evaluation, which are not part of the traditional enterprise, include the need for review and analysis of complete police reports and witness statements, assessment of the change in the clinical picture due to the setting in which the person is confined (i.e., correctional institution or hospital), and the fact that mental disorders may frequently be unrelated to particular offenses. It is a frequent misconception of the clinician who is not involved in forensic work that if a patient is mentally ill, the offense which is committed must be related to that mental illness. The forensic clinician must never assume that the symptom picture which occurs at the time of the evaluation is the same as the symptom picture present at the time of the offense. There may be deterioration, or restitution, with the patient appearing more disturbed, or more intact, than at some time in the past.

In doing forensic work, the somewhat uncomfortable role of "investigator" must be assumed by the clinician, with a willingness to involve oneself in interviewing witnesses, assessing physical evidence, and at times reading such documents as autopsy reports. An assessment of the relative contribution to criminal activity of both a mental illness and a personality style is often another dimension to be considered, as well as the "fit" between a particular patient's mental disorder and the crime committed.[2]

Because of the nonadversarial nature of the traditional clinical enterprise, most psychologists and psychiatrists, when first entering forensic work, do not consider the need to get "the total picture" and generally content themselves with performing an evaluation based on material presented by the patient alone, by the patient and his counsel, or by the government alone. In attempting to develop a

---

[1] See discussion in Chapter 1.
[2] See discussion in Chapter 2.

more comprehensive picture, it must become part of the forensic assessment to obtain as much data as possible on which to base one's conclusions. Indeed, if, from one's evaluation of the data available, one feels that there are certain essential parts which are not included, then this should be noted in the report, with a statement that the opinion could be more conclusive if those other documents were made available.

Once all of these sources of data are compiled, one must analyze the relative input from each source, and compare and contrast the impressions gleaned from these sources with those impressions generated by the more traditional clinical interview as well as by psychological testing. Only in cases where there is adequate "fit" between the objective data and the clinical data should an opinion be rendered. Where there appear to be discrepancies, one clearly needs to have further data or to investigate the situation in more detail.

The forensic clinician must constantly be alert to the matter of which issues can and cannot be answered. There will invariably be temptations, within the forensic setting, to render expert opinions on a wide variety of topics. The forensic clinician must continuously be aware of the limits of his or her expertise, and must distinguish among those questions which can legitimately be responded to, those which require more data than are provided, and those which should not be answered at all.

The clinician must constantly be on the alert for certain phrases which are "heavily loaded" or which may have totally different meanings in a court and in a traditional clinical assessment. Perhaps one of the best examples of this, because of its proximity to the language in many legal criteria, is "substantially impaired" — especially in reference to behavioral controls, or to mental or emotional processes.

Finally, it becomes critical for the expert to state his or her opinion in its entirety, regardless of whether or not it comports with the position of the side retaining the expert. It is important to give not only the parts of one's opinion which are certain but also those parts that are doubtful or uncertain, and to be very "up front" about the assets and liabilities of a particular position.

THE FORENSIC REPORT

In what follows, we will attempt to outline the dimensions of a comprehensive forensic examination, taking into account many of the factors noted in the preceding discussion as well as throughout this book.

Initially, it is important to outline the specific assessment devices used, including the various psychological tests given, the clinical interviews, and the social service histories taken — along with their dates, as well as the referrals to other professionals for follow-up evaluation, when applicable.

The next area that must be dealt with concerns the factual statement of the case. Within this area, one needs to note that frequently a mere statement of facts from the police report is not sufficient. Very often, these reports are rather scanty, somewhat skeletal, and do not provide much of the information needed for careful assessment.

EXAMPLE:

In a recent case, a woman was apprehended for an armed robbery of a police "decoy." The woman had walked up to the man, who was playing the part of a "wino," and removed his wallet. It was noted in the police report that she turned down the street and was apprehended by the two police officers watching her. Subsequent information which became available, in this case from the defense counsel following his interview of one of the codefendants, was that the woman had her face smeared in an exceedingly bizarre fashion with lipstick and was shouting curses at unknown people. Clearly, this additional piece of information was quite critical in determining the patient's mental status at the time of an alleged offense.

In addition, then, to the police report, other objective sources of data regarding the patient's behavior at the time of an alleged offense must be included. Some of these would be interviews with witnesses to the crime and interviews with family, friends, employers, teachers, and other people in the patient's environment who may have had contact with him or her in the period of time around the alleged offense. This becomes particularly critical since, as noted before, a patient's mental status may well change from the time of the offense to the time of the examination, and it is always crucial to evaluate and compare the mental state as noted by observers at the time of the offense with the mental state as revealed by current assessment and testing. If hospital records are available, especially those involving previous psychiatric contacts, these could be exceedingly valuable. In addition, presentence, parole, and probation reports are frequently very helpful. Also, since the patient is often being evaluated within a correctional setting, it is important to have access to the medical/ psychiatric record from that correctional setting. Frequently, anecdotal notations, contact with psychiatric staff, and incident reports of the correctional staff are very important in giving a picture of the chronology of the patient's behavior from the time of arrest to the time of evaluation. Whenever possible, the correctional staff who have been involved with that particular patient should be interviewed, especially if their entries in the patient's record appear to be of some significance.

The next area to be considered is the patient's own version of the alleged offense, with a continual comparison and contrast between the patient's version and the official version of the offense. It should be noted in the report whether these agree or disagree, and whether there appear to be distortions consistent with some particular mental disorder evident in the patient's presentation of the crime. Of course, on occasion the patient denies any involvement whatsoever in the alleged offense, and at such times interviews with the patient about the allegations have to deal with the official version of the crime and how the patient assesses that version. Also, concomitant with the review of the institution's records should be the patient's own evaluation of his/her experience within the correctional setting — whether or not there have been altercations, whether or not there have been assaults against the patient (homosexual or otherwise), and any other behaviors that may be noteworthy. This section of the examination is an exceedingly critical one and should be a continual source of input into the next section of the examination which is more traditional: namely, the mental status examination and history taking.

As in any comprehensive evaluation, mental status should include such dimensions as manner of dress; degree of cooperation; orientation; assessment of memory, attention, and perception; and evaluation of the patient's affect, of his or her speech quality, of the presence or absence of any delusions or hallucinations, and of the presence or absence of any suicidal ideation.

In considering the social history, of course, detailed analyses must be made of the patient's early childhood, including relationships with parents and siblings, the impact of any major events, and the presence of any serious illnesses or injuries. Evaluation of the latency period should include an assessment of the patient's school performance and of the general nature of his or her interpersonal style, whether the patient was very outgoing or primarily introverted. The kinds of activities in which the patient was involved during this period, as well as the quality of involvement, must be assessed not only from interview with the patient but, as noted before, from as many secondary sources as possible.

In describing the adolescent years, certainly many of these same dimensions are important, but one must also pay attention to various identity concerns, the nature of sexual experimentation, sexual object choice, and involvement in drugs and alcohol.

Depending on the age of the patient, similar assessments would follow for the periods of young adulthood, adulthood, middle age, and in certain cases, older ages. In assessing the sexual and marital pattern, one would want to know the nature of the relationships and the patient's perception of the personality of the spouse; if divorces or separations were involved, the patients's perception of the reasons for such occurrences is often diagnostic in itself.

As part of the social history, an assessment of the patient's educational and vocational history is necessary, along with an evaluation of the nature of the patient's involvement, if any, in military service. If the patient was in military service, specific attention should be paid to the patient's ability to cope with authority, the extent of disciplinary actions against the patient, any psychiatric assessment made and the nature of the patient's discharge.

Drug and alcohol abuse must also be considered again with a chronological emphasis. The history and extent of such involvement should be detailed and, if drugs are involved the nature of the drugs abused.

The next area that has to be carefully assessed is the patient's criminal history, both as a juvenile and as an adult. Here, one should not only depend on the patient's input but also make an independent assessment; this can usually be arrived at from parole and probation reports which often describe the pattern of criminal behavior. Many impressions can be gleaned from a patient's police record, including the nature of acting out (violent or nonviolent, property directed or person directed) as well as the chronology. There often appears, in police reports, a cluster of crimes around a particular date or a period during which the crimes seem to begin. This is frequently an important piece of information and can be used in further inquiry of the patient, to determine why that particular period of time appears to be so important in his or her life.

In a similar manner, a psychiatric history must be obtained, not only of the patient but also of members of the patient's family. If the patient is willing to give consent, then hospital records from other institutions should be obtained.

The next part of the evaluation is applicable primarily in crimes where there appears to be evidence of unprovoked violence or of violent overreaction to circumstances that could best be described as minor irritants. This represents a formal assessment of the concept of episodic dyscontrol syndrome or, as it is referred to in DSM III,[3] "intermittent explosive disorder." Many dimensions are considered, and perhaps the best description of the dimensions which should be evaluated in screening for episodic dyscontrol syndrome is contained in the recent work of Russell Monroe, M.D.[4] Monroe specifies a number of criteria and, in fact, has developed what is called a "dyscontrol scale," in which various aspects of the dyscontrol syndrome are rated by the patient, in terms of how frequently or infrequently he or she experiences them. Such questions may be asked of the patient either in an informal manner or as a formal test, with the examiner stating the item and the patient responding by discussing the frequency or lack of frequency of that particular event. Clearly, a high score on the dyscontrol scale does not indicate that the patient suffers from episodic dyscontrol syndrome, but it certainly does represent a screening device which suggests the need for further neurological and/or neuropsychological investigation.

---

[3] *Diagnostic and Statistical Manual of Mental Disorders* (3rd ed.). Washington, D.C.: American Psychiatric Association, 1980.

[4] Monroe, R. *Brain Dysfunction in Aggressive Criminals.* Cambridge, Mass.: D. C. Heath, 1978.

The next section of the evaluation should deal with the psychological tests administered. A comprehensive battery should be utilized, including both projective and objective tests, and some instruments to assess, if only in a screening capacity, the possibility of central nervous system impairment. Also some tests to assess the issue of malingering need to be included, most frequently the Minnesota Multiphasic Personality Inventory, in which the validity scales and the subtle-obvious dichotomy discussed in Chapter 1 may be utilized. In addition to the MMPI, some of the more commonly used tests for a forensic assessment battery would include the Wechsler Adult Intelligence Scale, the Projective Drawings, the Rorschach, the Thematic Apperception Test, the Sentence Completion Test, and any of a variety of screening devices for central nervous system impairment (e.g., Bender Visual Motor Gestalt, Memory for Designs Test, Benton Visual Retention Test). If any of these tests, or indeed the history, suggests the need for further workup, then more comprehensive neuropsychological techniques, such as the Halstead-Reitan Neuropsychological Test Battery or the Luria-Nebraska Neuropsychological Battery, should be utilized.

In describing the results of the testing, one should include not only the findings of the tests but the "test-taking attitude," the patient's ability to concentrate on the materials presented, and any other behavioral observations which would be relevant to the manner in which the tests were completed. In assessing the results of the psychological tests, one must always place them within the context, as already noted, of the genuineness or lack of genuineness (deception) in the test findings and the implications that those dimensions may have for the rest of the assessment. One needs to be exceedingly careful about the inferences drawn from the testing, staying relatively close to the data at hand and not making unwarranted inferences or sweeping generalizations. The test results, like the results of the clinical interview, must all "fit" the statement of facts in order for a case to be made for the involvement of a mental disorder in the particular crime. The mere fact that an individual shows evidence of a mental disorder does not in and of itself generalize to the patient's behavior at the time of the offense. On occasions, however, certain patterns of test responses may provide (as noted in Chapter 4) a microcosmic parallel to the actual events occurring at the time of the offense. When such a situation occurs, it is very helpful to correlate the test findings with the objective data and reveal, step by step, how the two coincide.

Finally, in the summary section of the evaluation, the issues of competency and criminal responsibility must be addressed, with the specific criteria for each legal test being discussed, as well as the way in which the patient's behavior and inferences drawn from clinical interview and from psychological testing "fit" those particular criteria. If, in addition to the opinions on competency and criminal responsibility, the court has requested some recommendations for treatment, these may also be included in the summary section.

In closing, what we have attempted to describe in this chapter are not only the constraints of which the forensic clinician must be aware and the dimensions which he or she must take into account, but also the specific outline of a forensic evaluation which, if followed, can result in a comprehensive and accurate assessment of the forensic issues involved.

Suggested Readings

Cooke, G. (Ed.). *The Role of the Forensic Psychologist.* Springfield, Ill.: Charles C. Thomas, 1980.

Gutheil, T. and Applebaum, P. *Clinical Handbook of Psychiatry and the Law.* New York: McGraw-Hill, 1982.

Halleck, S. *Psychiatry and the Dilemmas of Crime.* New York: Harper & Row, 1967.

Halleck, S. *Law in the Practice of Psychiatry.* New York: Plenum, 1981.

Robitscher, J. *Pursuit of Agreement — Psychiatry and Law.* New York: J. B. Lippincott, 1966.

Sadoff, R. *Forensic Psychiatry.* Springfield, Ill.: Charles C. Thomas, 1979.

Schwitzgebel, R.L. and Schwitzgebel, R.K. *Law and Psychological Practice.* New York: John Wiley and Sons, 1980.

Slovenko, R. *Psychiatry and Law.* Boston: Little, Brown, 1973.

Stone, A. *Mental Health and the Law.* New York: Jason Aronson, 1976.

Ziskin, J. *Coping with Psychiatric and Psychological Testimony.* Beverly Hills, California, Law and Psychology Press, 1981.

Appendix A
Criminal Responsibility

November 20, 1982

Mr. Howard Moss
Assistant U.S. Attorney
U.S. Attorney's Office — 5th floor
District of Columbia Courthouse
500 Indiana Avenue, N.W.
Washington, D.C. 20001

Dear Mr. Moss:

Pursuant to your referral, I examined Mr. H. R. at Central Hospital on two occasions: October 18, 1982 and October 20, 1982. In addition to clinical interview and history taking, I administered the following psychological tests: Wechsler Adult Intelligence Scale, Projective Drawings, Bender Gestalt, Graham-Kendall Memory for Designs Test, the Rorschach, and the Monroe Dyscontrol Scale.

In addition, I reviewed the documents that you provided for me, including the factual summary of the case; the defendant's psychiatric records from the army; presentence reports from 1979; psychiatric reports from the Federal Correctional Institution in Terre Haute, Indiana; hospital records from Southern State Hospital from July 31, 1981 to August 25, 1981; reports from the probation office covering the period from July 30, 1981 to November 10, 1981; hospital records from Eastern Regional State Hospital from August 29, 1981 to October 6, 1981; reports from the Division of Forensic Services, including the hospitalization records at Central Hospital; and a report from Dr. F. C. In addition, I interviewed the following individuals who had personal knowledge of, or contact with, Mr. R.: Mrs. C. R., the defendant's mother; L. P., the victim of the assault; J. T., one of the bank tellers who was present at the time of the bank robbery; and Dr. P. D., Mr. R.'s treating psychiatrist during his stay at the Southern State Hospital.

Review of the statement of facts reveals that on August 21, 1981, the defendant, while on a pass from Southern State Hospital, arrived at the home of L. P., who had known Mr. R.'s mother. Mr. R. told Mr. P. that he had come to pick up some clothes which he had left at the house, and Mr. P. took him to the area where the clothing was stored. Apparently, Mr. R. decided not to take the clothing and went with Mr. P. into the kitchen; he then allegedly grabbed Mr. P. and demanded his car keys, his money, and a gun. He also allegedly picked up a knife that was laying on the counter and slashed at Mr. P., during the course of the struggle cutting the cord of a wall telephone in the kitchen. Mr. R. then, during the course of the struggle, cut Mr. P. from his ear to his esophagus. The defendant Mr. R. ordered Mr. P. to remain on the floor, but Mr. P. ran from the room, got his gun, and fired a shot at the defendant. Mr. R. fled from the house, taking some money, identification cards, and some keys. He returned to Southern State Hospital, telling the staff that he had been visiting his mother and had lost track of time. He also indicated that he was working and had in that manner obtained the lacerations on his hand. Four days later, a man identifying himself as L. P. called Central Savings Bank to inquire about his account. He asked about the bank's closing time and the maximum cash withdrawal policy, and was instructed to come into the bank for the withdrawal. On that same day, Mr. R. was discharged from Southern State Hospital for disciplinary reasons, having to do with his repetitive sexual acting out on the ward. That same afternoon, the defendant came to the bank and filled out a withdrawal slip on Mr. P.'s account for $6,000. He was then arrested by police officers when he presented the withdrawal slip and Mr. P.'s identification card to the teller. At the time of the arrest, on Mr. R. were found Mr. P.'s identification card, Social Security card, insurance cards, and papers on which Mr. R. appeared to have practiced Mr. P.'s signature.

Mr. R.'s version of the alleged offense is quite different from the statement of facts. He indicated that he was fully aware of the fact that he was charged with assault with intent to kill, armed robbery, destruction of property, and forgery. He explained, during interview that "they say I took a knife to someone's throat and robbed him of $50." He further indicated, "They said I tore the telephone line off and tried to pass off a bank teller's slip to get money, and that I forged the guy's name." Mr. R. denied the charges, stating rather that he went to Mr. P.'s home to pick up his clothes since he used to rent a room in Mr. P.'s house. He indicated that Mr. P. had accused him of stealing his coins and that "he attacked me with a knife." He indicated that this was the reason he got cuts on his hand and that he was able to get the knife away from Mr. P. He stated that he did not take any money from Mr. P. but "maybe I did accidentally cut the phone line." Regarding the forgery charge, Mr. R. explained, "I thought I could get the money." He indicated that he had Mr. P.'s health insurance cards, but that this was unintentional. He stated that Mr. P. had been showing them to him, that he had stuck the cards in a book he was carrying, and that in his attempt to escape from the fight, he grabbed his book but did not know that Mr.

P.'s cards were in it. Mr. R. indicated that he had been at Southern State Hospital and had been on pass that very day. He indicated that he was hallucinating at the time of the offense, and that voices were telling him to "shut up" and that his parole had been violated. He stated that his brother used to tell him to "shut up" also; that he had heard his brother's voice saying, "You stole the coin"; and that he may have mixed up his brother's voice with Mr. P.'s voice. Mr. R. indicated that he had been drinking and was "pretty high," and also that he had smoked two or three joints of marijuana and was "feeling woozy" at the time of the assault. He stated that he felt scared when the voices were telling him to "shut up, H." but insisted that he did not attack Mr. P. and that he was merely defending himself. He did describe the content of his auditory hallucination as being primarily ideas of reference, with the voices commenting on his behavior. He mentioned that while he was in the federal prison facility, he was frightened by the voices, thinking that people could hear them and that they would be broadcast over the television set.

Interview with the various witnesses in the case reveals a number of important observations: Mrs. C. R., the defendant's mother, indicated that her son had a great number of sexual problems, consistently exposing himself and grabbing at women, which resulted in his expulsion from Southern State Hospital. She indicated that on occasion he had grabbed her by the throat, but that this was primarily associated with his being intoxicated. Mrs. R. was asked what her son's specific behaviors were when he responded to auditory hallucinations, and she indicated that he "acted like he was scared of everybody." She stated most emphatically that he did not get violent when responding to auditory hallucinations but tended to become violent when he drank. In short, it would appear from the observations of this one witness at least that even when Mr. R. was hallucinating, his behavior tended to be one of seclusion and withdrawal, associated with feelings of fright, rather than aggressive or violent acting out.

Mr. L. P., the victim of the alleged assault, is a former Central City policeman and was asked, during the course of interview, whether in his professional career as a policeman he had had the opportunity to transport patients to mental hospitals for purposes of emergency commitment. He indicated that he had, both to Eastern and to Western Hospital. He indicated that he had transported such patients "hundreds of times." When asked whether Mr. R.'s behavior at the time of the offense resembled in any way psychotic episodes which Mr. P. had observed, Mr. P. emphatically denied this, stating, "I never saw him look crazy." He indicated that Mr. R. had come to his door, asking for his clothes, and after looking at a box of his clothes, had indicated that he did not want them and then "yoked me and tore the telephone off the wall." Mr. P. indicated that at that point Mr. R. grabbed the knife and "started slicing away," and severed several tendons in Mr. P.'s hands. He indicated that while Mr. R. was choking him, he stated, "I want money, the keys to your car, and a gun." He stated that Mr. R. told him not to get up, or he would "cut me more." It was Mr. P.'s observation, based on his years on the police force, that Mr. R. was "not crazy" but "seemed under the influence of drugs."

Interview with Ms. J. T., one of the bank tellers who observed Mr. R. at the time of the robbery, indicated that Mr. R. looked "nervous" but did not appear to be out of touch with reality, and certainly did not appear to be responding to any bizarre or unusual voices or visions.

Finally, an interview with Dr. P. D., Mr. R.'s treating psychiatrist at Southern State Hospital, revealed that the only significant indications of Mr. R.'s mental disorder were his sexual acting out and one instance of an acute paranoid reaction, which Dr. D. indicated that Mr. R. was "talked out of." At no time, according to Dr. D., was there any observation of Mr. R. hallucinating or any evidence that he ever acted out in a violent manner in response to his mental disorder. Dr. D. was interviewed about removing Mr. R. from medication, and he indicated that he did this because of the very apparent side effects that Mr. R. was experiencing from the medication. He stated that following Mr. R.'s removal from the medication, he was "more in contact, more alert, and more engaged with reality." In short, according to Mr. R.'s treating psychiatrist, on or about the time of the offense, Mr. R. was far from acting in a psychotic manner but was more reality oriented than he had been earlier in his hospitalization while he was still on medication. In addition, Dr. D. indicated that the removal of Mr. R. from medication had resulted in a resolution of the disturbing side effects.

In summary, then, interviews with all of these witnesses who observed Mr. R. around the time of the alleged offenses cast some doubt on the report of the patient that he was hallucinating and that a possible response to those hallucinations was violent acting out. That is, there is no evidence in any of the interviews with the witnesses that he was hallucinating, and in fact, according to his mother, when he did hallucinate, he would tend to become seclusive and withdrawn rather than violent. The violent behavior only appeared to be precipitated by involvement in drugs and alcohol.

It should further be noted that at the conclusion of the examination with Mr. R., he inquired of the present examiner what his opinion was, and when the preliminary opinion was told to Mr. R., he insisted quite emphatically that he was mentally ill at the time of the offense and that his proof of this is that had he not been mentally ill, "I should have run out of the house, but the voices told me to stay and pick things up; I was not thinking too clearly at the time." In short, even in Mr. R.'s own accounting of the alleged offense, there is little if anything to suggest that he was acting in response to a command hallucination or to any paranoid delusion.

Mr. R. indicated that following his arrest, he was briefly placed in the Central City Jail and was then sent on personal recognizance to Eastern Regional State Hospital, where he remained for two months. He indicated that he did very well in the Eastern program until his federal parole officer came for him, since he had violated parole, in reference to his earlier federal charge. He indicated that he was then sent back to the Central City Jail for six months, where he took medication for a period of time; he was subsequently transferred to Lewisburg, Pennsylvania; Atlanta, Georgia; El Reno, Oklahoma; and Terre Haute, Indiana — a series of federal prison facilities. Mr. R. indicated that those transfers "kept making my condition worse." He indicated that he was off medication for three months, and he was not brought back to the Central City Jail until April of 1982. He stated that during that period of being transferred from one institution to another, "my mind completely flipped out and I couldn't remember people whom I had known for two years." He indicated that shortly after his return to the Central City Jail, his treating physician from forensic services placed him back on medication — Navane, Lithium, Thorazine, and Cogentin — and he was transferred from the jail to Central Hospital. Mr. R. appeared very positive towards his experience there, stating that he was doing "real good" though he followed this up with a rather bizarre, psychotic comment that at Central Hospital it is "Spain in my brain."

Review of the medical records from the Central City Jail revealed that Mr. R. was first seen in the jail when he was arrested on a charge of an unauthorized use of a motor vehicle in 1979. During April of 1979, he was described as suffering from alcohol abuse and being depressed, but showing no evidence of an active psychosis. He was found competent to stand trial, was treated with antidepressants, and in a final report to the court, was regarded as a danger to himself, considered to be in need of treatment, and diagnosed primarily as a drug abuser.

The medical records then resume in August of 1981, following his arrest on the current charge. Within seven days of the offense, Mr. R. was described in a forensic services evaluation as being competent to stand trial, though showing some signs of mental illness. Following his return to the Central City Jail, after his brief stay at Eastern, he was placed on Navane, a major tranquilizer, and his mental illness was described as being in remission. Affect was described as frequently silly and inappropriate, and it appeared that he was experiencing auditory hallucinations and demonstrating loosening of associations. According to the jail records, he was transferred to the federal prison system in January of 1982, and when he was returned in March of 1982, he was described as markedly deteriorated and regressed, and he was again placed on a major tranquilizer, on this occasion Mellaril, 100 milligrams twice daily. In May of 1982, he was felt to be far too burdened with anxiety to be regarded as competent to stand trial but, at the same time, was felt to be "nonproductive" in relationship to the alleged series of offenses.

During this period of time, he was frequently described as walking around, staring into space, carrying on incoherent conversations, laughing and crying, and shaking continuously. At the time of his transfer to Central Hospital, he was described as hallucinating, withdrawn, paranoid, depressed, and regressed. He was subsequently described as experiencing auditory hallucinations and being preoccupied, but eventually the frequency of the auditory hallucinations appeared to decrease, and Mr. R. appeared to show steady signs of improving. He nevertheless expressed trouble controlling his mind, and was observed to put paper plugs in his ears to block out the voices.

Mental status revealed a neatly dressed, cooperative, well-oriented young man, whose attention, perception, and memory were generally intact. However, his affective responding was notably blunted, with occasional outbursts of inappropriate laughter. His speech was halting, at times confused, and he would repeatedly show evidence of blocking, losing his thought in the middle of a sentence. There would be occasional intrusions of peculiar language, such as "undernourished sensory perceptions." Mr. R. denied current delusional thinking, but did speak of ideas of reference in the past, as noted earlier, especially in reference to the television set broadcasting his thoughts. He described prior experiences of auditory hallucinations, again of people talking to him from the television set. He denied any visual hallucinations, with the exception of "acid trips," and also denied any olfactory, gustatory, or tactile hallucinations. He did describe, in reference to his drug and alcohol usage, both withdrawal reactions from LSD, during which he would experience visual hallucinations, and delirium tremens on three occasions, during withdrawal from alcohol.

Regarding history, Mr. R. was born in Baltimore, Maryland, on April 15, 1955, the oldest of three siblings. He indicated that when he was 3 years of age his father left the family, and his mother, being unable to care for the children, eventually placed them in an orphanage. Mr. R. appeared very vague as to the reasons why he was placed in an orphanage, stating that he generally had a good relationship with his mother, though he had very few memories of his early relationship with her. He was aware of the fact that she had both a serious alcohol problem and, apparently, a mental disorder, having been at Eastern Regional Hospital and currently taking medication as an outpatient. It became clear that the early experience of deprivation did result in much of the blocking that Mr. R. experienced when attempting to talk about his early childhood. He indicated that he was placed in an institution called the Eastern Orphanage and eventually went to another facility in Baltimore where he remained until the age of 18. He stated that he had "a rough time and I got very lonely." He described some peripheral friends, but a generally lonely upbringing, while he attended school in Baltimore. He indicated that his grades in school were generally adequate until the eleventh grade, at which time he became involved with LSD, PCP, marijuana, and alcohol. He stated that he generally liked school and described himself as "a straight A student who was interested in his classes." Despite his interest in school, he stated that he became so involved in drugs that he dropped out in the eleventh grade and never completed high school, though he eventually did receive a high school equivalency degree. He described himself during his adolescence as being heavily into drugs, though he did not regard the drugs as creating any serious behavioral problems. He stated that he had no girl friend because he was "too busy tripping," and denied any sexual involvement with either women or men during the course of adolescence. He stated that after leaving school, he went to work in maintenance at a shopping mall just outside the Baltimore area and lived with his mother briefly at that time, though he found this "rough" because of the cramped quarters. He then stated that he joined the army and that he was only in the army for eight weeks when he was "kicked out of basic training" because of the fact that he was sniffing glue. He stated that he returned home, briefly obtaining a job as a lifeguard and then in landscaping. He indicated that he lived with a girl for a five-month period of time, but that she left him, again with Mr. R. being unaware of the reasons for her leaving. He worked some other construction jobs and eventually enlisted in the navy in October 1976. He stated that he was only in the navy for six months and at that point received an honorable discharge due to psychiatric problems. He eventually went to Los Angeles, where he lived and attended college, studying accounting. He stated that he returned to Baltimore in 1978, lived with his brother, and obtained a job at a restaurant doing bookkeeping. In 1979, he was arrested for unauthorized use of a motor vehicle, which began his current series of involvements with correctional institutions and mental hospitals. He indicated that he was married for two months, during the period of time that he was back in Baltimore, but that following his arrest on the auto theft, his wife left him.

According to Mr. R., he only had two prior charges — one of unauthorized use of a motor vehicle and one of unlawful entry — before he was arrested on the current series of charges. However, according to the probation report dated July 25, 1979, there are also two disorderly conduct charges, a charge of unlawful entry in 1976, and a charge of rape which was eventually changed to assault with a deadly weapon during the period of time that he was in Los Angeles, California. In 1979, as a result of his repeated acting out and the fact that he was rearrested within five days of a probation report suggesting that he seek therapy at Southern State Hospital, his probation was revoked, and he was sentenced under the Federal Youth Corrections Act.

As noted, his mother had been hospitalized at Eastern Regional Hospital, apparently suffering from auditory hallucinations, according to the patient. He also indicated that his sister was briefly hospitalized at Gage County Hospital, but Mr. R. did not know the reasons for that hospitalization.

Regarding his own psychiatric history, as noted earlier his first contact was in February of 1977, when he was examined at the naval hospital, following some rather bizarre, confused, and "drifty" behavior on the boat on which he was stationed. Psychiatric examination at that point described Mr. R. as circumstantial, with loosened associations and inappropriate laughter, though he denied hallucinatory phenomena. He was diagnosed as a schizoid personality, or simple schizophrenic, and was consistently noted to be wandering into unauthorized spaces. A subsequent psychiatric evaluation described him as speaking in a monotone and manifesting muted affect; this resulted in an eventual diagnosis of an acute situational reaction in a schizoid personality. It is noteworthy that within that same naval record, Mr. R. wrote a rather grandiose letter, inappropriately contesting the navy's desire to discharge him.

His next hospitalization was from April of 1980 to August of 1981 at the federal psychiatric hospital at Terre Haute, Indiana. Upon admission, Mr. R. was diagnosed as paranoid schizophrenic in partial remission, reporting ideas of reference, feelings of persecution, and what is described as a history of visual and auditory hallucinations, though it is unclear from the previous records just what this "history" refers to. He was placed on Thorazine, 400 milligrams per day. In August of 1980, he was described as not manifesting any overtly psychotic symptoms, and in September of 1980, he was taken off medication and transferred to the regular penitentiary, having received "maximum hospital benefits." He apparently deteriorated in the general population, for in February of 1981, he was referred back to the psychiatric hospital. As that point he was described as depressed; preoccupied; showing impaired memory, inappropriate affect, and psychomotor retardation; and responding to auditory hallucinations. Psychological testing, however, did not reveal the presence of an active psychosis, and in April of 1981, parole was recommended, but it was strongly felt that he should have psychiatric follow-up on an inpatient basis. In July of 1981, he was described as suffering from a schizoid personality disorder, and the first indication of his sexual acting out with female employees is noted in the record. He is described as showing flattened affect, as well as poor insight and judgment, and he carried a final diagnosis of paranoid schizophrenia in moderate remission.

Shortly after his discharge from Terre Haute, as already noted, Mr. R. signed into Southern State Hospital in Baltimore as a condition of his parole, remaining there from July 31, 1981 to August 25, 1981. Here, however, the clinical picture was somewhat different. He was described as preoccupied and detached from reality, with flattening of affect, perfunctory mechanical behavior, and much denial. His thought was impoverished, he appeared depressed, and there was much evidence of thought blocking and preoccupation with sexual matters.

As noted previously when the medication was reduced and eventually discontinued, he was described as alert and responsive. There are several examples in the chart of Mr. R. demonstrating inappropriate sexual behavior, including exposing himself to a female patient and masturbating in front of a female staff psychologist. It is noteworthy, and consistent with the previously noted interview with Dr. D., that on the day of the alleged offense, there is no evidence of psychotic behavior that is consistent with the hallucinations which Mr. R. delineated. He was certainly described as sexually preoccupied, and the only element that appeared psychotic was the level of denial regarding this very sexual acting out.

As noted, Mr. R. was discharged from the Southern State Hospital for disciplinary reasons related to this sexual acting out on August 25, 1981 and was arrested on that same day at the attempted bank robbery. Four days later, he was admitted as a condition of release on bond to Eastern Regional Hospital. In an admission note dated August 31, he was described as neatly dressed, anxious, "spacey," and again showing inappropriate sexual behavior, "masturbating during the admission interview." His affect was inappropriate, but there was no loosening of association or flight of ideas, though some paranoid delusions appeared to resurface. He was treated with Navane and, at the time of discharge, was described as anxious, depressed, superficial, and sarcastic. Progress notes reveal observations of confusion, depression, tangentiality, irrelevant conversations, agitation, inappropriate affect, and poor insight, but no delusions. However, later in that admission, the delusions and hallucinations appeared to surface once more.

As noted, Mr. R. was removed from Southern State Hospital by federal marshals, and at the time of his return to the Terre Haute federal prison facility, he was described as having shown a gross deterioration and being blank, with impaired motility, blocking, severe impairment in speech, suspiciousness, describing ideas of reference, and some auditory hallucinations. His concentration was poor, his cognition and judgment were grossly impaired, and he was diagnosed as suffering from schizophrenia, catatonic type. He was returned to the Central City Jail in March of 1982 and later transferred to Central Hospital in April of 1982.

From the point of view of neurological history, Mr. R. reported many head injuries and one incident of having been knocked unconscious. He also described a variety of symptoms suggestive of neurological involvement, including severe headaches, pathological intoxication, sudden mood changes, impulsive running away, periods of mental confusion, and periods of stupor and staring, but during the subsequent interview, he indicated that many of the symptoms which he described were "inaccurate." In addition, the Monroe Dyscontrol Scale revealed Mr. R.'s personal rating of his own propensity for dyscontrol as exceedingly slight.

On the current battery of psychological testing, Mr. R. obtains a verbal IQ of 103, a performance IQ of 91, and a resultant full scale IQ of 97, placing him within the average range of intellectual functioning. It is noteworthy that there is a great deal of scatter among Mr. R.'s subtest scaled scores, especially on the performance subtests. There are continual intrusions of manifestations of anxiety, blocking, and inappropriate thought processes. While his fund of general information is somewhat above average, even here one sees the evidence of his current mental disorder and his looseness of associations. For instance, when asked who Madame Curie was, he initially stated, "She's a spy; no, that's Mata Hari. Madame Curie was a scientist, but she must have been a prostitute too because she had a madame before her name." Mr. R.'s skills in the areas of concentration, attention, and short-term rote learning are generally average or above average, and his vocabulary skills are within the average range, though here again there is some loosening of associations and some concrete thinking, suggestive of the current psychotic process. Mr. R.'s capacity to appreciate the appropriate responses to social situations is generally intact, but in terms of translating these understandings into action, there is a marked decrement, frequently intruded upon by his impulsivity. He does show some impairment in his capacity for abstract thinking as well, again consistent with the current presence of a psychosis. His capacity to separate essential from nonessential details, in a task of visual concentration, is above average, but as already noted, his ability to manipulate social situations in an appropriate manner is exceedingly poor, consisting of confused and inadequate sequences of behavior. His perceptual motor coordination is in the average to above-average range, except in tasks requiring rapid learning and concentration, at which time his anxiety intrudes in a rather dramatic manner.

On the Projective Drawings, Mr. R. reveals a generally intact self-image, but there is a marked rigidity of defenses noted. Great attention is paid to small details, which suggests an attempt to utilize an obsessive reconstitution following a psychotic episode. There is clear evidence of sexual conflicts in his execution of the female drawings, as well as many repetitions of intrusive unconscious material. There is an obsessive quality in his continual attempt to both admit into consciousness, and defend against, certain unconscious material which is laden with sexual conflicts. He shows, in his own self-image, rather inadequate defenses and a lessened ability to cope with the world around him.

Consistent with the self-report on the Monroe Dyscontrol Scale, the screening tests for central nervous system dysfunction are basically negative, tending to contraindicate, at least on the basis of these instruments, any central nervous system involvement.

Mr. R.'s reality testing at the present time is very tenuous and suggests many internal preoccupations at the expense of his ability to actively interact with, and participate in, his environment. There is evidence of much rather poorly controlled inner hostility and an exceedingly immature level of relating to other people. Similarly, his fantasies are quite immature and primitive, suggesting a very regressed level of psychological development at present. Perhaps what is most disturbing is the fact that even Mr. R.'s rather tenuous contact with reality is maintained by the use of exceedingly rigid and brittle defense mechanisms. That is, he would have the capacity to look far more overtly disturbed were he not attempting to repress and deny as much as he is.

Several of Mr. R.'s attempts to defend against his inner chaotic world by use of abstraction continually fail, and stirring up of unconscious material continually results in a loss of reality testing, contaminated thought processes highly consistent with a psychosis, confabulation, and intrusions into consciousness of hostile impulses. He attempts to control these hostile impulses by utilizing obsessive defenses, but this is frequently ineffective. At times Mr. R. is capable of seeing reality but is unable to describe it adequately. Even when his contact with reality is adequate, there are intrusions of exceedingly regressive and hostile impulses.

In summary then, the current evaluation suggests that there is little doubt that H. R. is at the present time a rather seriously disturbed and indeed overtly psychotic individual. His defenses against the underlying psychosis are exceedingly brittle and fragile, and it appears that it would take very little stress to precipitate a rather gross deterioration in his already overstressed defensive systems. However, generalizing backward from the time of the current evaluation to the time of the alleged offense, and inferring that exactly the same state of mind existed at that time, would appear to be totally unwarranted. All of the interviews with people who observed Mr. R. around the time of the alleged offense fail to confirm the presence of any of the current symptomatology at the time the offense was committed. That is, the victim of the assault himself, Mr. R.'s treating physician, and the bank teller all failed to confirm the presence of any symptoms of an overt psychotic process, with the exception of sexual acting out. Even Mr. R.'s mother spoke about his behavior becoming seclusive and withdrawn, not assaultive, when he became psychotic. Indeed, his behavior, as psychotic as it is, at Central Hospital is characterized by an absence of any hostile and destructive acting out. It appears, then, even according to Mr. R.'s own subjective perception of his "falling apart" following the commission of the offense, and after having been shuttled from one federal institution to another without medication, that the gross deterioration currently noted followed the offense, rather than being present at the time of the offense. As closely as one is able to infer from the records, the seriousness of the deterioration was not noted until Mr. R.'s readmission to the federal psychiatric facility at Terre Haute in January of 1982, at which time he was diagnosed as catatonic schizophrenic.

Therefore, it seems most likely that the acute deterioration followed the commission of the offense by several months and was diagnosed first at that time, namely, in January of 1982. It thus appears that what Mr. R. is most likely doing is retrospectively interpreting his experiences of August 1981 in the light of his current mental deterioration. The overwhelming objective evidence from outside sources is that Mr. R. was not acting in a bizarre fashion at the time of the alleged offenses at all. Therefore, it is my opinion that while Mr. R. was suffering from a mental disease around the time of the offense, a disease which has been diagnosed by Southern State Hospital as "atypical psychosis," at the time of the offense this psychosis did not substantially impair Mr. R.'s understanding of the wrongfulness of his behavior or his ability to conform his behavior to the requirements of the law. In fact, whatever psychosis Mr. R. was suffering from at that time was not characterized by command hallucinations or by any propensity to act out in a violent manner. Therefore, while he was suffering from a psychotic condition, this condition cannot be regarded as causally related to his behavior at the time of the offense. Rather, as noted, it appears that Mr. R. is reconstructing his previous experience in light of his subsequent psychological deterioration. At the present time, it is my opinion that Mr. R. is indeed suffering from a paranoid schizophrenic psychosis, but that this psychosis developed several months following the commission of the alleged offense.

I trust the above analysis is of some assistance to you. If I may be of further help, please do not hesitate to call on me.

Very truly yours,

David L. Shapiro Ph.D.

Appendix B
Criminal Responsibility

April 12, 1982

Ms. Barbara Sears
Staff Attorney
Public Defender Service
451 Indiana Avenue, N.W.
Washington, D.C. 20001

Dear Ms. Sears:

Pursuant to your referral, I examined your client, Mr. T., at Central Hospital on February 3 and February 17, 1982, for a total of five hours; in addition to clinical interview and history taking, I administered the following psychological tests: Bender Gestalt, Graham-Kendall Memory for Designs Test, Thematic Apperception Test, Sentence Completion Test, Projective Drawings, and the Minnesota Multiphasic Personality Inventory. I also utilized the psychological test protocols that had been administered by the staff of forensic services, specifically Dr. G., who provided the protocols for the Wechsler Adult Intelligence Scale, the Bender Gestalt, and the Rorschach. In addition to this, I reviewed the complete medical record at Central Hospital, as well as interviewing the patient's grandmother.

Review of the police report reveals that on September 1, 1981, the complainant, while asleep in an upstairs bedroom, was awakened by the sound of breaking glass, and as she went to investigate, she discovered the suspect coming up the stairs towards her armed with a rifle. She barricaded herself and her two children in the bedroom, but the suspect broke down the door and entered the room. Once in the room, he wanted to know the whereabouts of her daughter. He was told where she might be and left to look for her. By this time the police had been called, and they eventually responded and arrested Mr. T. He indicated to the police that he had the weapon because he needed to use it on the complainant so that she would tell him where her daughter was. Recovered from Mr. T. was a loaded .22-caliber rifle, along with 135 rounds of ammunition.

The complaining witnesses in this case are Mr. T.'s uncle, and his aunt; the young woman named Sarah is apparently Mr. T.'s cousin. There were many bitter feelings of Mr. T.'s uncle towards him because of the great amount of time that Mr. T.'s grandmother (that is, the uncle's mother) spent taking care of him. The grandmother did so because of the very traumatic circumstances under which Mr. T. was raised. However, Mr. T.'s uncle could only see the attention that his mother paid to Mr. T. as "pampering."

In discussing the alleged offense, Mr. T. does not deny any of it, but justifies his actions in terms of an exceedingly extensive delusional system surrounding an imagined relationship between himself and Sarah, and the fact that his aunt and uncle are attempting to harm Sarah and that he (Mr. T.) had to rescue her.

Mr. T. was very frank in describing his hallucinatory experiences prior to, at the time of, and since the alleged offense, and saw their involvement in his motivation for the offense. However, it is noteworthy that at no time did Mr. T. view these hallucinations as evidence of a mental disturbance. Mr. T. indicated on interview that he trusted the voices, though he was aware that some were trustworthy and others were not. He indicated that the voices told him that Sarah was interested in him, and that he therefore became interested in her and considered her as a girl friend. In point of fact, there was no such relationship between Sarah and Mr. T. Mr. T. then indicated that "other voices came along" and threatened him, and he said that he did not know how the latter set of voices "got her name." He indicated that the voices would threaten him and make threatening statements about Sarah; that the voices were going to try to break them up; and that "the voices wanted part of my body, my heart." He indicated that the latter set of voices — "the evil set" — wanted him to give up Sarah. He indicated that he knew that there was mutual love between them because of a dream that he had had, and that he felt that he and Sarah were being threatened by the voices. He indicated that he was not getting along well with his uncle and, in some way, identified his uncle with the evil voices. He stated that he came to Baltimore looking for Sarah, and he indicated that his uncle would not tell him where she was and would not talk with him. This further convinced him that his uncle was involved with the voices in one way or another, and he concluded that Sarah was in the house and was in trouble. He viewed his breaking into the house as an attempt to rescue Sarah from his uncle and from the evil voices. He regarded them as "life-threatening voices."

Even as Mr. T. described the offense, he was rather defensive, as already noted, never recognizing that the voices were a possible symptom of a mental disorder. He also failed to discuss the fact that there had been a previous attempt to enter his uncle's house, approximately two months prior to the current offense, which resulted in his being hospitalized at Eastern Regional Hospital, an incident which Mr. T. was very evasive about and tried to avoid discussing.

Mr. T. described a variety of hallucinatory experiences in addition to the voices mentioned. He indicated that he would see light coming at him "in the shape of check marks," coming out of the sky towards his face and hitting him, but that "I don't feel it." He also discussed what he called "seepage" which he defined as pinprick sensations, coming out of the air, which diffused through his skin into his body. He indicated that they would come in contact with his skin and would actually penetrate his skin, so that he always felt a need to scratch himself. He also spoke about the feeling that somebody was reading his brain thoughts, a sensation that had been a rather consistent one since December of 1980. The phenomena of seepage and the "light checks" he dated to May of 1981.

Regarding any previous criminal record, Mr. T. denied having any juvenile record, but did indicate that while in the state of Missouri in 1978, he was charged with a failure to appear for a traffic violation. He indicated that he had a variety of speeding offenses for which he had paid fines. He also indicated that he had a charge of passing bad checks in South Carolina in 1980, for which he eventually made restitution. Other than that, there are only the trespassing charge of July of 1981 and the current charge from September of 1981.

Mr. T. indicated that he was arrested at the time of the September offense and remained in jail until the third week in October. He described having trouble in jail because he did not get treatment for his hallucinations. He indicated that the hallucinations stopped after a month of treatment with psychotropic medication at Central Hospital.

Mr. T. was born in Columbia, South Carolina, on March 26, 1955, an only child. He indicated that his parents are alive but separated when he was approximately 20 years of age. He was somewhat evasive and defensive in discussing his early childhood, for he did not indicate the amount of turbulence and trauma which was noted in the interview with his grandmother. According to Mr. T.'s account, his parents "had their fights," and there were occasional "hard times and troubles." He indicated that there was some physical violence but that he was not hit very often. Once again, this stands in rather sharp contrast to the picture of his childhood painted by his grandmother, who indicated that on many occasions Mr. T. needed to come to live with her. The patient's father was an accountant and his mother a librarian, and Mr. T. described them as being basically a middle class family. Mr. T. indicated that he had an epileptic condition, which he described as a series of absence states, until the age of 12. He indicated that this was characterized primarily by a twitching of his tongue, but he denied any significant loss of awareness and stated that he had never had any tonic-clonic symptoms. He indicated that he had been on medication for the epileptic condition but was unaware of what the medication was. He denied any spatial distortions, any headaches, and any déjà or jamais vu experiences; he also denied a variety of temporal lobe phenomena. Mr. T. described only one head injury, a very recent one, in which he hit his head and blacked out. He denied any symptoms of pathological intoxication, and stated that he basically drank very little and occasionally smoked marijuana, but he denied the influence of any drugs at the time of the offense.

Mr. T. indicated that when he was quite young, his family moved to the Baltimore area, and he attended both kindergarten and the first grade in Baltimore. He said his family then moved back to Columbia, South Carolina, where he completed high school. He indicated that he did not do so well in school, primarily because of a lack of motivation, but that he had a fair number of friends in school. He indicated that during adolescence, he would use marijuana occasionally and would drink occasionally, but "nothing heavy." He indicated that he had one girl friend and that he was "really close to her," but that he didn't have "much of a sex life." He indicated that the girl "wouldn't let me go all the way." He denied any homosexual encounters, and stated that he has never been married and has no children. Mr. T. was never in the military service. Following his graduation from high school, he went to a technical institute in South Carolina, but he indicated that he "messed around, missed classes, and dropped out." He then moved around the country, doing odd jobs, and this was apparently the period of time that he went to Missouri. He returned to South Carolina and, apparently since December of 1980, has been experiencing these various hallucinations.

Mr. T. denied any previous psychiatric contact for himself, though he indicated that his mother had some recent psychiatric contact. He appeared to become very distressed when asked about this, stating that his mother "doesn't want him to talk about it."

As Mr. T. indicated, he was admitted to Central Hospital on October 19, 1981 and was described at that point as hallucinating, being very anxious, and showing loosening of associations; he was diagnosed at that time as paranoid schizophrenic. On the day of admission, he was placed on Thorazine, 75 milligrams intramuscularly and 100 milligrams orally, as needed for agitation. Several days later, his medication was changed to Stelazine, 5 milligrams three times daily, and Haldol, 10 milligrams intramuscularly. In November of 1981, the Stelazine was increased to 5 milligrams four times a day. He was also placed on observation for violent behavior and had to be secluded on several occasions. The Stelazine dosage was increased to 10 milligrams four times daily towards the end of November and in early December of 1981. Thorazine, 50 milligrams, was added to the Stelazine on December 10, and on December 14, the Stelazine was cut back to 10 milligrams three times a day. The Thorazine and Stelazine were both discontinued on January 11, and on January 22, Mr. T. was apparently placed on a maintenance dosage of Thorazine, 200 milligrams three times daily and 100 milligrams at bedtime.

Throughout the course of the hospitalization, his behavior is characterized as confused, agitated, and hostile, with evidence of hallucinations, ideas of reference, and many delusional ideas such as his need to place calls to the FBI. Mr. T. was also described on occasions as suspicious, hostile, uncooperative, withdrawn, and at times depressed.

The first forensic services screening examination described him as grossly delusional, manifesting loose associations, pressured speech, and thoughts of being persecuted. A full competency evaluation was recommended. On October 7, 1981, Mr. T. was found incompetent to stand trail because of his looseness of associations, delusional thinking, persecutory ideation, and flight of ideas. At that time, it was also the opinion of the examining psychiatrist that he was most likely "productive." On November 5, 1981, he was again regarded as incompetent because of the powerful impact of his delusional thinking, which rendered him unable to cope with his criminal proceedings in any way other than that dictated by his delusions. Finally, in an evaluation dated December 29, he was noted to show blunted affect, as well as some residual evidence of hallucinations and loose associations, but he was found competent to stand trial.

The current battery of psychological testing generally reveals an individual in a rather unstable remission from a previous acute psychotic episode. Throughout the testing, there is evidence of defensiveness, evasiveness, and an attempt to "seal over" a serious underlying disturbance.

On the Wechsler Adult Intelligence Scale, Mr. T. obtains a verbal IQ of 86, a performance IQ of 74, and a resultant full scale IQ of 78, placing him within the borderline range of intellectual functioning. It was noted that he consistently had difficulty focusing his attention on the tasks so that his efficient performance was often compromised. This borderline range of intellectual functioning was regarded as significantly depressed below his true potential due to the influence of the schizophrenic thought disorder. There are a variety of peculiarities in his thought processes and many difficulties in his ability to respond adequately to social situations. A number of these dimensions suggest that there is still a powerful, though somewhat controlled, schizophrenic process at the present time. During the course of the testing he was tremulous, anxious, depressed, distractible, and frequently unable to focus on the test stimuli.

While the screening tests for central nervous system dysfunction are basically intact, once again the distractibility, especially when the memory task is presented, compromises his scores significantly.

The projective testing is also characterized by an exceeding constriction and some difficulty in handling emotionally charged situations. Mr. T. basically tries to avoid such situations, but when he is unable to do so, he may have a tendency to get "swamped" by the affective stimulation and be unable to respond in a reality oriented manner. Certainly, the picture that emerges from the projective techniques is of a remitting psychosis with many peculiarities in language and reasoning, and an exceedingly fragile defensive structure.

The defensiveness pervades the rest of the testing, in which he remains vague and evasive about a variety of family interactions, but also manifests the extreme instability of these defenses, with a breakthrough of some exceedingly peculiar, bizarre, and sadistic underlying ideation.

Finally, on the Minnesota Multiphasic Personality Inventory, despite his attempt to deny a mental disorder, he presents a picture that is consistent with a serious disturbance, characterized by anxiety, agitation, and a florid thought disorder.

In summary, then, at the present time, Mr. T. appears to be in remission — albeit an exceedingly unstable, fragile, and brittle remission — from a serious psychotic disorder.

Nevertheless, at the present time, Mr. T. is well aware of the charges against him, has both a factual and a rational understanding of the proceedings, and appears able to assist counsel with a relative degree of rational understanding in the preparation and implementation of a defense. He understands the different pleas that he can enter and the consequences of those pleas. He is well aware of the roles of various court personnel. Therefore, it is my opinion that his mental illness is in a significant enough degree of remission for him to be considered competent to stand trial at the present time.

Regarding criminal responsibility, in my opinion there is ample evidence that Mr. T. was actively delusional at the time of the offense, and was acting on the basis of this delusional thinking and the associated hallucinations. Mr. T. stated that he did not even think about getting arrested and that he felt justified in his actions since he himself had previously tried to contact the police, in an attempt to get help to locate Sarah. He indicated that he had tried to file a missing persons report, but the police had told him that only the parents could file such a report. He indicated that he did not feel that there was any way to hold back on the impulse to rescue Sarah. He indicated that he had also made several contacts with the police about the threatening voices, but the police had merely told him to obtain psychiatric attention. He spoke of his need to get FCC equipment to scan people on the radio, because of the people who were picking up his thought waves. In short, all of these delusional thoughts around the time of the offense, in my opinion, lead to the conclusion that on or about September 1, 1981, Mr. T. was suffering from paranoid schizophrenia and, as a result of this mental disorder, lacked substantial capacity to appreciate the wrongfulness of his behavior and to conform his behavior to the requirements of the law. It is my opinion that the alleged offense, if committed by Mr. T., was the product of his mental illness.

I trust the above analysis is of some assistance to you. If I may be of further help, please do not hesitate to call on me.

Very Truly Yours,

David L. Shapiro Ph.D.

Appendix C
Personal Injury

February 22, 1982

Ms. Sarah Thomas
Attorney-at-Law
3000 Connecticut Avenue, N.W.
Washington, D.C. 20008

Dear Ms. Thomas:

Pursuant to your referral, I examined your client Ms. L. on January 26 and 29, and February 5, 1982. In addition to clinical interview and history taking, I administered the following psychological tests: Thematic Apperception Test, Rorschach, Graham-Kendall Memory for Designs Test, Minnesota Multiphasic Personality Inventory, Bender Gestalt, Sentence Completion Test, Projective Drawings, and the Millon Clinical Multiaxial Inventory. In addition, I reviewed the test results obtained by Dr. D. on the Wechsler Adult Intelligence Scale, which he had administered as part of a comprehensive neuropsychological test battery.

I also reviewed, prior to preparation of this report, the following documents relating to Ms. L.'s examination and treatment following her accident: physical examination and radiological report from D.C. General Hospital, dated September 29, 1979; an ENT evaluation performed by Dr. M., dated January 27, 1981; the report of an audiogram from Central Memorial Hospital; an opthalmological examination by Dr. S., dated July 8, 1981; a psychiatric evaluation by Dr. W., dated December 24, 1980; evaluations by her treating psychologist Dr. P., dated March 31 and November 1, 1980; a report of electroencephalography from the Division of Neurology at Sibley Hospital, dated March 31, 1981; and a neurological consultation by Dr. R., dated March 30, 1981.

As you know, the general conclusion to be derived from this large volume of medical and psychiatric reports is that while Ms. L. suffered initially from a number of symptoms consistent with postconcussional syndrome, it appears that many of the symptoms have continued long past the point where one would expect them, in the absence of other neurological or physical findings.

Accordingly, many of the physicians involved feel that there is a functional or psychiatric overlay which appears to be prolonging the physical complaints. Indeed, this is reflected most accurately in the reports of Dr. W. and Dr. P., both of whom have diagnosed Ms. L. as suffering from a posttraumatic neurosis. In the opinion of both Dr. W. and Dr. P., Ms. L. is severely disabled by her emotional condition. This is certainly consistent with the fact that until very recently, Ms. L. has been completely nonfunctional, being unable to leave her home, go shopping, do housework, cook, or socialize in any way, without severe anxiety, confusion, and fainting spells.

Over the course of three weeks, I examined Ms. L. for a series of evaluations, and during the course of those evaluations, she continually appeared neatly dressed, cooperative, and well oriented. Attention, perception, and memory were generally intact; affect was appropriate; speech, coherent; and there was no evidence of delusions or hallucinations. There was also no evidence of suicidal ideation.

Ms. L. related a feeling that she was "out of control." She was aware of a number of symptoms that she had had prior to the accident, which appear to have been significantly exacerbated by the accident, as well as a number of symptoms that have occurred since the accident.

In the former category, Ms. L. recalled that she had been dyslexic all throughout childhood, having difficulties in reading, spelling, and arithmetic, often seeing her numbers and letters backward. She indicated that she had gained a good deal of control over this prior to the accident, but has noticed a distinctive worsening of this condition since the accident. She indicated that although it has improved somewhat, the control she can exert over this condition has certainly not been restored to the level which existed prior to the accident. She indicated that one of the ways in which she had learned to cope with her problem was by putting her finger on each word and color coding lines that she was reading. She indicated that this had helped substantially, but since the time of the accident, she feels that she had lost this degree of control over the reading difficulty. In fact, immediately after the accident, Ms. L. indicated, "I couldn't retain anything; I was in a fog."

Ms. L. also indicated that she felt very frustrated, "like a child out of control." This appeared to be a return to early feelings which she had as a child, for she stated that she had an "awful homelife . . . an adventure in yecch." Ms. L. indicated that she basically forced herself to overcome her early traumatic experiences, feeling that she "had one life to live and I won't be dragged down." She recalls always having been squeamish about death after her mother committed suicide. She indicated that since the accident, she has been unable to keep the suicide out of her mind any longer and has become obsessed with death. She stated that she is unable to sleep and wakes up screaming, reliving the accident and wondering as she awakes, "Am I dead yet?" As she was describing this feeling, Ms. L. broke into tears during the course of the evaluation. She indicated that she could not stop thinking about her mother committing suicide and that while this has diminished somewhat, it is still present and, whenever she thinks of it she will spontaneously start vomiting and then faint.

She indicated that prior to the accident, she had suffered from a spastic stomach, but once again, she had learned to control it somewhat. She indicated that soon after the accident, she was unable to enter an automobile, would vomit, and would lose bladder control. She became terrified about the fact that her husband might find her "passed out on the floor." This exacerbation of the earlier symptoms, coupled with the fainting spells, was something that Ms. L. had not experienced prior to the accident.

Ms. L. also indicated that she had had some hives when she was growing up, but at the present time is experiencing what she calls "internal hives." She indicated that any kind of tightness around her, such as tight fitting clothing, will give her internal pain, resulting in constant attention to her breathing and heartbeat, and a terror that she will stop breathing and die.

Ms. L. had also been aware, prior to the accident, of a feeling of sadness that "my father didn't love me." She indicated that she had worked through that feeling, to the point where it made her feel "sad, but never slowed me down." She indicated that she is now totally incapable of dealing with these feelings and can become exceedingly upset by her feeling that there is no support forthcoming from her father.

She also described a worsening of her vision since the accident and the fact that she was unable to draw until quite recently, her occupation, of course, being that of an artist.

Ms. L. also recounted a number of very disturbing symptoms which she has experienced since the time of the accident. As already noted she has become obsessed with death, and will frequently experience fainting and vomiting, none of which occurred prior to the accident. She also indicated severe anxiety about driving, though she does state that this has improved somewhat. She experienced a tremendous fear of going out of her own home and became very seclusive following the accident, but she indicated that this is slowly improving. Ms. L. indicated that even when she was a passenger in a car, she would experience severe anxiety and break out into cold sweats. Her fear of going out of the home had to do with the fact that she was afraid that she would vomit, have diarrhea, or pass out in the presence of other people. She found herself exceedingly distractible in social situations, being unable to screen out background noise, and finding that when she heard a variety of noises, she would grow nauseated and need to vomit. She indicated that because she was unable to screen out background noise from what people were saying, she frequently missed what people said and would become very upset by this, and she eventually terminated many of her social contacts.

Ms. L. felt unable to make any decisions whatsoever, feeling that her mind just wouldn't work. She felt obsessively tied in knots, unable to decide one course of action as opposed to another.

She suffered from headaches, insomnia, and rather prolonged sexual dysfunction, stating, "It makes me nauseous to think of it." She admitted that the sexual dysfunction has created a good deal of tension in her marriage and that she feels very guilty about it. Once again, it should be noted that Ms. L. indicated that prior to the accident, her sexual adjustment with her husband had been quite satisfactory and that the only difficulties they ever experienced occurred because of "differences in schedule." However, none of the intense revulsion which she currently experiences was ever present prior to the accident.

Ms. L. also spoke about severe depression arising since the time of the accident, about "feeling like my head is going to explode" and that "all of the sadness is coming back — everything at once." This refers, once again, to many of the depressing memories she had of her childhood, which she had successfully been able to overcome. She also indicated that she finds herself totally lacking in confidence, motivation, and energy, and will experience affective swings, independent of external circumstances.

Ms. L. also described a variety of symptoms which could be consistent with some neurological problem, though, as noted earlier previous neurological consultations were basically negative. She spoke of a loss of balance, as well as memory problems, blurring of vision, and the fact that she would "bump into things on my right side."

In reference to history, Ms. L. was born in Boston, Massachusetts, on July 10, 1948, the oldest of four siblings. She recalled her childhood as being an exceedingly volatile and violent one, with much fighting between her parents and a large number of physical separations. She recalls not only verbal but physical abuse, with her parents frequently hitting each other. When she was 10 years old, the family moved to Washington, and the violence continued, with her parents throwing tables and chairs around the house. She indicated that she had a congenital digestive disease when she was very young, but had apparently grown out of it.

She indicated that her father would "hit me harder than I could take it" and that she would frequently bleed from his beatings. She felt that she was singled out and that her siblings "didn't get it as bad as I did." She remembered many attempts on her mother's part to commit suicide, her first memory being when she was 4 years of age. With the exception of the congenital digestive problem, Ms. L. indicated that she did not have any serious illnesses or injuries as a child.

Ms. L. stated that because of her reading problem, she hated school, and that she was frequently punished by her father due to her difficulty in concentration and her poor grades in school. However, she indicated that she had a large circle of friends and had become involved in her artwork at a very young age. Ms. L. recalls a number of suicide attempts on her mother's part during her early school years, and one particularly "horrifying" time when she was 10 years of age. Ms. L. indicated that when she was 13, she ran away from home and went to Boston to live with her grandparents for a year.

It was while Ms. L. was at summer camp, at age 13, that her mother committed suicide. She indicated that there appeared to be much paranoid ideation on her mother's part, with her mother stating such things as, "There are detectives following me." She said that her father drove to summer camp and told her, in the automobile, that her mother had committed suicide. She indicated that she had a "feeling of death" which came back to her at the time that she was in the automobile accident. After her mother's death, her father asked her to move back to Washington to take care of her younger siblings. Her father remarried, and Ms. L.'s stepmother refused to live in the same home that the father had previously lived in, which resulted in her father's buying another house. It was apparently around this period of time that Ms. L. started to build her defenses against the shattering experiences of her childhood. She described herself as being "a stone wall" and becoming heavily involved with her peers, trying to forget her family. Ms. L. indicated that her stepmother had beaten her badly on one occasion and that she had again run away to Boston; she stated that "I learned to deal with it by staying away from it."

At the age of 17, Ms. L. became pregnant, and her stepmother arranged an illegal abortion for her which was again an exceedingly traumatic experience. However, Ms. L. indicated that she was able to suppress the memory of that until after the accident, from which time she has continually had nightmares about the abortion.

Ms. L. returned to the Washington area and did graduate from high school, passing her courses, though she indicated that her grades were not good. She worked for approximately one year and decided then that she wanted to go to college. She started attending the University of Maryland, obtained an apartment of her own, decided that she was "determined to do well," and did in fact make the dean's list. She indicated that she had a large number of friends and became a "flower child." She remained in college until 1972, describing it as "a wonderful experience." She started dating her husband in 1972, but went to Israel for four months on an archaeological dig. She returned to the United States, taught school for one year, and then married her husband. She has been a special education teacher in the Washington, D.C., school system until the time of her accident. She described a basically stable marriage, with her only feeling about difficulties being the fact that she was "more adventurous" than her husband. She also described, as previously noted, an adequate sexual adjustment until the time of the accident. There is very little evidence of drug or alcohol abuse, Ms. L. stating that she occasionally drank beer, had smoked marijuana occasionally, and on one occasion, had taken LSD.

Ms. L. indicated that there had been a number of prior contacts with psychiatrists and psychologists for evaluation in reference to her school difficulties. None of these appeared to be long term, involving psychotherapy, until the time that she started to see Dr. P., following the accident.

As noted, although Ms. L. indicated that she has been suffering from a number of symptoms, some of which seem consistent with neurological disorders, neurological evaluations have suggested a good deal of functional overlay and elaboration to the symptoms.

Ms. L., for instance, has described uncontrollable shaking which occurs on occasion since the accident, fainting spells, stomach cramps, vertigo, and feeling as if she is "totally drunk" even though she has not been drinking. She also has had dizzy spells and finds herself having an exceedingly "short fuse." She indicated that the slightest things set her off and that she will slam doors in anger. She stated that since the time of the accident, she has had mood swings apparently unrelated to any external precipitants, as well as the confusional episodes described. She has spoken about a ringing in her ears, but the audiological examination apparently failed to confirm any definite basis for this. She did describe a number of spatial distortions that accompanied the headaches and dizzy spells, which she characterized as "seeing one and a half objects." She described a number of autonomic changes, also without apparent external precipitants, such as diarrhea, problems with bladder control, sudden stomachaches, sweating, palpitations, and a feeling that "everything is rushing." Since the time of the accident, she has also noted sudden attacks of panic, for no apparent reason, during which she will break into tears. Immediately following the accident, she experienced frequently the altered state of consciousness called jamais vu, though she has indicated that this is gradually remitting. Immediately after the accident, she also described herself as having fugue states, though once again, these appear to be decreasing. There was also significant distortion of her body image: she stated that she did not want anybody to see her because she felt that she "looked like a hippopotamus." As noted earlier there were disturbances in both recent and remote memory, but these appear to have been pretty much resolved.

Psychological testing indicates that Ms. L. is presenting herself in an honest and forthright manner, attempting neither to exaggerate her symptomatology nor to deny its significance. There is no evidence whatsoever of malingering.

On the Wechsler Adult Intelligence Scale, Ms. L. obtains a verbal IQ of 97, a performance IQ of 112, and a resultant full scale IQ of 102, placing her within the average range of intellectual functioning. There is a good deal of scatter on her subtest scaled scores, suggesting the intrusion of significant amounts of anxiety which are interfering with her optimal intellectual functioning. There is no evidence of any pathological intrusions in her thought processes; this is consistent with the fact that there is no ongoing psychotic process. While many of her scaled scores are average or well above average, there appear to be consistent difficulties in tasks which involve sustained attention, concentration, short-term memory, and learning. This is, of course, consistent with her own self-report of confusion and difficulty in concentrating on matters in her day-to-day life.

Her fantasy productions are pervaded by a sense of depression and some degree of avoidance of emotionally arousing affect. When confronted with these emotionally stimulating situations, Ms. L. does appear to utilize some degree of distancing mechanisms, consistent with her adjustment prior to the accident. It appears that her psychotherapy has indeed assisted her in rebuilding this defensive structure.

Her reality testing is certainly very well intact, as noted, indicating no signs whatsoever of any psychotic process. She presents herself as a highly intuitive and creative individual who, at the present time, appears to be more in tune with her inner experience than with her reactions to the world around her. Consistent with the results of the other testing, on the Rorschach test there is ample and pervasive evidence of her serious depression at the present time, coupled with a sense of passivity; that is, she feels overwhelmed and unable to cope with her feelings of depression. She experiences the world as a terribly dangerous place and feels very much at loose ends in coping with affective stimulation. This inability to react effectively when a situation calls for an emotional response tends to make Ms. L. feel even more depressed and more incapable of coping with the demands of interpersonal situations. One of the reasons she finds it so difficult to deal with emotional stimulation is that this stirs up early memories of hurt and anger, and she feels that her defensive structure at present is not adequate to contain these feelings as it could prior to the accident. She also finds herself approaching interpersonal situations in a somewhat childlike manner, feeling unable to cope with object relationships in a mature and adult fashion. This once again represents a regression to early childhood modes of coping with the world, in my opinion, as a result of the shattering of her defensive structures since the accident.

In summary then, Ms. L. appears to be a young woman who had a series of exceedingly traumatic experiences in her childhood, with which she learned to cope by using a variety of defense mechanisms, and who indeed was performing at an exceedingly high level. The accident shattered her defensive structures, and threw her back to a series of more primitive defense mechanisms and a far more regressed manner of dealing with the environment around her. She appears to have made substantial progress in psychotherapy up to this point, but given the degree of disorganization, anxiety, and depression at present, it is my opinion that she will need to be involved in psychotherapy for a substantial period of time before she is able to regain the level of coping and adjustment which she had prior to the accident. In my opinion, intensive psychotherapy for a period of three to four years more would be the absolute minimum necessary to restore Ms. L. to her previous level of functioning.

Thank you for this most interesting referral. If I may be of further assistance, please do not hesitate to call on me.

Very Truly Yours,

David L. Shapiro Ph.D.

Appendix D
Child Custody

NAME: W. K.
DOB: 10-5-65
AGE: 15-8

TESTS ADMINISTERED:

Clinical Interviews:
W. K. (2 sessions)
Mr. and Mrs. N. (2 sessions)
Mr. and Mrs. K. (2 sessions)
Consultation with Mr. S.
Counselor, Smith Junior High School, Washington D.C.
Review of Previous Testing (10-1-79)
Minnesota Multiphasic Personality Inventory
Thematic Apperception Test
Projective Drawings
Bender Visual Motor Gestalt Test
Graham-Kendall Memory for Designs Test
Sentence Completion Test
Rorschach Psychodiagnostic Test
Wechsler Intelligence Scale for Children (revised form)

DATES OF EVALUATION:

May 22, 1981
June 5, 1981
June 11, 1981

W. was referred for psychological evaluation by his mother and father, who have been separated for five years and, more recently, divorced. W.'s grades in school have been deteriorating progressively, and an earnest effort was being made on the part of both parents to have W. evaluated, to determine what (if any) relationship his poor academic performance has to the ongoing visitation problems, and to work out an arrangement which would be most beneficial for him. Both Mrs. N.

and Mr. K. recognize the need for such an examination, and have indicated that they will respect the recommendation regardless of the findings.

The interviews with Mr. and Mrs. N., and with Mr. and Mrs. K., created one definite and overriding impression in this examiner's opinion: namely, that both sets of parents are genuinely interested in W.'s welfare and are earnestly committed to working out an arrangement which would be best for his emotional growth and development. There is no clear indication of any serious deficit in parenting on either side; the evaluation, therefore, is based primarily on an assessment of W.'s current needs and how they "fit in" to the different environments within which he may be placed.

In the interviews with Mr. and Mrs. N., it was continually stressed that the primary concern was for W. to be happy, and that Mrs. N. was basically appealing for help at this point because previous attempts to work with W.'s problems have, in her opinion, not been successful. Mrs. N. made reference, both in interview and in a letter that she sent, to a behavior modification program which she had set up on the advice of the school psychologist and which she felt had not worked out. Mrs. N. was quite concerned about the fact that W. sees his father "just for good times," for fun and games, and that no value is placed on education. She expressed concern that her ex-husband tells the children to lie to her and that he is instilling in them a generally irresponsible attitude; she stated her feeling that she and Mr. N. can provide a more stable atmosphere within which W. can grow up. While there had apparently been some previous emphasis on W. being able to go to college, Mrs. N. indicated that at the present time, her primary concern is with W.'s happiness and that she does not care whether or not he attends college; she stated quite bluntly, "If I am damaging him, let him go; I hold no grudges."

Interview with Mr. K. indicated in a similar manner that he wanted W. to be happy. In his view, his ex-wife treated life too seriously, and he felt that she was holding up standards that were too much for W. to attain. He indicated that his son was "a success to me already." He described his impression that W. was under continual pressure to succeed at home, and that this created great tension and anger in his son. Mr. K. spoke about wanting to have a chance to "straighten him out" since he felt that his son had feelings which were "tearing him up." Mr. K. shared with this examiner his impression that his son was afraid to talk to his mother about the fact that he did not want to go to college, since he felt that she was insistent on his attending college. Mr. K. stated that while he would not insist on W. going through with college, he would "have to do his best in school." He described W. as withdrawn following the divorce and said that for the first day or two that W. is with him, he appears withdrawn but then "comes out of his shell" and is "the happy kid he used to be."

Interview with W. himself revealed a rather hesitant, somewhat withdrawn, boy who had difficulty expressing himself directly. He did speak about the fact that his mother would get very angry about his poor grades and that "she got good grades and is always comparing me." W. became quite tearful when describing the separation and divorce; he stated that he feels close to both parents but has great difficulty talking about his feelings. W. stated that he got along "OK" with his mother, but he was far more positive when describing his relaxed relationship with his father. He stated that he frequently feels tense and "uptight" at home. He stated that while he was aware that his mother and father did not get along, he was totally taken by surprise by the separation and divorce. According to W., his grades remained at a decent level even for a year or two following the separation, and it is only within the past two years that his grades have apparently fallen off. He stated that when he was younger, he always looked forward to coming home, in contrast to the feeling of tension that he experiences now. He described being very much interested in "mechanical stuff" like his father. He stated that at this point in his life he would far prefer to be a mechanic than to go to college. He seemed quite comfortable in describing his father, but stated that he was unable to describe very much about his mother or his relationship with her husband.

Review of the previous psychological evaluation revealed an impression that there was definite emotional interference with W.'s intellectual efficiency, and that he had a great need to deal therapeutically with much of the anger he felt regarding the separation and divorce. Apparently, W. was very briefly in therapy with the school psychologist, but this treatment was terminated.

On the current battery of psychological testing, W. presents himself as a young man who has many of the typical feelings and attitudes of an adolescent, with an overlay of great dissatisfaction with the current way in which his family life is structured. There are continual themes of being pressured at home, resulting in a feeling of low self-esteem, a feeling that he is "not good enough," and an attitude of "just giving up." This appears to substantiate W.'s verbal statements that he has a hard time expressing his feelings, and it appears that much of his poor schoolwork relates to this low self-esteem and to the feeling that he is "not good enough." W. is able to recognize the happiness that can come from a warm and intimate relationship, but at the present time, he is unable to related himself to that experience. He experiences much blocking and confusion in his thinking when dealing with conflicts between men and women, and for that reason tends to avoid interpersonal relationships, perceiving them as fraught with pain and unhappiness.

In the Projective Drawings, W. presents himself as an exceedingly frightened, inadequate, anxious, and insecure young man, who has very great difficulty dealing with the emotional turmoil of adolescence. He experiences himself at the present time as somewhat isolated and empty, having no sense of any real roots. In the kinetic family drawings, he perceives interaction with his mother as generally a passive one, while the interaction portrayed with his father is a more active one.

The Sentence Completion Test reveals much identification with his father, a wish that he could live with him, and a sense that somehow his father is "bigger than life." He experiences a good deal of blocking in terms of any negative affective experiences, feelings about his mother, heterosexual relationships, and anything suggesting a lack of ability or a failure in a given area.

While W.'s Rorschach reveals no evidence whatsoever of any serious disturbance in reality testing, it does present the picture of a young man who exerts rather tight control over his feelings, allowing little affect or fantasy into his life. When he does become emotionally stirred up, this very rapidly turns to the strong feelings of anger about the divorce which he has never fully worked through. A secondary theme on the Rorschach appears to be some uncertainty and ambivalence about heterosexual relationships, with these most likely being normal adolescent feelings intensified by the uncertainties about such relationships engendered by the divorce.

SUMMARY AND RECOMMENDATIONS

Both verbally and nonverbally, W. has been expressing a desire to be with his father. His current scores on the Wechsler Intelligence Scale for Children have shown some deterioration over the test scores two years ago, indicating that the emotional problems and underlying anger continue to take their toll on his intellectual efficiency. W. is constantly feeling very angry about the situation and, in the current setting, feels unable to express these angry feelings directly, most likely expressing some of the hostility passively through the lack of achievement. It is felt that basically W. needs, at this point, more "breathing room" to decide what he really wants for himself. Currently, W. does not know what he wants, feeling continually confused and torn by the welter of angry feelings within himself. He experiences too many pressures pulling him in different directions. It is my opinion that for a trial period, to be determined by his parents, probably most realistically to coincide with one school year (i.e., approximately 8 to 9 months), W. should be placed in the custody of his father with ample visitation to his mother's home. He should continue in the school he presently attends, to maintain some sense of continuity. One of the goals that this may accomplish is that with the greater distance from his mother, W. may be able to perceive her in a more realistic light so that she is no longer continually "the bad guy"; by the same token, by living with his father, W. will be able to start relating to him as a human being and to stop dealing with him as "bigger than life," and continually on a pedestal. The difference in settings will also be more or less in the nature of an experiment to see whether W.'s grades can indeed improve, since they appear to have deteriorated continually over the course of the past several years. Certainly, at the end of this trial period, the positive and negative factors will have to be weighed to determine what the future course of action is to be. Finally, whatever setting W. is in, it is my strong opinion that continued counseling and/or psychotherapy is essential to enable him to work through some of the unresolved angry and hurt feelings that W. has never really been able to express.

David L. Shapiro Ph.D.

Appendix E
Follow-up Evaluation
8/20/82

NAME: W. K.   DOB: 10-5-65

                                   AGE: 16-10

TEST ADMINISTERED:

Thermatic Apperception Test
Millon Clinical Multiaxial Inventory
Minnesota Multiphasic Personality Inventory
Projective Drawings
Rorschach Psychodiagnostic Test
Wechsler Adult Intelligence Scale (revised)

W. was reexamined approximately one year following his initial examination, in accordance with the order of the court, to provide an updated observation of his current functioning.

On the Wechsler Adult Intelligence Scale, W. obtains a verbal IQ of 126, a performance IQ of 104, and a resultant full scale IQ of 118, placing him within the bright-normal range of intellectual functioning. It is important to note that his verbal IQ has increased nine points since the earlier testing, while the performance IQ remains essentially stable. This has resulted in an increment of six points in his full scale IQ.

Given the facts that the timed nature of most of the performance tasks tends to induce anxiety and that the only verbal subtests which are somewhat depressed are those which are highly susceptible to anxiety, it appears that there has been a definite improvement in W.'s intellectual functioning, with the exception of those items which bear the imprint of anxiety during the course of testing. Overall, it appears that W. is moving in an upward direction toward the scores which he obtained when he was tested initially in the school system.

From the point of view of personality functioning, several themes are currently apparent. There is still evidence of W.'s perception of the situation between his parents as a highly conflict-laden one. Nevertheless, there are some subtle signs that W.'s perception of his mother is becoming more realistic. This contrasts somewhat with the impressions noted in the initial evaluation one year ago, in which father was seen as "bigger than life" and on a pedestal, and mother was seen as everything that was wrong in life. It will be recalled that the recommendation reached in that initial evaluation was partially for the purpose of enabling W. to develop a more realistic appraisal of both parents. He has accomplished this to some degree. The testing reveals more ability on W.'s part to empathize with his mother's position and more ability to articulate those feelings, coupled with some indications that he is able to perceive men and women experiencing things together, sharing feelings, and generally acting in unison, rather than continually being at odds. W. has certainly become more in touch with the feelings that he has long been suppressing and appears able to deal with these feelings in a more constructive manner than he did one year ago.

On the other hand, it appears that W.'s relationship to his father has not substantially changed from the perceptions of a year ago. That is, to a great extent, W. still does tend to place his father on a pedestal and at times presents himself as rather defensive, minimizing and smoothing over many feelings that he may have. At times, W. shows an intense resistance to admitting that there could be anything at all that is not perfect in his current situation. He tries to appear outwardly controlled when he is having many strong feelings internally.

In becoming more aware of his feelings, W. has also become more consciously aware of some of his anxiety and, in so doing, has appeared to show some maturation developmentally. There are indications that W. is able at times to "look his fright in the face" and acknowledge it, though at other times, depending on the circumstances, he does try to deny the impact of these feelings.

In summary, then, there have been a variety of changes noted in W. over the course of the past year, including improvement in his intellectual functioning, greater maturity in his ability to relate to other people, and more ability to empathize with and articulate his feelings about his mother; however, at the same time, there is some degree of resistance in acknowledging any negative feelings that he may currently have.

David L. Shapiro Ph.D.

Subject Index

Adoption
  and evaluation of adoptive family, 109
  Uniform Adoption Act, 108
  and waiver of parental consent, 108
Alcohol
  and delerium tremens, 63
  and insanity defense, 62–64
American Bar Association Commission on
    the Mentally Disabled, 23
American Law Institute Model Penal Code,
    28, 36
American Psychological Association Code of
    Ethics, 132

Bazelon, Judge David, 31, 165–166
Best interests of the child, standards for,
    102–103
Bifurcated Trial, 45–46
  constitutional problems in, 45–46
  and jury issues, 47

Child abuse and neglect, and emotional
    abuse, 110–111
Child custody evaluations
  and "family systems approach," 107–108
  guidelines for conducting evaluations,
    99–102, 105
  and joint custody, 107
  and need for objectivity, 106
  and payment arrangements, 107
  and psychological vs. biological parent,
    109–110
  and visitation, 105–106
Civil Commitment
  and alternative commitment models,
    158–159
  and the criminal justice system, 159–160
  and dangerousness, 157–158
  and juveniles, 167–168
  and required level of proof, 161–162

Competency
  and amnesia, 18–20
  competency to stand trial and mental
    illness, 4
  criteria for, 1–10
  distinction from criminal responsibility,
    1
  and long-term incompetence, 20–24
  and malingering, 12–18
  and medication, 10–11
The Criminal Personality, 44
Criminal responsibility
  abolition of insanity defense, 41–45
  American Law Institute Model Penal
    Code, 28
  Blocker Case, 32
  conducting of evaluations, 51–62, 69–70
  distinction from competency, 1, 28
  Durham Test, 28, 31
  instruction to expert witnesses, 33–35
  irresistible impulse, 28, 29, 30
  McDonald Standard, 31
  McNaughten Standard, 20, 28, 30
  preparation of reports, 181–189
  Sua Sponte insanity defense, 49–50
  Washington Standard, 33
Cross examination
  and contingent fees, 95–96
  and generalizations, 90
  and isolation of symptoms, 94–95
  and issue of "planning," 92–93
  and knowledge of wrongfulness, 93
  and "normality," 91–92, 94
  preparation for, 79–82, 97–98
  and validity of psychological testing, 81-
    81–83
  ways of responding to, 81–82
Culpable and Mentally Disabled, 43
  mentally disabled, neither culpable nor
    innocent, 43

Case Index